Made Flesh

John's Gospel, Mission and the Global Church

Andy McCullough

malcolm down

PUBLISHING

First published 2024 by Malcolm Down Publishing Ltd.
www.malcolmdown.co.uk

28 27 26 25 24   7 6 5 4 3 2 1

The right of Andrew McCullough to be identified as the author of this
work has been asserted by him in accordance with the Copyright,
Designs and Patents Act 1988.

British Library Cataloguing in Publication Data
A catalogue record for this book is available from the British Library.

ISBN 978-1-915046-75-8

Cover design by Esther Kotecha
Art direction by Sarah Grace

Printed in the UK

Endorsements

Shalom, peace, harmony, unity, all describe the ultimate objective of the Christian life. Maturity in Christ is the narrow way to that objective. By John's hand, Jesus describes his relationship with the Father as a singularity, invites us into that divine union, and sends us into the world as witnesses after his example, just as the Father sent Him—in unity (John 17:18-26). Andy McCullough masterfully illustrates what that witness looks like. Not a homogenous uniformity but unity in glorious diversity. A harmony created from counterpointed tension where followers from every tribe, language, nation, and people bring their contextual relationship with God into the family of God. Weaving in voices from across World Christianity, McCullough scores an orchestral tapestry upon the pages of John's gospel, amplifying the harmonic opus that is the Body of Christ . . . *Made Flesh*: an essential read for the future of the global Church and her missions.

Dr Jay Mātenga, Aotearoa New Zealand

As an African who has spent a number of years in the West, this book impacted me more than I expected. Having read only the introduction, I found myself feeling quite emotional because of Andy's positive understanding of difference. He is very perceptive as he explains different cultures and the way they see the various stories in the Gospels. In particular, the walk through the last supper, death and resurrection of Jesus is marvellous. Glory to Jesus and His Bride, the Church, comes through so beautifully and makes one want to shout for joy. Breathtaking! May we be inspired to go as Jesus commanded; to 'go to the margins, not the centre, at the feet of the world, not its head, in the midst of the secular, not the hallowed.' An outstanding project!

Angela Kemm, South Africa

Andy's own words come to life revealing to us the beauty of the eternal Word made flesh. As we read John's gospel and the stories we think we know so well, Andy turns on the light and shows us a picture rich with symbols which draw us into the mystical union of the seen and unseen. Andy reminds us what a personal and generous God we have. Just like God 'translated' himself into human personhood for us to better understand him, he continues to translate himself into our cultures, contexts and needs. Andy's anecdotes and references from around the world are delightful and refreshing, reminding us that we are part of a beautiful and diverse family. We have so much to learn from every member of Christ's culturally rich body. Thank you, Andy for this glimpse of Christ's global bride.

Kayra Akpınar, Türkiye

Andy's book is incredibly thought-provoking and insightful. His exposure to multiple cultures and willingness to listen has brought forth amazing revelations that are extremely relevant in today's world.

I have been on a journey to navigate my faith in Jesus within my Indian culture. Coming from a Hindu family, I have had to discover Him without the trappings of the West. Sometimes I succeeded, but often I made mistakes—primarily by rejecting cultural practices as though they were evil.

Andy's book has given language to my search and learnings, stimulating me to seek Him further within my Eastern culture. It will inspire you too. People and cultures are different, and Andy's approach of genuine respect is refreshing.

Andy says, "The first thing Philip does is to find Nathanael under his fig tree and share the good news. He does not disrespect Nathanael. He does not rubbish, hate, or mock. He does not argue or disprove." Brilliant!

Nathanael was a seeker under the fig tree, like many Indians.
"As Philips, we too turn to those who are sitting under the fig trees of the world, respectful of their searches, their spirituality, their longings." This encouragement has further challenged my approach to seekers in India. The Word becomes flesh to different individuals in different ways. In this quest for contextualization, many from the West have attempted to contextualize the gospel for Hindus. Perhaps a better way is to ask a Hindu-background believer to contextualize Jesus within their own culture.

Made Flesh will surely make of you a better listener and propel you toward an empathetic mission.

Samir Deokuliar, India

Made Flesh is one of the most refreshing commentaries on the Gospel of John you will read today. It makes the entire book come pleasantly alive in many unexpected ways. Andy McCullough has been courageous in his approach, engaging John through the eyes and voices of Christians worldwide. You will wonder how you have managed to read John so far without the insight that Andy brings out. I cannot recommend it enough.

Dr Harvey Kwiyani, Malawi and UK

Andy McCullough has served the Global Church well with this work. Thoroughly researched, this book is timely, prophetic and practical. Timely, in that it speaks to issues requiring our urgent attention. Prophetic, in that it asks discerning questions and seeks to lead us to biblical and contextually aware answers. It is practical in that, true to its theme, the real-world examples and global voices point us toward concrete applications in our lives and churches for today. I doubt anyone can read this book without having their reading of John's Gospel enriched and deepened. Page after page of penetrating and at times even startling insights resonate at multiple levels with the heart and experience of an African pastor. I was immensely blessed by each chapter. *Made Flesh* challenges both how we read Scripture and how we do mission and in so doing addresses two of the most important questions facing believers today.

Mbonisi Malaba, Zimbabwe and Kenya

Contents

Abbreviations of Ancient Sources   4

Introduction   5

1. Flesh (John 1:1-14)   19
2. Fig (John 1:48)   37
3. Wine (John 2:1-11)   43
4. Margins (John Chapters 3 to 9)   55
5. Wind (John 3:1-15)   65
6. World (John 3:16)   79
7. Woman (John 4:1-42)   91
8. Shepherd (John Chapters 6 to 10)   109
9. Accused (John 8:1-11)   127
10. Light (John Chapters 8 and 9)   139
11. Friendship (John 11:1-54)   151
12. Donkey (John 12:12-15)   165
13. Feet (John 13:1-17)   177
14. Paraclete (John Chapters 14 to 16)   195
15. Garden (John 18:1-27)   211
16. Exchange (John 19:1-37)   221
17. Commission (John Chapters 20 and 21)   243

Bibliography   261

Abbreviations of Ancient Sources

b. Yoma	*Babylonian Talmud, Tractate Yoma.*
b. Git	*Babylonian Talmud, Tractate Gittin.*
b. Sanh.	*Babylonian Talmud, Tractate Sanhedrin.*
b. Suk.	*Babylonian Talmud, Tractate Sukkah.*
Cher.	Philo of Alexandria, *On the Cherubim.*
Eccles. R.	*Ecclesiastes Rabbah.*
Lam. R.	*Lamentations Rabbah.*
Leg. All.	Philo of Alexandria, *Allegorical Interpretation.*

Introduction

The Puncak Jaya mountain peak is the highest point between the Himalayas and the Andes. It's on the island of Papua, and the people who live in this remotest of regions speak the Damal language.

When the first missionaries to the Damal (now Amungme) people tried to communicate John 1:29, 'the Lamb of God, who takes away the sin of the world', they hit a major roadblock. There is no word for lamb or sheep in Damal. This concept, this animal, did not exist for them! Their equivalent, a domestic animal used for sacrifice, was the pig. Could Jesus really be explained as 'the pig of God'? An English rendering of the Damal translation of John 1:29 reads like this:

> Having said that and spent the night, Jesus came to where John was. Having seen him coming, John said, 'Look at that man. I see exactly that he is the Creator's sheep-pig. He is the one who will completely wipe out all the evil deeds of those who live in the place of real people.'

When I tell this story to my Middle Eastern friends, they are in equal measures amused and horrified.

I wonder what John himself would have thought?

But it's not just the Damal; we are all limited by our own culture and language. We all have blind spots. And the Word, who 'became flesh' (John 1:14) has condescended to allow himself to be imprisoned within our own cultural captivities, reduced by our own linguistic limitations, mis-perceived thanks to our own inherent blind spots.

However, when the Global Church comes together, as the strengths of diversity overcome the weaknesses of homogeneity, we round out each other's blind spots, we see more of the complete picture of Christ. We need each other – God intended it that way.

This is my third book. I know my books are not super-easy to read, I admit it. But I am trying, in my own small way, to help my readers to change the way they think, to expand the way they see the world. If all I was offering in what follows was a smattering of global voices, some exotic flavours to season an already-formed and untouchable reading of John's Gospel, then it would be an easier read, but a dishonest one. I'm hoping for more than that. My appeal to you is that you show honour to the voices and perspectives that are introduced here, that you listen, *really* listen, to opinions that may seem so different from what you are familiar with, and that you prayerfully keep putting your own heart in the frame. Yes, interrogate this reading – you must. But also, allow this reading to interrogate you.

Encounters with other perspectives can change you, and enrich your knowledge of God, if you will allow them to.

I remember sitting spell-bound, open-mouthed, in a plush Turkish hotel as a wise Armenian pastor taught through Matthew, showing us the relational friction between the disciples, and how Peter walking on the water wasn't heroic but arrogant. In a group-orientated culture, his constantly trying to outshine the other disciples was shameful, which is why Jesus told him to get back in the boat with the others!

I had the privilege of spending a couple of days with leaders of Chinese house churches learning about their principles of prayer and faith, and in particular being struck by their emphasis on simple, daily obedience to the leading of the Holy Spirit.

Where Western leadership seemed to be about complexity, their simplicity stuck me as refreshingly biblical.

I've never been the same after spending several months living in Pune, India, and reading 1 Samuel together with a South Indian guy who seemed to take the Bible literally, miracles and all, and heard the voice of God like Samuel did. To this day, when I read Samuel, I hear his voice!

Together with many other leaders, I was pinned to my seat as an Indonesian pastor told stories of persecution and revival, replete with photos on PowerPoint of machete wounds and burned-down church buildings. It felt very far away from English experience, but very close to the book of Acts.

I've sat in Soweto in the house of a young Zulu church leader listening to him talk about race and forgiveness and liberation theology. He spoke about Galatians in a way I hadn't considered before, talking about freedom and fruit as more communal than individual, and the inadequacy of an individualistic gospel freedom to enact justice and societal change.

Reading the story of Ruth with a room of Muslim Syrian refugee women in Athens changed that story for me forever – in their faces I could see her resilience, her will to life, her indefatigability. That experience provoked me to study Ruth in Middle Eastern perspective for my Master's thesis.

Grilling an Egyptian pastor over dinner about his family-based deliverance ministry has changed the way I pray for people to this day; he saw deliverance from evil spirits to be necessary not just for the individual, but for the family of which they were a part.

Time spent in Bethlehem with Palestinian Christians has utterly transformed my understanding of Christmas, which is more barbed wire than tinsel – as I wrote about in *The Bethlehem Story*.[1]

In each of these cases, and countless others besides, the perspective, the lived experience, the point of view of sisters and brothers from nations other than my own enriched, challenged,

---

1. McCullough, *The Bethlehem Story*.

broadened out how I understood the Bible. Sure, it would be possible to take each of these moments and view them as an exotic adornment to my otherwise fixed dogmas. But it's never been like that for me. I've chosen, I think intuitively and from a young age, to allow encounters like this to *shift my centre*. Maybe it comes from having lived in different places. But it's also been a theologically driven lifestyle choice, a deeply held conviction. I choose to see diverse voices as authoritative. Why, after all, should my perspective be more valid than someone else's? Many of these friends are just as qualified, if not more, than I am. Just as prayerful, usually more, than me. Just as experienced, if not more, than myself. They know God. They read Scripture. What could it possibly be, other than white arrogance, that would stop me listening, not just inclining my ear but *really listening* to other voices, other perspectives?

And then come books. I love Christian books. But it is staggering to me how many Christians in English-speaking countries like the UK, the US, South Africa and Australia only read Christian books written by white men. It is utterly unfair – unjust – how much theology, how many Bible commentaries on the shelves of pastors around the world come from Europe or America. It presents as objective, as scientific, but it is just as narrow as if you only ever went to the BBC for your news, or to your best friend, who has the same blind spots as you, for advice.

Not just narrow, dangerous. It may be that only ever reading within the same tradition makes you feel safe, but actually it's the opposite. Rehoboam's friends, with whom he grew up, shared the same blind spots as he did, and told him what he wanted to hear. The advice was wrong, but the echo-chamber of familiar voices made it impossible for Rehoboam to hear anything else (1 Kings 12:8). 'Homogeneity, whatever form it takes, is slow death', writes

Harvey Kwiyani (Malawi).[2] Perspectives from across the global family of Christ add resilience, depth, wisdom, colour, and rescue us from the tyranny of being subsumed into our own cultural moment. 'One thumb alone does not kill headlice', as the East African proverb says.

Theology, and missiology, that has been developed in the West by exclusively white voices misses so much. It dismisses much pre-West historical theology. It misunderstands key cultural elements in Scripture, as books like *Misreading Scripture with Western Eyes*[3] have shown. It does not speak to the needs and longings, to the realities and challenges of the majority of Christians, who are not white, and who do not live in the West. And yet, as is a common theme with whiteness, it does not acknowledge its own particularity, its own inadequacy, its own shortcomings.

For people who love the Bible, there should be loads of ideas in this book to delight your heart and stimulate your imagination. Biblical interpretation is not a closed book, we haven't arrived, and contemporary Western theology is neither the peak nor the summation of revelation. But, more importantly, theology exclusively from the Global North is insufficient to understand John's Gospel. If you only read North Atlantic commentaries on John, there is a great deal of great import that will be missed.

For instance, it's widely accepted that John is writing actual eyewitness history, but *at the same time* writing symbolically, poetically, with great artistry. Where Western scholarship has struggled to hold both of these in tension the Indian Church, for example, with her 2,000-year tradition of cherishing John, has the tools to help.

Rodriguez (Mexico) writes about theology as *flor y canto* (flower and song), with an emphasis on poetry and beauty:

---

2. Kwiyani, *Multicultural Kingdom*, p. 95.
3. Richards and O'Brien, *Misreading Scripture with Western Eyes*.

'According to this worldview, the deepest recesses of being human can only be expressed in the metaphor of poetry and beauty. While it recognizes the significance of reason and logic, this particular worldview takes seriously the affect, the intuitive, and the aesthetic.'[4] John's Gospel certainly meets this standard, with inimitable artistry, a depth of emotion and rich symbolism. Bauckham (England) would give equal emphasis to both metaphorical and historiographical functions of the text: 'The writer of John's Gospel is constantly putting two things together ... He tells stories such that they have more meanings than the literal one.'[5]

As an example, when the blood and water flow from Jesus' side on the cross, the literal 'Western' reading has been that this is a proof of death – that blood and plasma separate after death. This is not untrue, of course. But centuries of tradition have read this incident allegorically, metaphorically, theologically – the sacraments of blood (the eucharist) and water (baptism), or the promised gift of the Spirit in the water, as promised in 4:14 and 7:37-39. Rather than rubbishing this outright, we must consider that John has been referring to water in both symbolic and literal ways throughout his gospel. This subterranean watercourse throughout John, which surfaces in chapter 4 by a real well talking about spiritual thirst, in chapter 7 when Jesus announces that '"Out of his heart will flow rivers of living water." Now this he said about the Spirit' (vv. 38-39) now resurfaces in the body of Jesus, as water and blood will pour from his side. Literal and figurative waters intermingle. Stephen Moore (Ireland) writes:

This water is neither simply material and literal, since it is symbolic, nor fully spiritual and figurative, since it is physical ... Literality and figurality intermingle in the flow from Jesus'

4. Rodriguez, 'Tripuenteando: Journey toward Identity, the Academy, and Solidarity', p. 75.
5. Bauckham, *Gospel of Glory*, Kindle location 2585.

side, each contaminating the other, which is to say that we cannot keep the literal clearly separate from the figurative in the end.[6]

Indeed, we reflect, Jesus is the Word made flesh, he is both divine and human, both spirit and flesh, both God and man, from heaven and from earth. He makes the invisible visible, the distant near, the incomprehensible accessible. In Jesus, the distance between heaven and earth is dissolved. It is no surprise, then, that in Jesus physical and spiritual realities intermingle. It is no surprise that beyond every literal layer of meaning lies a figurative layer. The body of Christ is a paradox, a vessel for both literal and spiritual water, a portal between heaven and earth.

Unlike the three Synoptic Gospels (Matthew, Mark, Luke), John does not have a moment where Jesus inaugurates the Lord's Supper as a sacrament. But throughout John, Jesus is *embodying* this tradition rather than just talking about it. He says, 'I am the true vine' (John 15:1) and he also miraculously provides wine at a wedding in John 2. He says, 'I am the bread of life' (John 6:35) and in John 6 he feeds 5,000 hungry people with miracle bread. He is Word 'become flesh' (John 1:14), and he is constantly making his words flesh to real people in specific situations. He never leaves truth in the abstract, in the theoretical, he *makes it flesh*. He says, 'I am the light of the world' (John 8:12) and then in John 9 he heals a man born blind. He says, 'I am the resurrection and the life' (John 11:25) and he raises his friend Lazarus from the dead.

John was writing for a global audience. He wrote later than the other apostles, when Christianity was rapidly becoming a global movement. He saw beyond just Greek and Jewish audiences. If tradition is to be trusted, most of the apostles had made it to

---

6. Moore, 'Are there Impurities in the Living Water that the Johannine Jesus Dispenses?', p. 290.

far-flung lands. Thomas was already in India. Consider John's 'of the world' statements: 'light of the world (8:12), 'Saviour of the world' (4:42), 'Lamb of God, who takes away the sin of the world' (1:29), 'For God so loved the world' (3:16), 'the bread of God . . . who comes down from heaven and gives life to the world' (6:33) . . . he is reaching further, appealing wider. Consider Nathanael in John 1, sitting under the fig tree. Fig trees are universally sacred. John would almost certainly have been aware of Egyptian reverence for this tree, Roman myths about this tree, and even the Buddhist image of Buddha sitting under the banyan (a species of fig) receiving enlightenment. The calling of Nathanael, and Jesus' comment, 'Before Philip called you, when you were under the fig tree, I saw you' (John 1:48) reaches beyond the boundaries of Israel and appeals to the search for meaning embedded in innumerable cultures and religions. Such ideas as light, bread, water, shepherd, life are strong universal symbols, and resonate deeply with people from so many parts of the world. John's writing at multiple levels simultaneously means that this book speaks to lots of different kinds of people at the same time. This continues to prove true today. The Church is more global than she has ever been, and John is more widely resonant than it has ever been.

John has a huge amount to teach us about mission. The powerful scene, on the Sunday evening, where Jesus appears to his disciples and commissions them, 'As the Father has sent me, even so I am sending you' (John 20:21) frames the whole book as an example to be emulated. As Jesus was Word made flesh, an embodied communication from God, so should our mission be incarnational, up-close and personal, local and specific. As Jesus washed feet,[7] so should we. As Jesus focused on the margins of society, so should we. As Jesus dialogued with different people, contextualising his approach to the various characters with whom

---

7. See John 13.

he engaged (he spoke differently for example, to Nicodemus in chapter 3 and the Samaritan woman in chapter 4), so should we. The Global Church in the twenty-first century has lots to say about mission. The greatest energy for mission, and therefore missiology (the study of mission), is in the Global South. That's why I'm trying to reflect on mission using John's Gospel, but in global perspective, as well as just reflect on John's Gospel in global perspective. We must at all costs avoid outdated modes of cross-cultural sending that smack of colonialism and defunct ways of approaching mission that are out of sync with global realities.

De-Westernising, or decolonising your theology (talking about God) or your ecclesiology (talking about the Church) or your missiology (talking about mission) is an immersive and holistic journey. It's not just a matter of new technique. It's not just a matter of supplementing interpretation. We are longing for a transformed view of Jesus, a bigger view of God, a changed narrative to live out. This one book won't do it, but like with all my writing, I'm hoping to introduce you to voices, ideas, schools of thought which you can pursue afterwards. There's no point recruiting people for mission if you are not working to equip them. But equipping people for mission is primarily about *attitude* and *perspective*. I pray this little book touches both. As the mighty John Mbiti (Kenya) wrote:

> Theologians from the new (or younger) churches have made their pilgrimages to the theological learning of the older churches. We had no alternative. We have eaten theology with you; we have drunk theology with you; we have dreamed theology with you. But it has all been one-sided; it has all been in a sense your theology . . . We know you theologically. The question is do you know us theologically? Would you like to know us theologically?[8]

---

8. Mbiti, 'Theological impotence and the universality of the Church', pp. 16-17.

Jesus is searching for his bride, and she is global. Jesus is introduced as the bridegroom (3:29), and he takes on the responsibility of the failed bridegroom at the wedding in Cana, he provides wine. When he travels to Samaria, we find Jesus and a Samaritan woman standing by a well, a re-hashing of the common Old Testament type-scene where the potential groom travels to a far country, boy meets girl by a well, one of them draws water, they go and tell the wider family and there is a feast – which always happens when a young groom is searching for his bride (Moses, Isaac, Jacob). Jesus is searching for his bride, the Church, throughout John, a bride which must include Samaria. The vocative, 'O woman', with which he addresses her is used six times throughout John, always to a woman who is without a husband, as Jesus repeatedly, symbolically seeks out his bride, the Church.[9] Christ will not have many brides, only the one, but she will be a bride made up of all nations.

The Latin-American Church loves John for his focus on the margins, on the disinherited. As the new Temple, the enfleshed dwelling place of God, Jesus goes to those who could never come to the Jerusalem temple. He creates access.

The Chinese Church delights in the portrayal of Jesus as the 'Word' and of Jesus as the 'Way', both ideas which resonate with the Chinese appreciation of the search for wisdom.

First Nations churches appeal to the concrete in John. 'Without physicality, there is no sustenance,' writes Sylvia Marcos (Mexico).[10] Aboriginal communities have long related to God in tangible, everyday ways rather than abstract or theoretical doctrine. John's presentation of Jesus as flesh and blood, down-to-earth, one who weeps and thirsts and bleeds is appealing to many from these communities.

---

9. 2:4; 4:21; 8:10; 19:26; 20:13; 20:15.
10. Marcos, 'Teologia India: A Context Theology', p. 273.

The Middle Eastern Church loves John's use of symbols. For example, the use of the number seven, to which we will refer throughout this book, is artistry and symmetry, as well as a vehicle for theological import, which delights the hearts of Middle Eastern readers.

The Postcolonial Church, wherever she is found, recognises John's engagement with the tyranny of empire. The colonial power of Rome is present throughout the book, for example Biju Chacko (India) recognises the colonial renaming of the Sea of Galilee as the Sea of Tiberias (6:1) as a clue to the background of empire throughout John's sixth chapter. Where Caesar has failed to provide bread and left the people hungry, Jesus provides bread, and so they want to make him king. Jesus is a non-violent seditionist of sorts, crucified between two seditionists. The Creedal statement, 'Suffered under Pontius Pilate'[11] has a tone of empire, as Pilate represents the brutally violent Roman occupying power.[12]

As we will see, different aspects of John's Jesus resonate deeply with different parts of the Global Church. Cultural resonance is so important, as D.T. Niles (Sri Lanka) has written:

The gospel is like a seed and you have to sow it. When you sow the seed of the gospel in Palestine, a plant that can be called Palestinian Christianity grows. When you sow it in Rome, a plant of Roman Christianity grows. You sow the gospel in Great Britain and you get British Christianity. The seed of the gospel is later brought to America and a plant grows of American Christianity. Now when missionaries came to our lands they brought not only the seed of the gospel, but their own plant of Christianity, flowerpot

---

11. See www.catholic.org/prayers/prayer.php?p=220 (accessed 12.4.24).
12. Cruchley, 'Turning Whiteness Purple', p. 247.

included! So, what we have to do is to break the flowerpot, take out the seed of the gospel, sow it in our own cultural soil, and let our own version of Christianity grow.[13]

Lamin Sanneh (Gambia), who has written magisterially on the emergence of a world Christianity in recent decades, speaks of this 'irruption' and what it means for 'a new day of human solidarity':

> Third World Christianity irrupted on the basis of a new indigenous anthropology of mother tongue literacy, ethnic empowerment, esthetic adaptation, and . . . of being driven by a striving for justice, trust and reconciliation. Christianity became the faith of the oppressed and dispossessed who as objects of Western colonial supremacy had been left as without hope and without history . . . We find ourselves today at the junction between the waning of the West's global authority and the rising demands for justice and equality of once colonized and oppressed societies, with a challenge to acknowledge Christianity's unprecedented pluralist expression without the split burden of territorial conquest or cultural exclusiveness. A new day of human solidarity has dawned, with much in it to challenge and encourage.[14]

This little book will probably fail to achieve these goals. My Global North readers will be offended that it goes too far, my Global South readers, that it does not go far enough. For some it is ten years too late, for others, ten years ahead of its time. It's limited by virtue of being written in the English language, and by virtue of being written by me, with all my limitations and blind spots. It

---

13. Niles, *Upon the Earth*, p. 61.
14. Sanneh, 'Should Christianity be Missionary? An Appraisal and an Agenda', pp. 96-97.

does not claim to be a commentary, or in any way comprehensive. There are absolutely key works on John that I have not read, and absolutely essential observations about the text that I have not noticed.

When John, in his final verse, says that 'I suppose that the world itself could not contain the books that would be written' (21:25), he is surely thinking about the global reach of the gospel, the Christ for all nations which he has been presenting, the multiple languages and innumerable generations who would claim Jesus as Lord and write about him. 'World' is an important word for John, which he develops throughout his Gospel, from its first mention in 1:9 to this point in 21:25. Jesus' global impact is front and centre. This universality is something I have discovered as I have researched this book. John – infinitely translatable – speaks in the languages of the whole world to the cares and concerns of the whole world. And there is certainly a tension between this global resonance and the limited specificity of any one book, of any one articulation in any one language at any one time for any one purpose. It's into that space in-between the universal and the local that I'm writing, as John himself prophesied.

Chapter One

Flesh

(John 1:1-14)

In the beginning was the Word ...and the
Word became flesh and dwelt among us ...
(John 1:1,14)

John's inspired choice of 'Word' (Greek: *logos*) in his opening sentence has resulted in the spilling of gallons of ink over two millennia. Immediately, he captivates both Jews and Greeks. Immediately, he is appealing to the broadest of audiences, to the whole world. It's important when we read John that we remember he was writing for the whole world.

For readers of Jewish heritage, there would be an instant resonance with Greek translation of the Old Testament. 'In the beginning' is exactly how Genesis starts. The first five verses of the prologue are rich with Genesis language (beginning, life, light, God), and the last five verses (vv. 14-18) are replete with Exodus language (dwelt, glory, Moses, law). 'One of the functions of the prologue', writes Bauckham (England), 'is to indicate to readers how, starting with the Old Testament, they should read the story of Jesus.'[15]

For readers with a Hellenistic education and view of the world, 'In the beginning was the *logos*' would equally capture

---

15. Bauckham, *Gospel of Glory,* p. 50.

their attention. *Logos* was a weighted, freighted word, present right through the everyday systems of life and being. It was the fundamental principle, the basic building block of life. Greek readers, from the first verse, would feel – this is written for us!

St. John has thus established common ground with all his readers. If they are Jews they will recognise and assent to the familiar doctrine of the Old Testament concerning the Word of God. If they are Greeks they will recognise and assent to the declaration that the ultimate reality is Mind expressing itself. To both alike he has announced in language easily received that the subject for which he is claiming their attention is the ultimate and supreme principle of the universe.[16]

John, therefore, is modelling something important about communication of the gospel. If Jesus is indeed good news for everyone – 'Saviour of the world', 'Light of the world', 'Lamb of God, who takes away the sin of the world' then he must be articulated in a way that is meaningful for the world. Keller (USA) puts it like this, 'As soon as you choose words, you are contextualising, and you become more accessible to some people and less so to others. There is no universal presentation of the gospel for all people.'[17]

Today, many around the world would speak of the global resonance of John's writing. In India, the key themes throughout the Gospel of life (*jiva*), light (*jyoti*), truth (*satya*), witness (*sakshi*), and world (*lokam*) reverberate with lived realities. Thomaskutty (India) explains that John is a 'gospel with an Indian spirit'.[18] In the Arab World, John's portrayal of religious leaders

---

16. Temple, *Readings in St. John's Gospel*, p. 3.
17. Keller, *Center Church*, p. 94.
18. Thomaskutty, 'The Gospel of John', p. 129.

holding on to state-backed power and oppressive purity laws is instantly recognisable. For marginal and excluded people everywhere, the time and care Jesus gives to ordinary and even despised people, to women and the sick and the poor is attractive. To people in colonial and postcolonial contexts, the presence of the Roman Empire throughout John truly chimes with the fears and frustrations they experience.

We can learn from John how to communicate this good news in a way that it will be accessible to people from many different backgrounds.

I wonder what you think of when you imagine 'in the beginning'. I think of silence, nothingness, emptiness. And yet, John tells us, 'In the beginning was the Word' (John 1:1). God was talking, even when there was no one to talk to. God had a comment, even when there was nothing on which to make comment. God is a noisy God! This, too, is important for our view of mission. Mission originates in the person of God. He has something to say. We call this the *Missio Dei*, the mission of God. Mission is not something he gives us to do, something intrinsically human. God had a great purpose, one overall story arc through creation, redemption, judgement and ultimately new creation. We are invited to participate in *his* mission, to join him in what *he* has always been doing, to tune in to what *he* has always been saying.

With God it is never 'no comment'. God has something to say about the great aching agonies of every generation in every place. Whether it is the climate emergency, or the refugee crisis, or the darkness in the soul of humankind, God has a word. And God's comment, as we shall see, ultimately becomes flesh in Jesus. God's message is concentrated and pressed together and given human life in Jesus. Jesus is, and always has been, God's word to a broken world.

Michael Amaladoss (India), in his classic *The Asian Jesus,* discusses whether or not, in an Indian context, it is appropriate to call Jesus an *avatar*. In Hindu thought, avatars are incarnations of divinity, gods among us in human form. And although this is a very different idea from the once-for-all, fully-God-fully-man, born-to-die Christ, laid in a manger in the margins of the world, Amaladoss concludes that it is impossible for someone from a Hindu background *not* to consider Jesus, in some sense, an avatar.

Indians looking on Jesus will spontaneously consider him an avatar. It is an Indian religio-cultural entry point to explore our experience of Jesus as a human-divine person. By considering Jesus an avatar my aim is not to compare him with Hindu avatars. I am taking avatar as an image which has a general meaning of 'divine manifestation'. It implies more a descent than an ascent. It is not simply the divinization of the human. By looking on Jesus as an avatar, the term avatar itself will be taking on a new connotation in the Christian context...

I think that the Indian approach can escape the Greek dichotomous one that separates God from the human and then does not know how to put them together. Not that it would find it more easy to understand and explain the mystery of Jesus Christ, the divine-human. At least it would look at it differently.[19]

Logos, dao and the Chinese Bible

John's choice of *logos*, a pagan, Hellenistic word, to describe Jesus has given generations of Bible translators permission to explore equivalent ideas in the languages of the world. A great example is the Chinese idea of *dao,* or *tao. Dao* has pervaded a Chinese worldview, from ancient times to today, and although

---

19. Amaladoss, *The Asian Jesus*, Kindle location 2036.

its meaning has varied in emphasis according to various schools of thought across the generations, the idea of *dao* has remained foundational. For Laozi, in the classic text *Daodejing*, the *dao* was the primordial principle of all creativity and materiality. For Confucius, the *dao* seems to have been more akin to 'The Way', wise principles and guidelines of life. In both of these senses, there is resonance with the first-century idea of *logos* as well as substantial overlap with John's articulation of Jesus, both as 'In the beginning was the *logos*' (1:1) and later, as 'the way, and the truth, and the life' (14:6). K.K. Yeo (China), wrestling with these ideas, asks:

> Can I, as a modern Bible interpreter, translate logos adequately into the Chinese word 'dao'? Does the word 'dao' in the Chinese Bible Union Version mean the Daoist cosmic dao or the Confucianist personhood/character dao, or a combination of both and more? Is the Chinese translation here limited, thereby betraying the original meaning of John's Gospel? And, is there a real possibility that the Chinese dao translation and interpretation – despite its potential limitations and its differences from Greek and Hebrew – has in fact a richer rendition of logos than the English translation 'Word'?[20]

The concept of *dao* is of course not enough. Like avatar, it has shortcomings, misleading connotations, and it needs redeeming and refilling with meaning if it is adequately to explain what Christians mean when they talk about Jesus. But that's also true of the English 'Word', which really feels quite weak and thin in comparison. And, indeed, even John's choice of *logos* in the first century was not without risk. All this tells us is that translation

---

20. Yeo, *What has Jerusalem to do with Beijing?*, p. 18.

is difficult, imperfect, yet essential. And Yeo, as an insider to Chinese culture, is much better equipped to wrestle with these ideas than me.[21]

'And the Word became flesh'

The incarnation (*carne* meaning meat or flesh in Latin) of the Word is a profound and unfathomable mystery, yet one which gives us a great deal to think about as we aspire to get better at communicating the Word ourselves. You see, with the Word becoming flesh, the conceptual was made concrete, the incomprehensible made accessible, the universal became specific, and the powerful rendered vulnerable. Let's consider these.

Conceptual made concrete (or invisible made visible)

Philip asks Jesus, 'Show us the Father, and it is enough for us' and Jesus replies, 'Whoever has seen me has seen the Father' (14:8-9). Jesus renders the Invisible One visible. He can be touched, and eaten with, and argued with and even harmed. When he weeps at the tomb of Lazarus, we know God to be weeping. When he moves towards the outcast, we see God to be moving. Jesus takes what we would otherwise only know conceptually, and he makes these truths about God concrete.

Jesus declares, 'I am the light of the world' and then he heals a blind man. He declares, 'I am the bread of life' and he miraculously feeds 5,000 people. He announces, 'I am the resurrection and the life' and then he raises his friend Lazarus from the dead. He says, 'I am the true vine' and he makes miraculous wine at a party. In each of these cases, he makes a claim which is cosmic and timeless and all-encompassing (like 'I am the light of the world'),

---

21. See also Wan, 'Tao – The Chinese Theology of God-Man'.

but then he *makes that word flesh* in an individual person's life, in a real situation. Timeless truth becomes local, personal, physical. Hungry bellies are filled. Eyes blind from birth are opened. It is easy to claim to bring life, but when Lazarus walks out of the tomb in front of many witnesses, that's a different story.

In John there are seven 'I am' statements with predicates – like the ones mentioned above (I am the . . .). The 'I am' formula comes from Exodus, when God revealed his name to Moses. 'I am' has sent you. In the book of Exodus, there are seven moments of divine self-revelation using this formula, for instance, 'I am the LORD, your healer' (Exodus 15:26), 'I the LORD your God am a jealous God' (Exodus 20:5). Seven is the divine number, the number of perfection and completeness. John loves the number seven, and with Jesus making seven 'I am' statements, he is being portrayed very clearly by the author as Israel's God in flesh, the God of Exodus come to deliver people from ultimate slavery – not just slavery to Pharoah but slavery to sin. When Nathanael meets Jesus, he is meeting Israel's God. When Thomas touches the wounds in Jesus' hands, he is touching God. When Judas kisses Jesus, he is kissing God.

There are also seven absolute 'I am' statements in John, those without a predicate which stand alone. These are sometimes lost in English translation, but stand out starkly in Greek because of their unusual construction. For example, when Jesus says, 'Truly, truly, I say to you, before Abraham was, I am' (8:58), his listeners immediately pick up stones to stone him, enraged at his blasphemy. And when, in the garden, those who have come to arrest him say that they are seeking Jesus of Nazareth, he replies, 'I am,' and they step back and fall to the ground (18:6). The use of the 'I am' formula indicates that Jesus is more than a revealer of God, he is the revelation of God. The seven-fold use suggests that he is the perfect, or complete revelation of God himself.

Yet alongside these seven plus seven 'I am' statements, there are also seven signs in John, seven miraculous and dramatic actions that point to his divine identity and forwards towards the cross. Jesus is committed both to word and action, to statement and sign, to declaration and delivery.

Few people can grasp abstract ideas. Most people think in pictures. We could talk about beauty for long enough and no one would be any the wiser; but, if we can point to a person and say, 'That is a beautiful person,' beauty becomes clear. We could talk about goodness for long enough and fail to arrive at a definition of it; but we all recognize a good deed when we see one. There is a sense in which *every word must become flesh*; every idea must be actualized in a person.[22]

When First Nations communities reflect on God, the idea of word become flesh is front and centre. This is because many indigenous ways of believing are less theoretical and more concrete. Even language in some Aboriginal communities is more physical than metaphysical, says Sylvia Marcos (Mexico): 'Belief and thought enact themselves through corporeality. Without physicality, there is no sustenance and foundational reality for ideas, beliefs, thoughts and especially for reflections on faith.'[23]

For Latin-American liberation theologian Rene Padilla (Ecuador), word becoming flesh gave permission to criticise any theology that was purely rationalistic or intellectual, any words not backed up by flesh:

God's *logos* became a historical person. The knowledge of this *logos* is therefore not merely an intellectual knowledge

22. Barclay, *Mark*, p. 100, italics mine.
23. Marcos, 'Teologia India', p. 273.

of ideas, rather it involves commitment, fellowship, and participation in a new way of life. Gospel truth is always truth to be lived out, not merely truth to be intellectually known.[24]

This idea was the beginning of what became liberation theology, whereby the enfleshedness of the gospel among the poor became a mark of authenticity, while any words that did not become flesh could not be a true reflection of the Word. If the Word is from God, it becomes flesh, that's what God-words do.

Incomprehensible made accessible (or far brought near)

Jesus is portrayed early on in John as the true Temple. In the Jerusalem temple complex, during the busy Passover festivities, he tells the crowd that the temple will be destroyed and then 'in three days I will raise it up'. The narrator then elaborates, 'He was speaking about the temple of his body' (2:21). God meets man in the temple. God can be accessed in the temple. God is worshipped in the temple. God dwells in the temple.

And yet, the physical temple in Jerusalem had limited access. The system of rules and boundaries, implemented by the religious elite in the city, actually excluded a large number of people. Physically disabled people were barred from access – so Jesus heals a crippled man in John 5. He couldn't come to the temple, so the Temple came to him, in the person of Christ. Non-Jews were not allowed to enter, so Jesus goes to meet a Samaritan woman. The blind could not enter, so Jesus goes to a blind man.

Stephen Motyer (England) observes about the crippled man in John 5, sitting in the shadow of the temple, 'and even though the temple is supposed to deal with the sin which had caused his condition, it has done him no good at all. Far from providing an answer, it has excluded him.'[25]

---

24. Padilla, 'Liberation Theology II', p. 15.
25. Motyer, 'Jesus and the Marginalised', p. 81.

Jesus has come to create access to God for the excluded. His mission is to the margins. He goes to those who cannot come. Which, indeed, is the message of the gospel. We cannot come to God, so God comes to us in Christ. Who in your town, in your nation, or across the world is unable to come? Then let's go to them! If they can't get to the gospel, then the gospel needs to get to them.

Universal made specific

Although John has shown us that the gospel is universal, that 'God so loved the world' (John 3:16), it is enacted in the specific, in the local. God is not a first-century Middle Eastern man, but 'in the Incarnation, God contextualized himself'[26] in a specific place at a specific time in history because word must become flesh and flesh must be local.

Most people live, move and have their being in their immediate locale, even though they may be influenced by global factors. What it means to be and to live as a Christian is enacted in the local. Here the concrete finds its manifestation. Just as Jesus of Nazareth lived a specific life in a particular cultural setting, so too most human beings do not live in some supra-cultural reality. The best of the local, then, is about the humanization process, our ways of becoming human.[27]

The dialogues of Jesus with different individuals in John illustrate this. Jesus talks to different individuals in different ways. He responds to their questions, he challenges their assumptions.

26. Padilla, *Mission Between the Times*, p. 83.
27. Schreiter, 'Globalization, Postmodernity and the New Catholicity', p. 26.

He does not have one standard way of 'sharing the gospel'. He listens. He interacts. It is dialogue, not monologue. To Nicodemus, he says, 'You must be born again' (John 3:7 – the only person to whom he is ever recorded saying this). Why? Because everything that Nicodemus had in life – his wealth, his status, his prestige – came to him through his family name. Jesus calls him to renounce everything that accrues to him through his first birth, to renounce his status and influence. To the Samaritan woman, Jesus answers her questions about ethnic identity and exclusion. To Pilate, Jesus talks about the nature of truth. We see him making the Word flesh to different individuals in different ways. This is a powerful example for us to follow.

This tension between the universal and the local is always present in mission. For example, in African Christianity there is ongoing heated debate about the use of wide-ranging languages, like English and French, versus the use of tribal languages, which are more narrow in scope. Some argue that to work across various groups in Africa, you need to use English. Others argue that the important thing is to incarnate and concentrate the gospel into each limited, local, tribal language.[28]

In our world, where postcolonialism is such a powerful reality, driving many of us to value our local and specific identities highly, Jesus' dialogues in John are an important example. He shows us that in talking to different people, different elements of the gospel ought to be emphasised. He shows us that the social location and questions of the Samaritan woman in John 4 are very different from the presenting issues for Nicodemus in John 3, or the blind man in John 9. He shows us that we ought to contextualise the gospel to different people in different ways. And he shows us how.

---

28. Harries, 'The Case Against English in Africa and the Majority World, and its Implication for Christian Mission Today'.

No one ever meets universal Christianity in itself; we only ever meet Christianity in a local form, and that means a historically, culturally conditioned form. We need not fear this; when God became man, He became historically, culturally conditioned man, in a particular time and place. What He became, we need not fear to be. There is nothing wrong with having local forms of Christianity – provided that we remember that they are local.[29]

What Andrew Walls (England), one of the fathers of today's World Christianity movement, is saying here is of utmost importance. There is no Christian Word without flesh. There is no supra-cultural gospel existing in the world of ideas without an earthed, specific presence. And some local expressions of Christianity are not more valid than others. The normal, the intended mode of Christianity is diverse enfleshment in the rich and various cultures of our world. The endless incarnation of Christianity is predicated on the once-for-all incarnation of Christ.

The beloved Archbishop Desmond Tutu (South Africa) writes of his own journey of discovery in this area:

Yes, contextualisation seemed a jargon term but it was basically calling us to take seriously the specificity, the scandal, of the Incarnation. God became a particular human being in a specific context dealing with the perplexities, the challenges and demands of that context. An authentic theology had to be equally specific.[30]

Powerful made vulnerable

As 'Word became flesh', we also see in John that flesh is vulnerable. We see nakedness, weakness, tears, betrayal, pain, wounds,

29. Walls, 'The American Dimension in the History of the Missionary Movement', p. 19.
30. Tutu, *Handbook of Theological Education in World Christianity*, p. xxii.

blood and death. The Word is not presented as indestructible, carved in stone by the hand of God as in Exodus, but rather God's love message to humanity is carved into his hands by the nails. Jesus did not come to shed the blood of his enemies, but to shed his blood *for* his enemies. Flesh by its very nature is soft and it bleeds. It scars. It dies. And Jesus' experience is fully human, is ultimately and paradigmatically human, so his flesh too will weep salt tears, will be stung by the whip, will be pierced by the spear.

Indeed, Word had to become flesh in order to suffer with us and in order to die for us. He needed skin so that the skin could be punctured. He needed blood so that it could pour out of him. He needed lungs so that they could stop breathing. If Word had not become flesh, there could be no sacrifice. For God to sacrifice a concept or a proxy would not have been redemptive. He needed to, was compelled to sacrifice 'his only Son' (3:16), so that the world 'might be saved through him' (3:17). For Kitamori's (Japan) *Theology of the Pain of God*:

Only the pain of God can deny fundamentally every sort of docetism.[31] It is now clear that the concept of the pain of God upholds the significance originally attached to the historical Jesus ... The whole life of Jesus was a way of pain.[32]

Making the Word flesh

John's Gospel will teach us how to go on making the Word flesh. As Christ offered people concrete truth, not merely concepts, so should we. People cannot see God but they can see us. We are his body, his hands and feet. They cannot touch God, or eat with him, or argue with him, but they can with us. And as Jesus went

---

31. Docetism denies the true humanity of Christ.
32. Kitamori, *Pain of God*, pp. 34, 43.

to those who could not come, we can do that too. For those in our world who cannot access the gospel, how can we take the gospel to them? To those in our towns who do not come to church, how can the Church go to them? Gospel witness must be up-close and personal, must be proximate and intimate, must reach to the margins of society. As Christ made the universal specific, and tailored responses to different people and various demographics, how can we incarnate the message into a particular group? How can we devote ourselves to a particular language, or immerse ourselves into a particular culture, all for the sake of the gospel? And as Christ modelled vulnerability and pain, so we too need to offer our cheeks to be slapped and our bodies as living sacrifices. We too risk rejection, criminal charges, scarring, even death.

Donald Senior (USA) argues:

> The Christological focus of the Fourth Gospel is the key to understanding its theology of mission . . . That Christology is universal, even cosmic in scope, not only because the evangelist dealt with a cosmopolitan milieu but because of his conviction about Christ's cosmic significance. The core of John's Christology is the affirmation that Jesus Christ is the unique revealer of God.[33]

Matthew Vellanickal (India) comments:

> For John, evangelization is the process of an ever-renewed incarnation of the Word of which Christ was the perfect expression in a given nation, in a particular place and time, through the sharing of the Christian experience. This is effected in dialogue with other religious experiences of the Word present in the world from the beginning. Hence

---

33. Senior, 'Johannine Theology of Mission', p. 283.

evangelization in John presupposes dialogue with other cultural and religious traditions.[34]

Schnackenburg (Germany) writes, 'All missionary work is in unbroken continuity with the mission of Jesus, and every missionary builds on the labours of his predecessors.'[35]

Likewise, John Stott (England) explains, 'All authentic mission is incarnational mission.'[36]

And Harvey Kwiyani (Malawi) reflects: 'Christianity is translatable enough to withstand being infinitely embedded in the cultures of each of the world's tribes. In fact, Christianity is most authentic and powerful when it is completely contextualized – when it looks and speaks local.'[37]

John Azumah (Ghana) explains that one of the major differences between Islam and Christianity is the Incarnation. Word becoming flesh provides a foundation for the translatability of the gospel, and the possibility of distinct lived experiences of faith in all the cultures of the world, in a way that is the polar opposite of Islam:

In Christianity, the doctrine of the Incarnation provides a theological warrant for translation. By his condescension to humanity and becoming flesh in the person of Jesus, God has demonstrated clearly that the Christian Gospel is not be quarantined in a particular culture or geographical location but translated or inculturated into every language and culture.[38]

As for me, I seek to write not merely as a theorist, but also as someone who is hands-on involved in church planting in various

---

34. Vellanickal, 'Evangelization in the Johannine Writings', p. 168.
35. Schnackenburg, *The Gospel According to St. John*, Volume 1, pp. 454-55.
36. Stott, *The Contemporary Christian*, p. 35.
37. Kwiyani, *Multicultural Kingdom*, p. 150.
38. Azumah, 'Incarnation and Translation in Islam and Christianity', p. 65.

places. To those who ask me to expand on these ideas, I often say, 'Come and see' (a phrase beloved of John, see 1:39, 46; 4:29). Come and see the churches we are planting, which look different in different languages and cultures. We are seeking, always imperfectly, to make the Word flesh in the varied contexts in which we serve. I do hope that the ideas in this book will serve, not just in theory, but in concrete, life-changing, specific, local ways.

'And dwelt among us'

The final phrase for our reflection is this one redolent with the glory of the desert God and his special tent, from the book of Exodus. The word translated *dwelt* is the Greek *eskinoesen*, from the verb *skenoo*, meaning to pitch a tent, and specifically the Old Testament tabernacle. It's not a normal Greek word, but rather one favoured by the Greek translators of the Old Testament – a special, religious word. The Hebrew *miskan* in Exodus 25:9 is taken and manipulated by the translators into *skene*. *Miskan*, the dwelling-place or tent of God, arises from the Hebrew root *s-k-n/ sakan*, which is used for God's dwelling with Israel (Exodus 25:8, 29:46, Zechariah 2:13). From this, eventually, came the word *shekina*, God's indwelling presence. So explains Rabbi Jonathan Sacks (Jewish-English):

> The verb 'to dwell' had never before been used in relation to God. The root sh-kh-n means a neighbour, someone who lives next door. God was about to become not just the force that moves the stars and changes the course of history, but also one who is close, a neighbour. It was from this root that the rabbis coined their name for the divine indwelling, God's presence that was always with the Jewish people, even in exile. They called it the Shekina.[39]

---

39. Sacks, *Leviticus*, pp. 11-12.

When John joins these ideas together in 1:14, we read 'and the Word became flesh and dwelt among us, and we have seen his glory'. The eternal Word pitching his tent among us, therefore, carries both a tone of neighbourliness, everyday proximity, a co-camper, but also hints of glory, the *shekina* presence of God, the special and particular divine indwelling in his own sacred sanctuary among the chosen people of God. Both are true of Christ. He chose to live in a tent of human flesh with its implied temporality, and one day our own mortal frames will be folded up and moved on to our permanent home. For now, this life is a desert pilgrimage, insubstantial, without foundations or walls of stone, and Christ enters in and journeys with us as Neighbour. And yet, there is a glory, a weight, a presence, a holiness that he bears and into which we too may enter. And so with mission. We pitch our tents among those we seek to reach, we are neighbours who live lightly, who are aware of the insubstantiality and finiteness of our frame, we are up-close and personal, with a visible, lived-out ordinary witness amongst those with whom we are camping. And yet, there is a glory with us, a weight to us, a light upon us. There is something different about our tents. There is an outshining of God through our lives. There is a treasure in our 'jars of clay' (2 Corinthians 4:7).

Chapter Two

Fig

(John 1:48)

By the fig and by the olive. And by Mount Sinai.

(Qur'an 95:1)

Nathanael sat in the deep shade of the ancient fig tree on a drowsy afternoon. Insects buzzed soothingly, contently even, in the thick air, air sweetened by the sugars of fallen fruit in various states of decomposition. Although there was not even a whisper of breeze, the fig's giant, flat leaves trembled preternaturally, as if shivering in the presence of the divine. And Nathanael, as earthily and unpretentiously religious as most people on the planet, had a sense that he was seen, that he was observed, that he was known. The hairs on the back of his neck stood up. The air around him became close. He could not articulate precisely the nature of the encounter, but it was real, and it stayed with him.

This story could have happened anywhere. Fig trees don't just carry symbolic meaning in the Jewish tradition, but around the globe. Fig trees, and their close relatives, are considered spiritual, are celebrated and revered in countless cultural traditions. There is no tree as globally sacred as the fig tree. Ever since Eden, where its leaves provided a covering for our first parents, the fig, across its 750 species, has maintained a unique place in the religious imagination. That's why this story, of Nathanael sitting under the fig tree, carries universal resonance.

Biologists call fig a 'primary source'. They sustain more biodiversity than other trees. They have always been foundational to whichever ecosystem they support.[40]

In Maasai tradition, God sent the first cattle to earth via the fig tree. One Indonesian origin story has the first parents carved from fig wood. Herodotus mentions that fig culture is as ancient as human culture. Fig is mentioned in 5,000-year-old Sumerian sources. Ancient Egyptian monks were fed on figs when they started their training. Vishnu, the Hindu god of gods, is depicted as a fig tree. Romulus and Remus were sheltered under a fig tree while suckled by the she-wolf. That secretive sect, the Druze, kiss the bark of the fig seeking blessing. The Bedouin settle their disagreements in fig-shade. Kikuyu women daub themselves in fig-sap when they want to get pregnant. Beneath the Banyan, a species of fig, Buddha found enlightenment, and to this day Buddhists plant Banyan trees near their temples. Mohammad said the fig was the one tree he wished to see in paradise, and there is a Sura in the Qu'ran named *Sura at-Tin* (The Fig). Christians have a long tradition of eating figs at Christmas – in the UK to this day 'figgy pudding' is eaten.

Sitting under the fig tree, then, is a universal picture of humankind's search for meaning. Readers in John's world from any background would have felt a deep connection with this story. This story is a signpost to all the cultures of the world.

Later, when Nathanael meets Jesus, the Saviour tells him, 'Before Philip called you, when you were under the fig tree, I saw you' (John 1:48). This statement by Christ becomes a powerful bridge into many traditions. Your spiritual experience, which you cannot define, I now explain to you. You felt seen? It was me who saw you. Your search for meaning has led you to me, Jesus tells him.

---

40. Shanahan, 'Tree of life: How figs built the world and will help save it'.

Instead of rubbishing or discounting previous superstitions as empty, or false, or demonic, Jesus affirms their authenticity, while simultaneously calling out their inadequacy. And so with the billions on our planet who apply to the fig tree, or its local equivalent, for blessing or meaning or power. Jesus sees them. And we Philips need to call them to come and meet him who can explain their search.

Is this what John meant when he wrote down these words? I believe it was. John could well have known about Buddha. It is well-documented that Palestine had interaction with India before John's time, through the networks the Persian Empire created. This picture of Nathanael sitting under the fig tree is so profoundly close to the soul of Buddhism, to Buddha receiving enlightenment under the Bodhi tree, and there is no reason why John could not have had this in his mind as he wrote. Either way, we must not underestimate the pluralistic context of the ancient Near East. Superstition, and in particular the approach to trees as centres of folk spirituality, is as old as humanity itself, and was certainly observable by John. Fig trees were endued with symbolic meaning, both within and without the Jewish tradition. Yes, 'when you were under the fig tree' speaks to Nathanael's earnest Judaism. Fig leaves have provided shelter and covering in the Abrahamic faiths as far back as Eden, when Adam and Eve sewed themselves coverings from fig leaves. Something deep in the human psyche, worked out through our worldwide family, still sees the fig as a refuge, a place of sanctuary, a connection back to our innocence lost. Yes, it speaks to Nathanael's Judaism, but also to something predating Judaism, something ancient and inescapable in our collective human memory. And so Jesus' words to Nathanael resonate across ages and continents as words to all truth-seekers, 'before ... while you were ... I saw you.'

This is important. Western readers of John, who may not have a particularly pluralistic day-to-day experience, do not think about John's multi-religious milieu. Indian Christian scholars, for whom competing religious claims are the air and water in which they live, help us to see that John was indeed wrestling with how to present Jesus, not just as Jewish Messiah, but as Saviour of the whole world. 'It is beyond a doubt that John's Gospel bears the stamp of an intercultural milieu', writes Chacko (India).[41] Palestine had been colonised multiple times, each empire leaving a footprint. First-century Jews like John were trilingual (Hebrew, Aramaic and Greek) and Latin was also prevalent. Evidence of cultural exchange eastwards into Asia seems to indicate that India and Judea had contact at least from the ninth century BCE, or even earlier.[42] In fact, then, John could easily have known about Buddha, and the similarities between Nathanael and Buddha could be more than coincidental.

'Nathanael, as a person who sits under the fig tree and is enlightened to recognize Jesus as the "Son of God" and the "King of Israel," resembles in many ways Buddha, who sat under the Bodhi tree in Bodh Gaya and was enlightened',[43] writes Thomaskutty (India). John certainly would have been aware of neighbouring Egypt's long history of reverence for the sycamore fig, another closely related fig species. The sycamore-fig, closely connected to the sacred city of Memphis, was regarded as a manifestation of the goddesses Nut, Isis and Hathor, who was even given the title 'Lady of the Sycamore-Fig'.[44] Some of the earliest Egyptian coffins were made from sycamore-fig wood, and these trees were planted in funerary gardens. In the *Book of the Dead* it is the tree that is called 'the tree of life'.[45]

John is portraying Jesus as having open arms to those from any tradition who have sought God, and to do so he chooses an

41. Chacko, *Intercultural Christology*, p. 135.
42. Matthew, 'Early Contacts', p. 158.
43. Thomaskutty, 'The Gospel of John', p. 149.
44. Azzazy and Ezzat, 'The Sycamore in Ancient Egypt', p. 209.
45. Evans, *God's Trees*, p. 37.

internationally prevalent symbol of humankind's search, the fig tree. It might be the equivalent today of Jesus saying, 'Before Philip called you, when you were Googling the meaning of life, I saw you.' This is not universalism. John is not approving fig-tree spirituality as adequate, or as able to save. He is not saying that all religions lead to God. But he is affirming the authenticity of the search, and even of the spiritual experiences one might have on the way. And yet, the role of Philips is essential, inviting Nathanaels to come and meet the One in whom all searches find their object.

Philip, for John, is an evangelist. Here, he witnesses to Nathanael. Later, some Greeks approach Philip for an introduction to Jesus (John 12:21). Philip, in John 1, has just been called by Jesus. The first thing he does is to find Nathanael under his fig tree and share the good news. He does not disrespect Nathanael. He does not rubbish or hate or mock. He does not argue or disprove. But he is persuaded that Jesus is the answer to all questions, that any spirituality is inadequate unless it leads to Christ, and that any journey starting under the fig tree must end under Calvary's tree. Philip the sharer invited Nathanael the seeker to meet Jesus the Saviour.

All searches find their goal in Jesus. Buddhism is a search for enlightenment: Jesus says, 'I am the light of the world' (John 8:12). Islam is a search for purity: Jesus is the Lamb of God who takes away the sins of the world. Chinese religions search for wisdom: Jesus is the Word made flesh. Folk religions search for power: Jesus rose from the dead, defeating the devil and his angels.

As Philips, we too turn to those who are sitting under the fig trees of the world, respectful of their searches, their spirituality, their longings. And we introduce them to Jesus, in whom all fears are stilled, all thirsts are quenched, and all tears wiped away.

Chapter Three

Wine

(John 2:1-11)

The Guest is God.

(Indian proverb)

In cultures with a high regard for hospitality, failure to provide is unforgivable. One goes into debt, draws on all one's connections and relationships, bankrupts oneself and one's family, rather than be considered stingy. Stinginess is *the* great shame, the end of the road socially. Even today, Middle Eastern TV shows often feature a stingy character, one who reneges on his obligations to his family and his community, a Scrooge, the darkest of villains.

In the Bible, godliness is often expressed as generosity, as fulfilment of social responsibilities, and failure in hospitality is always condemned.

One of the Old Testament expressions of this distinction is the contrast between the good eye (of a generous person) and the evil eye (of a stingy person). The eye is the window of the soul, and generosity reflects faith in the bounty of God. Hospitality is an act of faith – if I put others first, as I should, then God will provide. Should I run out, God will meet the need.

Elijah's demand on the widow of Zarephath's hospitality, one of the most vulnerable in society during a time of severe famine, came down to her faith in God, and was met with supernatural reward: 'The jar of flour was not spent, neither did the jug of oil become empty, according to the word of the LORD that he spoke by Elijah' (1 Kings 17:16).

Aquaro (USA) puts it like this: 'Hospitality, described as a "good eye," is the ultimate sign that one believes in the Unlimited Good of God. As a rule, those who are faithful to Yahweh are generous towards others, knowing that God will always provide enough good if they follow the Law.'[46] So Proverbs 22:9 is an example of this language:

> Whoever has a bountiful eye [a good eye] will be blessed,
> for he shares his bread with the poor.
>
> *(Proverbs 22:9)*

Evil eye belief is a large and complex area, but certainly one of the Old Testament uses of 'evil eye' language is in contrast to generosity – stinginess. Evil eye language is prevalent in the Old Testament, although it is often obscured by translation into English – which is understandable, since the evil eye does not mean much to most English readers. Consider these verses, for example:

> Do not eat the bread of a man who is stingy [has an evil eye];
> do not desire his delicacies
>
> *(Proverbs 23:6)*

> Take care lest there be an unworthy thought in your heart and you say, 'The seventh year, the year of release is near', and your eye look grudgingly [your eye be evil against] on your poor brother, and you give him nothing, and he cry to the LORD against you, and you be guilty of sin.
>
> *(Deuteronomy 15:9)*

---

46. Aquaro, *Death by Envy*, p. 29.

The bridegroom in John 2 who fails to provide sufficient wine for the week-long wedding celebrations is not someone to be pitied. He does not care about his family or his village. He is prepared to bring shame upon his community. He epitomises everything that is worst about humanity. He has an evil eye.

I don't think I am overstating this. Where hospitality and honour are intrinsically linked to godliness, 'My guest is the guest of God', as the culturally ubiquitous proverb from the Balkans through to India puts it, and failure in hospitality is a failure in service to God himself. It is to default on one's honour. Rihbany (Syria) writes of Middle Eastern hospitality: 'The person who fails to extend such hospitality brings reproach, not only upon himself, but upon his own clan and town.'[47] Abram in Genesis 18 showed perfect hospitality to strangers, contrasted with Sodom in Genesis 19, a city which treated strangers with contempt, showing not just neglect, but active anti-hospitality.

Maori missiologist Jay Matenga contrasts Industrial and Indigenous ways of life, where Industrial is shorthand for Global North individualist culture, and Indigenous means First Nations, communalist, Global South ways of being. He describes a web of values sustaining Indigenous life, which includes the values being threatened in this story, of responsibility, hospitality and generosity.

Peace, harmony, reconciliation, consensus, honour, submission to the collective are all part of the same core motivator in Indigenous worlds. Each people have their own words for it. For Maori it is kotahitanga (integrated unity), which is attained via a whole range of value commitments like aroha (loving kindness), manaakitanga (honouring others through generosity, hospitality, nurture etc.) and awhi (to embrace, include, support, cherish), among many others.[48]

---

47. Rihbany, The Syrian Christ, p. 146.
48. Matenga, The Emancipation of Indigenous Theologies in Light of the Rise of World Christianity, p. 4.

Throughout John, the extravagance associated with Jesus is an important theme, often contrasted with the stinginess of man. There are several examples of this, the Cana wedding being the first.

In 2:6, the abundance of Jesus' wine (six times two or three *metritas*),[49] contrasted with the stinginess of the bridegroom, who failed to provide.

In 6:7, the feeding of the 5,000, worth 200 *denarii* according to Philip's calculations.

In 12:5, Mary's pound of expensive ointment, which Judas, who was a thief, valued at 300 *denarii*.

In 19:39, Nicodemus brings 100 *litras* of spices, obscenely expensive.

In 21:11, there is a net full of large fish, 153 of them.

In 21:25, John suggests that if everything Jesus did were written down, 'the world itself could not contain' all the books written.

In all of these instances, human attempts to measure or budget or calculate are superseded by lavish divine superabundance.

Phanxicô Xaviê Văn Thuận Nguyễn (Vietnam) was a Catholic priest imprisoned for many years after the Communist takeover of South Vietnam in 1974. After his release he was made a cardinal and worked closely with John Paul II. In his wonderful book *Testimony of Hope* he starts off by saying that what he loves most about God are God's faults, chief among which is his 'ludicrous over-generosity'. His experience in prison was that his meagre rations were a sign of the gracious hospitality of God. He cites the wedding in Cana story as an example of God's unnecessary superabundance – the lavish, overflowing benefaction of God in Christ.[50]

This wedding, in the wine-growing region of Galilee, is a community affair. It is a chance for this village to show off

---

49. One measure *(metritis)* was equal to eight or nine imperial gallons. The six pots together held between 100 and 150 gallons, which is between 500 and 750 litres.
50. Nguyễn, *Testimony of Hope*.

its generosity, and particularly this year's vintage of wine, to the surrounding villages. It is a chance for prestige, not as an optional extra but as a duty. The hospitality failure brewing here is utterly scandalous. The village will lose face. The family will suffer profound loss. There is even some evidence that to run out of supplies at a wedding could lay the groom open to a lawsuit from the aggrieved relatives of the bride.[51] Marriage, after all, is business, a contract between two families. Shame, remember, is not an emotion but a demotion. It will impact the family's standing for generations; no one will do business with them, no one will marry their daughters. Pariah status is looming. And all because the bridegroom is bad. He does not care about his civic duty. He does not care about his family's honour. He is potentially sentencing his family to generations of untouchability. He is like Nabal, the arrogant fool, who failed to give hospitality to David's men.

And in the deepest of ironies, among the wedding guests to whom he fails to show respect, God is actually present, in Jesus. His insult to his guests is directly a sin against God, because God is among the guests. If he is a son of Nabal, the son of David with his followers has shown up expecting to be victualled. 1 Samuel 25 is being re-lived.

Do not neglect to show hospitality to strangers, for thereby some have entertained angels unawares.

(Hebrews 13:2)

At this wedding, the neglect is not just of angels, but of God himself, present in Christ.

The Bible's hallowing of hospitality speaks to our welcome of the stranger, our treatment of refugees, our care for the poor, our generosity. All of these are an extension of divine hospitality.

---

51. Carson, *John*, p. 169.

God is the Great Host, and the bounty of all creation is a sign of his abundant generosity. Whenever we are hosting, we represent God. Hospitality is sacred.

Into this context, the context of a looming tragedy, Jesus implements his first sign. Sometimes readers, not understanding what is at stake, see this sign as merely cosmetic, rather than the gracious saving of an undeserving, evil-eyed fool from a monstrous mess of his own making. This first sign is many things, one of which is Jesus intervening to save the whole wedding. This story is our story. We all, like this bridegroom, are selfish, steeped in dishonour, neglectful of our responsibilities. And Jesus, the very guest whom we have insulted, steps in to become a perfect host who takes responsibility, delivers us and redeems the whole situation.

Shame-removal

The bridegroom, then, when he is summoned by the master of the feast, takes the credit for what Jesus has done. Instead of condemnation, he receives congratulation. Instead of embarrassment, he receives aggrandisement. His story is our story. The good eye of Jesus looks into the evil eye of stingy, faithless humankind, and his lavish grace overcomes our failure. He turns our water into wine. He transforms dishonour into honour. Rather than this wedding becoming notorious as the wedding at which the wine ran out, it will be long famous as the wedding at which the good wine was saved until last.

John will repeatedly return to this theme of Jesus rescuing people from dishonour. 'Jesus turns water into wine at a wedding to solve a family's pressing problem in an honor-and-shame sociocultural context and to launch his public ministry' concludes Thomaskutty (India).[52]

---

52. Thomaskutty, 'The Gospel of John', p. 146.

Symbolism

John loves sixes and sevens. Seven is God's number, that of perfection, of rest, the number of the sacred. Six is man's number. We were created on the sixth day of the week (maybe that's why we love Fridays so much!). Six is the 'nearly, but not quite'. Never quite good enough. As hard as we try, we just can't make it to seven. It's the number of frustration, exhaustion, disappointment. Jesus will die on behalf of humankind on the sixth hour of the sixth day – representing humankind. This first sign is the first of seven signs in this gospel. Its firstness must be important to the picture that John is painting of Jesus. Here are some aspects to the story that show us its importance.

There are six stone water jars for the Jewish rites of purification (2:6). Ceremonial washing is part of every major religion, from the ablutions before prayer in Islam to the 120 million Hindus who bathe annually in the sacred Ganges river. In Judaism, ritual washing was extremely important. One rabbi imprisoned by the Romans chose to use his daily ration of water for washing rather than drinking, nearly dying of thirst as a result. The water jars are stone rather than clay because stone does not affect the purity of the water. So these jars symbolise the Old Covenant, a religion of washings and externals. And they are six in number, symbolising the human effort and energy involved in such ritual. The jars are filled 'to the brim' (2:7), reflecting the fact that the time of the Old Covenant is complete.

The water represents the old order of Jewish law and custom, which Jesus was to replace with something better ... the sheer quantity of water turned into wine then becomes symbolic of the lavish provision of the new age ... filling jars with such large capacity to the brim then indicates that the time for ceremonial purification is completely fulfilled.[53]

53. Carson, *John*, pp. 173-74.

Jesus will transform water for washing into wine for drinking. Not only does his generosity supersede the bridegroom's stinginess, but as wine is superior to water, so is the New Covenant superior to the old. As drinking is superior to washing, so is the New Covenant superior to the old. Water for washing has an external effect, whereas wine for drinking is efficacious on the inside. Washing is about lifestyle, while drinking is about life.

The prophets consistently connected wine to the Messianic age (see Jeremiah 31:12; Hosea 14:7; Amos 9:13-14). Most famously, Isaiah prophesied that the Messianic feast would be characterised by 'well-aged wine . . . well refined' (Isaiah 25:6). When Messiah comes, we will drink wine – and now Messiah is here! The Isaianic oracle continues, declaring 'and the Lord . . . will wipe away tears from all faces, and the reproach of his people he will take away' (Isaiah 25:8). The bridegroom of Cana has his tears wiped away, and his reproach (a powerful shame-word) removed by the miraculous intervention of Jesus.

Jesus will speak of wine. Most famously, 'This [wine] is the new covenant in my blood. Do this . . . in remembrance of me' (1 Corinthians 11:25). Do what? Drink!

More symbolism

All of this happens, in the way John crafts the narrative, on the seventh day. John's Gospel twice slows down to relate a full week, once at the beginning and once at the end of the book. There are seven days between 1:28 and 2:1, and then seven days between 12:1 and 20:1. The first week, and the last week.

The first week is clued in in 1:29, 'the next day'; 1:35, 'the next day'; 1:39 is day four (it was 'the tenth hour' – Jewish days were reckoned from sunset); 1:43 'the next day'; and then 2:1, 'On the third day' which, by inclusive reckoning, gets us to day seven.

John's Gospel relates a full week in chapter 1 – telling us what happens every day, and later a full week in Jesus' final week leading up to the cross. John's story starts with a full week – a new creation, a new Genesis. What Matthew had communicated by saying, 'the *genesis* of Jesus Christ' (see Matthew 1:18), John reinforces by signifying new creation. There is so much Genesis 1 language in John 1, light in darkness, the hovering Spirit, and the counting of seven days. There is energy, joy and newness. Jesus has come to create a new world.

Within this first week, between 1:29 and 51, John introduces a series of seven titles for Christ: Lamb of God, Chosen One of God,[54] Rabbi, Messiah, Son of God, King of Israel and Son of Man.

By stark contrast, John also slows down to relate the final week of Jesus Christ, leading up to his death. This week is full of darkness and night-time, of enemies and betrayal. This is a week of de-creation, a great unravelling. The gathered disciples are scattered now. Friends become enemies. Where Jesus had called Simon Peter with 'follow me' (Matthew 4:19) he now announces, 'Where I am going, you cannot follow me now, but you will follow afterwards' (13:36). Darkness reigns instead of light. There is a long night from chapters 13 to 18. John crafts an incredible parallelism between these two weeks. The first week began in Bethany-beyond-Jordan. The last week begins in another Bethany (12:1). The first week climaxes with the first sign (water into wine). The final week climaxes with the seventh and greatest sign (the resurrection of Jesus from the dead). In 2:4 Jesus declares, 'My hour has not yet come,' while in 13:1 and 17:1, he announces that his hour has indeed come. The first 'Son of Man' saying is in 1:51, and the final 'Son of Man' saying, in 13:31. In the first week Jesus is introduced as 'the Lamb of God,

---

54. A variant reading of 1:34, based on the LXX of Isaiah 42:1, which many scholars judge as original.

who takes away the sin of the world' (1:29). In the final week, the Lamb is sacrificed.

And on the seventh day of the first week, Jesus provides the best wine for men to drink, while at the final moment of the last week, men provide cheap, 'sour wine' for Jesus to drink (19:29). He gave us his best. We gave him our worst.

The whole of discipleship seems to take place between these two realities – the new has begun but the old is still being dismantled. One would normally say 'out with the old, then in with the new'. But John seems to craft his Gospel the other way around; in with the new, then eventually out with the old.

And then, on the eighth day of the final week, new creation. But not yet.

Gathering all of this together, we understand that at the wedding, Jesus is announcing through this sign that Day Seven has come. That God has come. That the things that belong to Day Six, the striving of the Old Covenant, are replaced by the advent of Rest. That Messiah, who inaugurates the season of celebration, of wiping away tears and shame-removal, who brings wine for drinking . . . Messiah has come. The Messianic age has begun.

When Jesus says to his mother, 'My hour has not yet come' (2:4), he is signalling the cross. 'My hour' is a phrase which consistently points to his death on the cross (7:30; 8:20; 12:23; 12:27; 13:1; 17:1). At this wedding, Jesus is actually thinking of his own wedding, the great and final wedding feast of the Lamb. As we will see later, John is suffused with bridegroom imagery, so it is appropriate for the first sign to take place at a wedding. Jesus is looking forward to his own wedding, when the glorious hospitality of God will be shown to all nations, and this bridegroom, the perfection of generosity, will never run out of wine.

'A wedding is a burst of joy, a celebration of the beginning of a new family, with new naming and the anticipation of new life. It resonates across cultures and generations.'[55] In other words, we see newness, family, celebration, abundance – all naturally and ordinarily evident at weddings, here infused with new meaning through Christ – the ideal context for a first sign. In addition, there is an intercultural element, as all cultures celebrate weddings. All communities experience, to some extent, the pressures of hospitality and provision for celebration at weddings, and this sign speaks to the destination of the gospel in all cultures. This story has power anywhere on the planet.

Even more symbolism

Reflecting a little further (and we remember that John had decades to reflect before he crafted his exquisite book), Jesus, who will later declare, 'I am the true vine' (15:1), will here offer wine to specific people in a specific moment. The Word made flesh, the Conceptual made concrete, the Cosmic made local. Grapes are harvested and crushed underfoot in order that wine might flow. And the life of Christ was harvested, plucked in its prime, and he was crushed in the winepress of God's wrath, pressed underfoot in order that the wine of his blood might flow (Revelation 14:19-20). Only John, among the four Gospels, does not have a specific scene detailing the sacrament of the Lord's Supper, but John's imagery of grapes and wine and blood, of drinking and generosity, make the same points in a different way.

We must not miss the violence involved in the manufacture of both bread and wine, the elements of the Eucharist. For bread to be made, the wheat is ground into flour, then repurposed into bread. For wine to be made, the grapes are crushed, and then repurposed into wine. In John's Gospel, Jesus will refer to himself both as 'the true vine' (15:1), and as 'a grain of wheat'

---

55. Ford, *John*, p. 67.

(12:24). In both cases, a crushing (death) and then a repurposing (resurrection) must occur to offer people bread to eat and wine to drink. Jesus, in this same Gospel, miraculously offers bread to the hungry, and miraculously provides wine at a wedding. The sacrament is not just explained in John, it is lived out.

And when we get to chapter 19, we see Jesus' side being pierced and the blood pouring out of him like wine from a barrel. He truly is the Bridegroom, the self-sacrificial host who provides for his guests at great cost to himself, the One who has truly saved the best wine until last.

Chapter Four

Margins
(John Chapters 3 to 9)

The most terrible poverty is loneliness …
(Mother Teresa)

John brings laser focus, especially in chapters 3 to 9, to Jesus' mission to the marginalised. What is clear in these chapters is more than a movement towards those who, because of their illness, disability, ethnicity, gender or perceived impurity, are outside of the reach of the temple system. There is also a rebuke of the very temple which is the cause of their marginalisation, as well as of those who perpetuate this system with its structural injustice. We will here see quite clearly both sides of the justice of God, the resisting of the proud and the embrace of the humble. Those who are too big are made a little smaller, and those who are too small are made bigger. It is both, it needs to be both. Otherwise the problems persist.

In these days of power-sensitivity, there has never been a greater need to understand not only *that* Jesus does this, but *how* he does it. Going to those who cannot come is an essential dynamic of the mission of God, and indeed of the gospel, but a radical overhaul of insiderness and outsiderness is also needed, or those from the margins will never find inclusion on the same footing of grace as those from the centre. Harper (African-

American) writes, 'If one's gospel falls mute when facing people who need good news the most – the impoverished, the oppressed, and the broken – then it's no gospel at all.'[56]

Jesus as the new Temple

In ancient Jerusalem, this inequality was never more clearly evident than in the accessibility of the Temple, a horizontal dynamic of proximity and exclusion of which John makes much. In 2:18-21, Jesus prophesies both the destruction of the old and its replacement by something very different in *himself*.

> So the Jews said to him, 'What sign do you show us for doing these things?' Jesus answered them, 'Destroy this temple, and in three days I will raise it up.' The Jews then said, 'It has taken forty-six years to build this temple, and will you raise it up in three days?' But he was speaking about the temple of his body.'

John writes and publishes after the destruction of the Jerusalem temple in AD 70, when the Romans had left not one stone upon another, when Herod's temple is no more. Jesus is heard to prophesy this very destruction, and to speak of its replacement – his own person, his own body. As we saw with 'dwelt among us' in 1:14, God has come to dwell among his people, not in a building of stone but in the flesh of Christ. Not in Jerusalem with its restrictions and rules, but in One who will go into the backstreets, who will go to Samaria. Jesus goes where the temple could never go. Instead of stark monologue he will engage in dialogue. Instead of otherising constraints, 'no Gentiles, no women, no cripples', he will go to those very people, he will heal and ennoble them, love and include them.

---

56. Harper, *The Very Good Gospel*, Kindle location 342.

And when in 4:21-24 he tells the Samaritan woman, 'Neither on this mountain nor in Jerusalem will you worship the Father . . . the Father is seeking [worshippers] . . . those who worship him must worship in spirit', he is announcing a new system, one that is no longer centred on Jerusalem, one that renders all places and all flesh equally sacred in Christ, where one geography does not trump another, where Jewish flesh is not more holy than Samaritan flesh, where men are not closer to God than women. This New Covenant ought to eradicate all the preferences of the old.

While mainstream theology has always held this interpretation – that Jesus becomes the new religious centre – American separation of Church and State and extreme individualism has de-politicised the temple institution, often making it only about spirituality. However, the Jerusalem temple and priestly apparatus were also economic and political entities and, in traditional societies like first-century Palestine, these realities could not be disentangled from one another.

> Insofar as tithes and offerings were paid to the Temple and priesthood, the latter were also economic institutions; indeed they stood at the centre of the economy of ancient Palestine. Insofar as the high priests were responsible for collecting the tribute to Rome, they were also politically central to the whole political economy of the Roman province of Judah.[57]

It's important to understand this. Jesus is not only transforming the way religion works, he has come to radically overhaul the way everything works. Christ as the new Temple has implications for economics and politics. A new kingdom, based not on merit but on

---

57. Horsley, *Jesus and Empire*, p. 10.

grace to the underserving will be one that champions weakness over strength, humility over pride, devotion over ability. Holiness will not be at its most holy in a sanctuary, shut away from people, but in the margins meeting human need. Knowledge of God will not be at its purest looking down from the Temple Mount onto the city below, but on the streets, among the great unwashed, Word made flesh. Jesus is changing all things.

Nicodemus vs the Samaritan woman

By means of a stark contrast between an insider and an outsider, placed next to each other in juxtaposition, John portrays this new reality. Nicodemus is male, the Samaritan woman is female – in the ancient world, a significant difference. He is an insider to holy Jerusalem, she is in despised Samaria. He is named, she is not named. He is extremely wealthy, she is far from rich. He is part of the ruling party, the elite, a Pharisee. Culturally, he is 'righteous'. She is the opposite of all of those things. And yet, despite all his advantages, Nicodemus is rebuked by Jesus for lack of understanding, while the woman is praised by Jesus for her faith. She very quickly believes and makes her witness public, while Nicodemus takes until the death of Christ at the end of John to publicly demonstrate faith. Here, then, in these two stories in chapters 3 and 4, we see a microcosm of the mission of Jesus. We see the hardness of the centre and the openness of the margins. We see a rebuke to all existing systems of privilege whereby this insider man would be preferred to this foreign woman. We see Jesus making a new world, where structural injustice is exposed to prophetic critique and found wanting. We see the coming of the kingdom of God.

The official's child

Geography in John, and particularly proximity to Jerusalem in Judea, is important, theologically freighted. This is nowhere clearer than in the healing of the official's son in 4:46-54. This account is bookended by the repeated phrase, 'Jesus had come out of [*ek tis*] Judea and into (*his tin*) Galilee.'[58] In fact, verse 54, which declares this healing to be 'the second sign that Jesus did', couches the importance of this sign in the horizontal movement of Jesus. Healing, a prerogative of the temple, is delivered to this child. He could not come to the temple, so the Temple came to him. John's seven signs start in the margins and get closer to Jerusalem as we move towards the climax.

Is the official a Gentile? Certainly, the parallel stories in Matthew 8:5-13 and Luke 7:1-10 are about a pagan Gentile military officer. Whether or not John's official is Gentile, he works for Herod Antipas, who collaborated closely with the Romans. Such collaborators were the targets of disdain, shunning, and often outright hatred. The power of the story is the distance, geographically and religiously, from the temple-centre. The account, like the wedding at Cana, emphasises the power of Jesus' word: 'The man believed the *word* that Jesus spoke to him' (John 4:50, italics mine), reminding us that Jesus is the creative Word, and that his word is authoritative and powerful as the Word of God.

The disabled man

Jesus' next encounter in the margins is with the disabled man in John 5. He has been lying in the shadow of the temple for thirty-eight years. He watches the joyful throng going up to worship, yet because of his disability he is forbidden from joining them. For

---

58. My translation.

pretty much his whole life, and certainly for as long as Herod's new temple has been being built, the very edifice supposedly representing the presence of God to him signifies the absence of God.

He is by the Sheep Gate, to the north of the temple complex, sitting by the pool where the shepherds, bringing their lambs up for sale, would wash them before selling them to pilgrims to be sacrificed in the temple courts. That's where the Lamb finds him. In a horrifying verse, we read that there are a multitude of sick bodies – 'blind, lame and paralysed' (v. 3) – lying around the pool in some macabre parody of today's photographs of the wealthy with their beautiful bodies lying around swimming pools in Los Angeles or Monaco. These discarded bodies and lives are piled up in the northern shadow of the tall walls of the temple where the sun never reaches, but now the Son has reached them.

> Jesus said to him, 'Get up, take up your bed, and walk.' And at once the man was healed, and he took up his bed and walked. Now that day was the Sabbath. So the Jews said to the man who had been healed, 'It is the Sabbath, and it is not lawful for you to take up your bed.'
>
> *(John 5:8-10)*

The very moment he is healed, he is rebuked for carrying his bedroll on the Sabbath. The very instant the reason for his exclusion is removed, insiders find another reason to marginalise him. The status quo, it seems, is determined not to admit him into its circle. This is the story of so many on the margins. Jesus tells him to get up, pick up his mat and walk. He does what the words of the Word instructed. And then he is told that the very thing he has done is unlawful. The Christian scene is littered with people who have heard Jesus tell them to do something – and their obedience was also their healing – who are subsequently excluded as unlawful. Consider women who have felt Jesus speak to them about leadership, only to be told that women should not lead, or people of colour in white-led spaces who have felt Jesus speak to them about certain initiatives, only to be rebuked as unlawful and told there is no place for them within their organisation or church.

Karen Kchatryan (Armenia) explains the number thirty-eight in this story thus:

The Mishna had 38 streams of works you can't do on the Sabbath. Thirty-eight! How long had the man been excluded from the temple? 38 years. John is showing us that the sign here is the breaking of exclusive religious tradition. The triumph of inclusion![59]

In all the explanations of the thirty-eight years I have come across, this is the most compelling to me. Although the Mishna was not collated as a written source for another 200 years, it represented oral traditions that were already in place. Healing of a chronic condition on the Sabbath was forbidden, on the grounds that treatment could just as easily take place before or after the Sabbath (*b. Yoma 84b*).[60]

In the big story of the world, humankind cannot come to God, so God comes to us in Jesus Christ. And in this man's story, we see this same reality.

---

59. Karen Kchatryan, unpublished sermon, Islamic World School of Leadership, 2017.
60. Reinhartz, 'The Gospel According to John', p. 168. Reinhartz writes more generally that such parallels between John's Gospel and Rabbinic literature, 'do not reveal any dependence or direct knowledge of rabbinic texts, all of which were dated to a period of at least two centuries after the completion of the Gospel. For this reason, John's similarities to some rabbinic traditions and his use of similar exegetical methods do not demonstrate dependence but rather help to establish the existence in the first century of beliefs, practices or methods that may otherwise be known only from much later Jewish texts ... *the similarities reflect ideas that were "in the air"*,' p. 155, italics mine.

And this was why the Jews were persecuting Jesus, because he was doing these things on the Sabbath. But Jesus answered them, 'My Father is working until now, and I am working.' This was why the Jews were seeking all the more to kill him, because not only was he breaking the Sabbath, but he was even calling God his own Father, making himself equal with God.

(John 5:16-18)

Some people say Jesus never claimed to be God. Or that the Gospel writers never claimed that Jesus was God. But John is very clear here.

No one was allowed to work on the Sabbath. But the Jews understood that there was one exception. Babies are born on the Sabbath. The sun rises and sets on the Sabbath. Crops continue to grow on the Sabbath. So who is making all these things happen? God! God is exempt.[61] By Jesus working on the Sabbath, he is making a claim – I am exempt! Why? Because I am God! That's what Jesus says in verse 17. That's what the Judaian elite understand in verse 18.

Women

In John's Gospel, the other clearly marginal group to whom Jesus is determined to relate is women. Women in John are so much more than one of the most vulnerable groups in society who need the protection and mercy of Christ. Yes, they are a cypher for the most marginal in John's world. But also, women in John are the strong, who despite their disadvantageous social location have much to bring to the new world that Jesus is building, oftentimes in the context of rebuke to the men.

---

61. Philo of Alexandria *(Cher. 86-890; Leg. All. 1.5-6)*.

In chapter 8 it is a woman who is dragged before Jesus accused of adultery (where is the man with whom the adultery took place?) by religiously elite men. At the cross, four named female disciples are present, juxtaposed with four unnamed male soldiers (and where are the male disciples?) (19:23-25). At the tomb, it is Mary who stands watching and waiting in the early morning, who is the first to see the risen Lord, who is apostle to the apostles. Where are the men?

Thus it is that the margins of the world ought not only to be our missional priority, but that they are also a critique of the centre, a rebuke to power, and the place where Christ is building his Church.

Lamin Sanneh (Gambia), writing about the rise of World Christianity in recent decades, compares it to Christ's focus on the margins over and above the simultaneous critique of what has been, in recent centuries, 'centre'.

World Christianity was thereby freed of the West's intellectual inhibitions to become the religion of the excluded, the oppressed, and the marginalized ... Third World Christianity irrupted on the basis of a new indigenous anthropology of mother tongue literacy, ethnic empowerment, esthetic adaptation, and ... of being driven by a striving for justice, trust and reconciliation. Christianity became the faith of the oppressed and dispossessed who as objects of Western colonial supremacy had been left as without hope and without history ... We find ourselves today at the junction between the waning of the West's global authority and the rising demands for justice and equality of once colonized and oppressed societies, with a challenge to acknowledge Christianity's unprecedented pluralist expression without the split burden of territorial conquest or cultural exclusiveness.[62]

---

62. Sanneh, 'Should Christianity be Missionary?', pp. 96-97.

Samuel George (India), writing on 'a disability-informed Christology' in the context of India, estimates that in India alone there are 70 million people with some kind of disability. Their reality is one of ostracism, social marginalisation, lack of access, poverty.

> 'Margin' is a dynamic reality. Beyond the notion of limits, margin also refers to 'frontiers' (as in 'new frontiers of knowledge,' 'on the verge of discovery,' or 'cutting edge'). It signifies a dynamic and creative space, which has a life beyond what those at the centre can ever imagine. In fact, its presence calls into question the centre's existence. Margin is a space of play but also of resistance, allowing some real voices – neglected or suppressed by the logic of the centre – to make themselves heard. It is here that 'life' happens, with its contingencies and uncertainties but also with its unexpected disclosures and surprises. 'Centring' theology on the margins, therefore, is a creative and dynamic yet full of surprises way of doing theology.[63]

Jesus' interest in the margins of the world arises not just from compassion for the dehumanised and mistreated, but also from a prophetic justice which rebukes the status quo, inverts and subverts the priorities of the world, and forges a new reality. His acts of healing speak as more than individual acts, but of the margins as the locus of transformation and recreation, the place where God is present and working. Jesus' focus, consistently, is on powerless people in disenfranchised spaces. And so should ours be.

---

63. George, 'Theological Education as Missional Formation', p. 14.

Chapter Five

Wind

(John 3:1-15)

If you want to speak to God, tell it to the wind.

(African proverb)

Some Christians seem preoccupied by power and influence in mission. They direct their prayers, their evangelism or their church-planting strategies towards those in the centre. Rather than constantly fishing out the mess downstream, they argue, we should aspire to transform what gets put into the river of culture upstream.

But is such a belief warranted by the mission of Jesus? Jesus who was born, not in the centres of power, but in a tiny village in the corner of the world. Jesus who was put to death by the elite, in the capital city of his people. Jesus who invested so much time and care into the downtrodden, the pariah, the socially disregarded.

Like the other Gospel writers, John makes Jesus' mission to the marginalised a major theme of his writing. Christ, declaring himself to be the new Temple, focuses on taking the temple to those who cannot come, on being the temple to those who are socially, ethnically or religiously barred from access. The Samaritan woman, the official's son, the crippled man, the woman caught in adultery, the blind man, all are marginalised, disregarded, dehumanised by the Jerusalem elite, and all are brought dignity by Jesus.

And yet this sequence of individual encounters and conversations (chapters 3-9) begins with Nicodemus. Nicodemus is different from the others. He is everything that they are not. He is wealthy, male, upstanding, powerful, privileged. He does have access to the corridors of power. It is important, therefore, to look carefully at how Jesus interacts with Nicodemus.

Who was Nicodemus?

> Now there was a man of the Pharisees named Nicodemus, a ruler of the Jews.
>
> *(John 3:1)*

This introduction tells us a huge amount. We know his name. He is part of the ruling party, meaning he comes from an influential family. He is a Pharisee, meaning he is particularly invested in ritual purity and Jewish religious tradition. He is elite. He is on home territory in Jerusalem. He holds, relative to Jesus whom he is approaching, higher status.

Compelling historical record from outside the Bible tells us about the ben Gurion family, one of whose sons was Nicodemus ben Gurion. It tells us that this family was one of the three most powerful families in all Jerusalem. They were obscenely rich. It is recorded that each of these three families was wealthy enough to keep the city in food and drink for ten years. Nicodemus, in modern terms, is a hereditary billionaire.[64]

In Global Church terms, I like to think of Nicodemus as representing North Atlantic Christianity; wealthy, comfortable, an

---

64. Bauckham, *Testimony of the Beloved Disciple*, p. 137, b. *Git.* 56a, *Lam. R.* 1.5.31, *Eccles R.* 7.12.1.

'insider' to inherited tradition and holding status in the worldwide Church. In this chapter, then, I'll be thinking primarily about how Jesus might dialogue with the Global North Church today.

Yet, before we delve into his dialogue with Jesus, let's compare Nicodemus in chapter 3 with the Samaritan woman in chapter 4. The contrast between these two characters is absolute: male-female, insider-outsider, named-unnamed, powerful-marginal, Jerusalem-Samaria. Yet wonderfully, Nicodemus will be rebuked by Jesus, whilst the woman is praised.

The dialogue

This man came to Jesus by night and said to him, 'Rabbi, we *know* that you are a teacher come from God, for no one can do these signs that you do unless God is with him.' Jesus answered him, 'Truly, truly, I say to you, unless one is born again he cannot *see* the kingdom of God.'

(John 3:2-3, italics mine)

Nicodemus says 'we know'. Jesus replies with 'you cannot see'. There is a difference between knowing and seeing. John's Gospel is about seeing. Knowing isn't enough. In fact, knowing can be an obstacle to seeing.

And, famously, Jesus speaks of being born again. Being born again, in this context, is about cost. New birth invalidates your first birth. Everything that Nicodemus has, his name, his position, his honour, accrues to him from his earthly family – from his father. Jesus is calling Nicodemus to renounce his earthly family, and associated status, in favour of a new birth. Jesus is not offering to baptise Nicodemus' power and influence and repurpose it for the kingdom of God. He is speaking of it as part of Nicodemus' old identity which must be discarded in favour of following Christ.

The Nicodemus story is John's version of the story of the rich young ruler, which is told in all three other Gospels. Approached by a man who has everything, Jesus is firm and clear about the cost of following him. Where we (who are often better evangelists than Jesus – the door he makes small (Matthew 7:13), we try to make as wide as possible) would have accepted and invited a profession of interest that did not count the cost, Jesus is quick to challenge. Nicodemus is the only person in John to whom Jesus says, 'You must be born again' because he is the person who stands to lose the most in renouncing his first birth.

The ubiquitous Middle Eastern axiom, 'A stone is weighty in its place' outlines this principle. It means that a person's honour is derived from their family, community, place in the order of things. And it implies that honour does not automatically go with you if you are to leave these things behind – that to leave one's 'place' to become a rolling stone or dislocated from one's family and community (the very thing that God called Abram to do), is to lose honour. There were no self-made men in the ancient Mediterranean. Reputation, status, wealth all accrue via family. Jesus is asking Nicodemus if he is ready to renounce everything that makes him who he is.

Today, we see counting the cost as inherent in a Muslim, for example, becoming a follower of Christ. Many expect to have to choose between their blood family and the family of God. When an idol-honouring Hindu turns to Christ, we expect them to remove their idols from their house and from their heart. But when it comes to the invisible strongholds of Western Europe, materialism or education or class or financial security, do we apply the same tests for born-again-ness? Surely, Nicodemus' social location within John's narrative indicates to us that the very people who need to be born again are those from moral, civilised, comfortable backgrounds. Their existing security and influence are not to be baptised into the kingdom. They are to be cut off, lest they prohibit those who hold them from being able to see. Privilege, then, is a form of blindness.

> Nicodemus said to him, 'How can a man be born when he is old? Can he enter a second time into his mother's womb and be born?' Jesus answered, 'Truly, truly, I say to you, unless one is born of water and the Spirit, he cannot enter the kingdom of God. That which is born of the flesh is flesh, and that which is born of the Spirit is spirit.
>
> *(John 3:4-6)*

Nicodemus now asks a 'how' question, and Jesus responds with another metaphor. Nicodemus, from the religious and cultural centre, is used to certainties. Religion in the centre can afford to think scientifically, with certainties, absolutes and confidence. The Nicodemuses of this world are purveyors of a neat and tidy domain, with straight lines and orderly rules. In the margins of the world, life is a lot messier, a lot more complex. Jesus, in dialogue, seeks to disciple Nicodemus out of his scientific, tidy worldview. 'The kingdom that you seek to enter,' explains the Christ, 'is not perceived through "how" questions. It can only truly be articulated through parable and metaphor and enigma. It is poetry, not prose. It is faith, not knowledge. It is about a person, not principles.' The blind man in chapter 9 asks a 'who' question rather than a 'how' question – this is much better!

Metaphor is an interface between evangelism and the sovereignty of God. Those who are given 'ears to hear' (Matthew 11:15) will perceive and believe. A metaphor is a word of grace to the elect and a word of judgement to the hardened.

Among the idols that authentic faith must resist are the idols of human thought concerning God. Living faith remains aware that the most subtle and sophisticated of all idolatries might actually be the one constructed by theologians who claim to know and understand God.[65]

Mission and the wind

Do not marvel that I said to you, 'You must be born again.' The wind blows where it wishes, and you hear its sound, but you do not know where it comes from or where it goes. So it is with everyone who is born of the Spirit.'

(John 3:7-8)

In this verse, Jesus analogises wind and the Holy Spirit. He emphasises unpredictability and invisibility. Wind, like the Holy Spirit, moves. It is powerful. It creates an effect – things are moved, things are shaken, things are blown completely away. It can't be seen, but it can be perceived, felt, discerned. There can be prevailing winds; trends, but also unpredictable shifts in direction. Wind interacts with context; the landscape redirects the wind and the wind erodes the landscape. Wind is outside of human control and beyond human bidding. The Sage expressed the human search for meaning as being like trying to shepherd the wind (Ecclesiastes 1:14) – futile!

Mission can be by the Spirit or by the flesh. 'That which is born of the flesh is flesh, and that which is born of the Spirit is spirit' (3:6). It is possible to emphasise the human factors involved in mission at the expense of the divine factors – something which happens a lot in books about mission. This activity of the flesh produces fruit of the flesh. The activity of the Spirit gives birth to spirit. What follows are some thoughts on mission flowing from these verses.

Firstly, it is possible to do mission by the flesh. When church planters think more about methodology, technique and resources

---

65. Johnson, *The Revelatory Body*, Kindle location 90.

than the sovereign prerogative of the Holy Spirit, this is mission by the flesh. When you plan more than pray. When you decide more than discern. When it's more about principle-ising than perceiving. When you depend on money more than the Messiah. It's possible to do mission by the flesh.

Lamin Sanneh (Gambia):

> We in the West are a confident and articulate people, and theology has served us well as a vehicle of our aspirations, desires, and goals. There is no shortage of theological books on all sorts of imaginable subjects, with how-to-do manuals instructing us about effective ministry, about how to fix our emotions, how to affirm our individual identity and promote our choices and preferences, about how to change society by political action, how to raise funds and build bigger churches, about investing in strategic coalitions, etc. All this language leaves us little time or space to listen to God with the chance that God may have something, and even something else to say to us, especially if that something else challenges what we want to hear.[66]

Secondly, mission in the flesh produces outcomes of the flesh. 'That which is born of the flesh is flesh, and that which is born of the Spirit is spirit' (3:6). Mission by the flesh produces flesh-sons. Those whose paradigm is 'leadership technique' raise leaders who are enslaved to said technique. Those who use money as a resource to build with end up building financially dependent disciples. Those who only think in terms of statistics and measurability will produce flavourless, factory-processed fruit. Those who commit their lives and ministries to the service of any given model will only produce results commensurate with

---

66. Sanneh, in conversation with Graham Hill, in Hill, *Salt, Light and a City*, pp. 56-57.

that model's promise. Just as Abraham spawned Ishmael through human effort, so those who entrust themselves to mission in the flesh will produce flesh-sons.

Thirdly, 'you do not know'. In this dialogue, Nicodemus started the conversation by saying, 'Rabbi, we know . . .' (v. 2). Jesus corrects him – 'you do not know'. In wealthy, educated Nicodemus, Jesus upends the idol of knowing. How much more in the West-sponsored, education-fuelled mission space! It is not possible to know how God will work. It is impossible to say what God will do. The wind blows where it pleases – you do not know where it comes from or where it goes.

It was impossible for Spirit-led Philip in Acts 8, Ananias in Acts 9, Peter in Acts 10 to predict or anticipate what God would do through their obedience. Through the Ethiopian the gospel entered Africa, through Paul it entered Asia, and through the centurion it entered Europe. No strategy, plan, leadership, programme, system or method could have engineered this. It was a sovereign move of God.

You do not know what God will do. You do not know how he will choose to work. You cannot know what will happen next. But that which is born of the Spirit is spirit. If the DNA of the gospel agent is obedience to the leading of the Holy Spirit, this DNA will carry to the next generation.

Fourthly, don't try to shepherd the wind. The writer of Ecclesiastes is emphatic: 'striving after wind' (Ecclesiastes 1:14) is futile, impossible, exhausting. Jesus makes it clear that the wind is completely unpredictable. The great initiative in mission belongs to the Spirit ('blows where it wishes' – note the personality of the Holy Spirit expressed here in 'wishes'), and our job is to perceive, discern, align, obey, respond. In this way, the fruit produced will be that of the Spirit, will belong to the Spirit, with its own life and energy and its own relationship with God.

And finally, a deft responsiveness to the Spirit is part of the decolonisation of mission. Colonial mission was resource-heavy, inflexible, laden with modernist assumptions, the 'white man's burden'. Its outputs were buildings and institutions and organisations, some of which have lasted for 100 years. There was nothing deft, nothing nimble, nothing responsive or reactive. Mission today can be similar; money-dependent, planning-heavy, model-driven, outcome-hungry. The responsiveness to the invisible, unpredictable, uncontrollable Spirit of which Christ speaks is very, very different. Mission in the Spirit is charismatically informed; prayer, prophecy, supernatural guidance is the norm, not the exception. It defers to proximity, with local practitioners, not distant headquarters empowered to make reactive decisions. It is sensitive to context as wind is sensitive to landscape. It is lightweight, divesting itself of power and privilege as a matter of course. It is entrepreneurial, exciting, dynamic, flexible, ready to be bent and blown by the Spirit in whatever direction he so chooses. Planning, control, measurability, method-reliance, these Western idols must be sought out and destroyed by modern-day Hezekiahs (2 Kings 18:4) because they lead people astray from naked dependence on the Holy Spirit.

The mechanics of the snake

Nicodemus persists in asking 'how' questions (3:9), and Jesus persists in being intentionally obtuse, dissimulative, hard to pin down. He's not always like this, of course – at times he is direct and matter of fact. But to each individual he brings the necessary challenge, and Nicodemus, like so many to whom everything has been handed on a silver platter, needs to be given some hard-to-digest truths in a format that require the hard work of chewing and thinking and responding. When Jesus compares himself to the snake in the wilderness, he is continuing to push into Nicodemus on the same theme.

> And as Moses lifted up the serpent in the wilderness, so must the Son of Man be lifted up, that whoever believes in him may have eternal life.
>
> *(John 3:14-15)*

The story is somewhat mysterious – which is probably why Jesus chooses it! Its placement here in the dialogue has often bamboozled commentators, but I think that's the whole point! Jesus is keeping Nicodemus, and others like him who think in a logical and reductive way, on his toes. Like a boxer, right hand, left hand, jab, Jesus is hitting Nicodemus' worldview from multiple unexpected directions.

In the story, recorded in Numbers 21, the people of Israel are bitten by poisonous snakes as judgement from God for grumbling against him and hence defaming him. Serpents, which spit venom from their mouths, are associated with slanderous speech. God is giving them a taste of their own medicine; the snake-tongued reap snakes. Moses, for their healing, is instructed to set up a bronze serpent on a pole, 'And if a serpent bit anyone, he would look at the bronze serpent and live' (Numbers 21:9). Thus, 'by confronting their own poisonous mouths in the image of the serpent, they receive healing'.[67]

How does it work? We don't know! This is not a story to be understood mechanically.

Jesus declares that the cross is going to be like this. He speaks of being lifted up (exaltation, honour, praise), but he is talking about the cross (shame, weakness, defeat). This ironic reversal

---

67. Aquaro, *Death by Envy*, p. 47.

will be significant in Nicodemus' own journey. Nicodemus, who is used to seeing the world through the lens of honour and status, is finally transformed by beholding the shame of the cross.

But as per human nature, the people make an idol out of a method. Just because it worked once in one place, doesn't mean it will work everywhere. Israel set up the bronze statue in the temple and made offerings to it. They even gave it a name – Nehushtan! This idolatry, or perception of God's once-used sovereign means of grace as somehow magical, is precisely what the Western Church commonly loves to do with methods, models, templates. King Hezekiah in 2 Kings 18:4 eventually destroyed Nehushtan in the course of cleansing the temple from idols. John Wesley (England), on this story, wrote, 'He said, this serpent, howsoever formerly honoured, and used by God as a sign of his grace, yet now it is nothing but a piece of brass which can do you neither good nor hurt.'[68]

The people of Jerusalem took what worked at one time in one place and set it up as a universal principle! This is such a danger for Europeans. Making an idol out of a method is the classic failing of Western missiologies. For example, numerous studies on Church Planting Movements analyse and principle-ise sovereign moves of God, subsequently making the point that if one applies these principles, then one can see a move of God. So argues David S. Lim (Philippines):

> Much of the missiology of movements has been written by Westerners, with a result that can tend to be dichotomistic and complex. I write as an Easterner, trying to harmonize different strategies and communicate them holistically and comprehensively. Movements don't have to be complicated, but it doesn't follow that they happen easily.[69]

68. Wesley, 2 Kings 18, www.studylight.org/commentaries/eng/wen/2-kings-18.html (accessed 7.3.24).
69. Lim, 'A Biblical Missiology', p. 80.

You cannot reverse engineer a work of God! This is the induction that Jesus is seeking to give Nicodemus into the hard-to-pin-down kingdom of God.

What happens to Nicodemus?

The conversation is finished, but we are left unsatisfied. What happens to Nicodemus? Most of John's dialogues are finely crafted and complete, with individuals speaking seven times and arriving at a destination. The Samaritan woman speaks seven times and ends with 'Can this be the Christ?' (4:29). The blind man speaks seven times, and goes from blindness to seeing. In the same chapter, the Pharisees speak seven times and go from seeing to blindness. In both interviews between Pilate and Jesus, Pilate speaks seven times and ends with a question both times – Pilate is Mr Question Mark. But Nicodemus has only spoken three times. His story is left unfinished, and the reader is left unclear. What happens to him?

He pops up briefly in chapter 7, as if to say, 'I'm still here.' John here changes his earlier designation of Nicodemus from 'Pharisee' and 'ruler' to that of 'Galilean' (see 7:52), suggesting that Nicodemus is on a journey away from the things that defined his old identity, or at least, he is drifting away from his former colleagues.

Later, in chapter 12, we read:

Nevertheless, many even of the authorities believed in him, but for fear of the Pharisees they did not confess it, so that they would not be put out of the synagogue; for they loved the glory that comes from man more than the glory that comes from God.

(John 12:42-43)

If this includes Nicodemus, we see that he is still not ready to pay the price. To be put out of the synagogue is to lose all of one's identity, one's standing in the Jewish world, yet these insider men are still not in a position to suffer this sentence. The blind man was put out of the synagogue for his faith in Christ, but again, those with more to lose in terms of status and reputation are understandably slower to arrive at this costly decision.

Finally, in chapter 19, we see that Nicodemus, who has been reflecting on Jesus' hard sayings since chapter 3, is finally in a place where he is prepared to go public.

> Nicodemus also, who earlier had come to Jesus by night, came bringing a mixture of myrrh and aloes, about seventy-five pounds in weight. So they took the body of Jesus and bound it in linen cloths with the spices, as is the burial custom of the Jews.
>
> *(John 19:39-40)*

Previously, Nicodemus came in the night. Now, he comes while it is still daytime. Sabbath starts at sundown, so it is still light when they move the body of Jesus. In order to carry the corpse and this significant weight of spices, Nicodemus would have brought with him several servants. In the cramped, festival-busy streets of Jerusalem, this is a public action. Nicodemus is watched, seen, and observed to be a follower of Jesus. His faith has come to full flower. He has counted the cost and deemed it worth paying. He is nailing his colours to the mast.

Nicodemus has seen the cross and is finally changed. He has understood the dishonour required of those who will follow a crucified Messiah. He has seen the glory of God is revealed through weakness and shame. People who are used to power are not converted through power, but through weakness. Otherwise we have the Simon the sorcerer scenario from Acts 8.

Simon is into power. He sees power. He 'converts' but with no real repentance. The idol of power is displaced only through weakness. The idol of status is undermined only through a revelation of the goodness of God in nakedness and dishonour. Throughout John, the marginalised have come to faith first, and only at the end does Nicodemus confess his faith publicly. There is a process to conversion – it takes time. We must allow people time to count the cost. I am increasingly suspicious of speedy conversions where worldviews are so distant from the gospel, where Western culture has diverged from Christian values there must be time for realignment. With Roland Allen, 'I do not trust spectacular things. Give me the seed growing secretly every time.'[70]

What ultimately happened to Nicodemus for choosing Christ? We would expect him to be struck off the synagogue register as per 12:42 and 9:34. We would expect him to lose his family fortune, his position on the council, his network and connections.

In fact, the Babylonian Talmud lists names of key Jewish elite who believed in Jesus and were sentenced to be put to death. Nicodemus' name is on this list.[71] When Nicodemus put his faith in Jesus, he lost his power and position. He may even have lost his life.

---

70. Allen, *The Ministry of the Spirit,* Kindle location 425.
71. *b. Sanh.* 43a. See Backham, *Testimony of the Beloved Disciple,* for discussion of this text, including, 'Nicodemus was a rare name among Jews. Even in the diaspora only two instances are known. The few instances among Palestinian Jews, known from Josephus and rabbinic traditions, can all confidently be assigned to the Gurion family, like all instances of Gurion or Guria before the second century. This was precisely the point of the use of such unusual names among the Jerusalem aristocracy: they were utterly distinctive of a particular family and so unmistakably identified members of that family', p. 172.

Chapter Six

World
(John 3:16)

If we wonder often, the gift of knowledge will come.
(Arapaho proverb)

When I planned this book, I didn't expect to write this chapter – it wasn't even on my radar. But as I've listened, *really* listened to Global South Christians' voices, there appears in the famous words of John 3:16 a truth that I had never noticed. God loves the planet. And care for our fragile world, and the justice implications of our environmental crisis, are an inescapable part of our response to his love. I find it staggering that in this verse, which so many evangelicals have seen as the most succinct gospel summary in Scripture, we can be so individualistic and anthropocentric as to miss that God loves the world, the earth, the Blue Planet which we call home.

In the Global North, where I live, care for the environment is something wealthy people do. It is middle-class morality. Ordinary working people can't afford to buy organic bananas, or fair-trade coffee, or an electric car. But in the Global South, for the billions who live in life-and-death subsistence proximity to fluctuations in temperature or sea-level or air quality or fish stocks or rainfall or soil quality, the question of whether or not God loves the world screams loud. In the North, eco-theology is a luxury for academics. In the South, it is grass-roots basic Christianity.

Our growing interconnectedness as a global body of Christ should alert us to the fact that environmental devastation is one of the clearest forms of inequality and injustice there is. Rich countries appropriate, destroy, profit and grow richer, while the impact is felt by the poorest among our brothers and sisters. Those most affected are the least responsible, and those most responsible are the least affected. Climate change is racist.

One of the things that happens when we listen, really listen, to our brothers and sisters in other parts of the world, is that we realise that there are major issues, huge areas of concern, of which we were not aware, about which we didn't care. And yet we realise that we are complicit, that by not caring we are part of the problem, and that if one part of the body is suffering, then the whole body suffers with it.[72] Pope Francis, who has been such a prophetic voice for change on these issues, directed that Christians should 'hear both the cry of the earth and the cry of the poor',[73] for the two are interconnected.

The world

Kapy Kaoma (Zambia) is one of those who argues that the incarnation of the Son of God – Word made flesh – is good news for all creation. On 3:16 he writes:

> Generally, this statement has been understood anthropocentrically. However, the Greek word employed for 'world' refers to the entire cosmos and not only to humanity.

---

72. See 1 Corinthians 12:26.
73. Pope Francis, *Laudato Si'*, 49. https://www.vatican.va/content/francesco/en/encyclicals/documents/papa-francesco_20150524_enciclica-laudato-si.html.

God's love is cosmic in expression – God loves the entire Creation – humans, non-humans and the physical world. It is the Cosmos that the Creator loves and Jesus redeemed to the glory of the triune God.[74]

While we might disagree with Dr Kaoma's direct linkage in meaning from the *Koine* (common) Greek *kosmos* to our modern English word *cosmic* – *kosmos* has a broad range of meanings in ancient (and, indeed, modern) Greek including 'the people in the world' – his point is thoroughly sound. Think of the semantic range of *monde* in French, which includes the planet and everything in it, its people, its systems of thought. 'God so loved the world' certainly does not exclusively mean 'God so loved humans'. And there are plenty of Scripture translations into languages which lack the nuance of English where one might effectively read, in John 3:16, 'God so loved the earth.'

Kaoma goes on to observe that Jesus' declaring himself to be the water of life – 'living water' (4:10) – is good news for all creation, not just humans, as all life needs water. And when, from the cross, water gushes forth from Jesus' pierced side onto the earth, Kaoma sees this as a symbol for the redemption of all creation through the death of the Saviour (19:34). For people whose livelihood depends on the earth being watered, one can see how this is an important reading.

Kosmos is a big word in John's Gospel. It has a universalising aspect: Saviour of the world, Light of the world, sins of the world. There are times when John means the unjust and broken systems and powers: 'You are not of the world' (15:19), 'Now is the judgement of this world; now will the ruler of this world be cast out' (12:31). Yet despite all this, 'God so loved the world'. The sending of the Son needs to be thought of not merely as a rescue

---

74. Kaoma, *The Earth,* pp. 284-285.

plan for humans, but a plan to redeem all creation. Jesus' analogy of himself as a grain of wheat which falls into the earth, in 12:24, suggests that in his burial he is planted into the very earth he came to save, absorbed into the bosom of 'mother earth', which accords with John's portrayal of the resurrection in a garden on the first day of the week, a new Eden, where a man and a woman face each other, and the man is mistaken for a gardener. John's new creation imagery is rich and bountiful. Metropolitan Geevarghese Mor Coorilos (India), discussing Orthodox theological perspectives on earth-care, argues that Fathers such as Gregory of Nyssa and St John of Damascus emphasised God's love for the earth:

> In Orthodox spirituality . . . the earth is depicted as a theological category, the medium of God's incarnation in Christ. God became 'earth' (an 'earthling') in Jesus Christ. It was matter that Jesus Christ assumed to become one with humanity and the universe – thus the church is meant to be the continuation of this incarnation. 'I shall not cease reverencing matter by means of which salvation has been achieved,' writes St. John of Damascus.[75]

This is where our themes coalesce – perspectives from the Global Church enrich our insight into Word become flesh and thence augment our view of human responsibility. Creation care, argue many of our sisters and brothers, is an indispensable aspect of Christian mission.

Dominion like the *Dominus*

Where did we go wrong? Our sisters and brothers from indigenous cultures tell us that we are interpreting and applying Genesis

---

75. Coorilos, 'Ecology and Mission: Some Orthodox Theological Perspectives', p. 142.

1:28 wrongly in the English-speaking world. 'Have dominion' seems to be a really unhelpful translation which plays into our sinful desire to 'dominate' – to possess and control, to use and abuse. Lynn White's watershed critique in 1967, 'The Historical Roots of our Ecologic Crisis'[76] really got the Church thinking. His observation was that Western Christianity 'is the most anthropocentric religion the world has ever seen', and was to blame for a worldview that saw nature as a resource to fuel industrial expansion (hence we talk about creation as 'natural *resources*').

If we must translate Genesis 1:28 as *dominion,* let us consider that this word comes from the same Latin root as *Dominus,* which of course is the Latin Church's title for the *Lord* Jesus Christ. His exercise of Lordship was to empty himself, to live among, to serve, to lay down his life. It was incarnational, kenotic. Human dominion over nature should not be dominating or dominant, but should replicate the *Dominus.* As the Creator stoops to wash the feet of his creatures in John 13, so should we humbly interact with our environment.[77] James Cone (African-American) wrote, 'The logic that led to slavery and segregation in the Americas, colonisation and apartheid in Africa, and the rule of white supremacy throughout the world, is the same one that leads to the exploitation of animals and the ravaging of nature.'[78]

In the same way, Christopher Wright (England) argues: 'Human rule in creation was never a licence to dominate, abuse, crush, waste or destroy. Those are the marks of *tyranny* manifesting itself in fallen human arrogance, not *kingship* modelled on God's character and behaviour.'[79] Furthermore, Mike Higton (England), writing in a book about de-centring whiteness in mission, makes a similar point to Cone. He describes 'self-possession'

---

76. White Jr, 'The Historical Roots of our Ecologic Crisis'.
77. Coorilos, 'Ecology and Mission: Some Orthodox Theological Perspectives', p. 142.
78. Cone, 'Whose Earth is it Anyway?', p. 23.
79. Wright, *The Great Story and the Great Commission,* p. 117.

as a recognisable foundation of whiteness: 'The self-possessed man stands at the centre of concentric circles of possession. He possesses himself, his feelings, his knowledge, his vocation, his estate and ultimately his empire.'[80]

'Dominion' in Genesis 1:28 has unfortunately played into a view of humankind's relationship with our environment which is exploitative, harmful, and us-centred. If we've got it so wrong, misunderstood our relationship with the earth so profoundly, where should we look for correction? Bible scholars from indigenous backgrounds, who are able to maximise their traditional heritages reimagined through the gospel, are great sources of wisdom and perspective. Rather than dominion, many now prefer the term 'guardianship.'

Guardianship

Ruth Valerio (England) argues that even 'stewardship' is not the best term, as it still implies a relationship above, superior to, or separate from living creation.[81] Guardianship is humbler, more intimate, more appreciative of the fact that humans are a part of their environment, interdependent and fully integrated into the *kosmos* which God so loves and into which he sent his Son. Jay Matenga, writing from Māori perspective (New Zealand – Aotearoa) explains:

> The word we use for guardianship is 'kaitaiakitanga,' from the root 'tiaki', which means to look after, nurture, care, protect, conserve, safeguard or save. Translators of the Māori Bible quite rightly interpreted Genesis 2:15, where the man was placed in the garden to tend and watch over

80. Higton, 'Beyond Theological Self-Possession', p. 15.
81. Valerio, 'Why We are Not Stewards of the Environment'.

it, as 'hei tiaki.' It is also what God does to our hearts and minds as we live in Christ Jesus, keeping us in perfect peace (Philippians 4:7, from Isaiah 26:3)...

Guardianship is an important role that only indigenous or local people can play. Visitors can participate, but the task lies with the locals. Guardianship carries an authority that is granted through successive generations of dwelling in and becoming a part of a space and its spirituality. That authority carries a responsibility for the care and wellbeing of that which we are charged to nurture. This is as much an important leadership perspective as it is a creation care perspective.[82]

Ama'amalele Tofaeno (Samoa) uses the Samoan concept of *aiga* to explain how all things are interconnected:

Samoans have a concept called *aiga*, which means 'family.' It's a powerful concept in Samoan social and spiritual life. Unlike the notion of family in much of the West, *aiga* doesn't just include immediate family. And *aiga* isn't only limited to extended family either. *Aiga* includes the whole family of creation. *Aiga* includes God, spiritual beings, humans, the whole earth, and all living creatures. *Aiga* is the 'household of life.'[83]

Sylvia Marcos (Mexico) writes, 'For Indigenous peoples, the world is not "out there," established outside of and apart from them. It is within them and even "through" them.'[84] Chief Seattle (Native American) famously said, 'We are but one thread within the web of life. Whatever we do to the web, we do to ourselves.' What if

---

82. Matenga, 'Indigenous Relationship Ecologies: Space, Spirituality and Sharing'.
83. Hill, *Salt, Light and a City,* 157. See Tofaeno, Ama'amalele, *Ecotheology: AIGA. The Household of God.*
84. Marcos, 'Teologia India', p. 277.

these indigenous perspectives on human interconnectedness with our environment are closer to what Moses meant when he wrote, 'God took the man and put him in the garden of Eden to work it and keep it' (Genesis 2:15)? Then John's 'God so loved the world, that he sent his only Son' (John 3:16) wouldn't force us to choose between the human and non-human world, because they are one. What if God so loved the world with its complex interconnected and delicate ecologies, the web of life within which humans are a part? What if he sent his Son into the earth to redeem the earth, sent into creation to redeem creation (including humans)? What if John 3:16 speaks of the taking of the Second Man and placing him into the garden, a repainting of Genesis 2:15? As Michael Amaladoss (India) wrote, 'The Lord has entrusted the earth to humanity. It is meant for all, not to be exploited unjustly by a few.'[85]

Abundant Africa is a development process funded by Tearfund bringing together Christian African voices to focus on the goal of an African 'restorative economy.' Their 2021 report brings together theological, cultural and practical perspectives in a significant way. Below I quote a section on the vital importance of 'land'.

Land is an important aspect of African identity. African soil carries our stories, our birth and our culture. It has also been the site of death, of dispossession and of disconnection...

In Eden our original purpose was to tend a garden fed by rivers. We lived in harmony with nature, and in Genesis 1, we see that God declared all creation to be very good. After the Fall, these relationships were broken, but God's work is restoration. He partners with us to care for, not extract from or destroy, all creation – from the soil to every person who lives and tends it.

---

85. Amaladoss, *The Asian Jesus,* Kindle location 1366.

Who owns and benefits from land, and natural resources both on land and in the ocean, is critical to creation flourishing – and is often disputed. Control of land was a key pillar of colonialism in Africa. In the twenty-first century this pursuit has continued in a different form as foreign investors and governments seek to acquire resource-rich African land. How much land? The lack of records and transparency makes it difficult to know, but for a sense of scale, in just five years nearly 2.5 million hectares of agricultural land from just five African countries were transferred in large-scale acquisitions. This is happening in the context of persistent land and border disputes, often driven by a complex interplay of historic disagreements, trauma, cycles of violence, cattle raiding, and competition for natural resources. Over 20 million people across Africa are separated from their land, living as refugees or Internally Displaced Persons.

And yet the land continues to hold deep spiritual meaning and economic significance. Seven out of ten Africans depend on agriculture for their livelihoods. But the life-giving quality of the land that our growing population relies on is under threat. Ecosystem destruction from human activities takes many forms. Deforestation. Mining. Extraction of fossil fuels. The result is fragmentation, biodiversity loss and degradation of the land that God made and we depend on – often while exploiting local communities.

The climate crisis is already exacerbating these threats . . . The dry seasons across the Sahel are getting longer, threatening a thousand-year-old tradition of pastoralism that over 20 million people rely on. The climate crisis threatens us all, but it affects people living in poverty the most.[86]

---

86. 'Abundant Africa: Our Decade to Shape the African Century' at https://abundant. africa (accessed 15.1.24).

As a Western Christian myself, it is important to listen humbly to such criticism. I think the really important learning here is that verses like John 3:16, which our children memorise in Sunday school, can be misread individualistically, anthropocentrically, and with a modernist view which detaches humans from the rest of the natural world. Dawn Nothwehr (USA) is a Franciscan theologian who writes a lot about eco-theology. She contends:

> Over the centuries Western theology's focus on sin became so intense that the wideness of God's saving mercy throughout the whole created world was by and large overlooked. Any connection between the cross of Christ and cosmic redemption came to seem esoteric. As a result, the natural world was ignored in doctrine, liturgical prayer, and ethical practice. *It is hard to take cosmic redemption seriously if redemption is only about forgiveness of humans.*[87]

Let's not forget the context of John 3:16. Jesus has been challenging Nicodemus' preconceived ideas about religion in a robust dialogue. Could the emphasis in this verse not be on the *world* as the locus of God's love? – Hey Nicodemus, God doesn't just love Jews. He doesn't just love men. In the next chapter you'll see how he loves a Samaritan woman. Hey Nicodemus, God doesn't just love humans. He loves the whole world.

Is your Jesus Saviour of the world?

John's Jesus is identified with the whole world, he is a global Jesus. He was sent because 'God so loved the world'. The cosmic scope of John's Jesus ought to be a litmus test for our Jesus.

---

87. Nothwehr, 'For the Salvation of the Cosmos', p. 69, italics mine.

How much does your image of Jesus belong to the whole world? Would he be good news to others in the way that he is good news to you? If not, he falls short of the standard John sets in his gospel.

A chauvinistic Jesus becomes good news to men and not to women. A white Jesus is not good news to the majority of the world's population. A Jesus who is for *us* and against *them* is not the Jesus of gospel portrayal – whether for Israel and against Palestine, or for Americans and against Iranians, or anywhere for the right wing and against the left. This Jesus fails to pass the bar John has set. A Jesus who only saves human souls is not good news to creation groaning. A Jesus who cares not about justice is not good news to 20 million Africans displaced from their land. 'For God so loved the world' becomes a radical benchmark for our perspectives on who God is and what he loves.

A world Jesus is for the whole world. A global Christ is for the whole globe. A cosmic Saviour is for the whole cosmos.

Chapter Seven

Woman
(John 4:1-42)

Cast no dirt into the well that gives you water.

(Korean proverb)

Pandita Ramabai Sarasvati was born into a Hindu Brahmin family in South India in 1858. She was an extraordinary woman. Reading John 4 was the trigger for her conversion to Christianity: 'I realised after reading the fourth chapter of St. John's Gospel, that Christ was truly the Divine Saviour he claimed to be, and no one but He could transform and uplift the downtrodden women of India. Thus my heart was drawn to the religion of Christ.'[88] Imagine her courage to convert as a woman from a religious high caste family in nineteenth-century India! She went on to become a significant activist for women's rights, including founding the Arya Mahila Samaj, an organisation advocating for women's education, and the Mukti Mission as a refuge for destitute women, children and disabled persons. She was the first woman to be awarded the titles of *Pandita* (teacher) and *Sarasvati* (goddess of wisdom). She also learned Greek and Hebrew and spent eighteen years completing a translation of the Bible into simple Marathi for people living in the rural areas of Maharashtra. She really was quite a lady!

---

88. Kaur, '4 Incredible Christian Women Who Changed India'.

'What good news for me a woman, a woman born in India among Brahmans who hold out no hope for the likes of me! The Bible declares that Christ did not reserve this great salvation for a particular caste or sex', she would later write.[89]

John 4 is well-beloved and oft-discussed, and rightly so. From the perspective of cross-cultural mission, this story carries layer upon layer of insight. Jesus crosses geographic, ethnic, religious and gender boundaries, as should we. Overcoming Judaian prejudice against Samaritans seems to have been a cornerstone of Jesus' ministry: Luke treats it at length throughout Luke and Acts, including such key moments as the parable of the good Samaritan and the revival through Philip's ministry. In John, the Samaritan woman is the epitome of the marginalisation dealt with throughout the section from chapter 3 to chapter 9. Jesus, having declared himself to be the new Temple, then proceeds to go to those who could never come to the temple: the Samaritan woman, prohibited through ethnicity and gender, is a prime example. Jesus goes to those who cannot come. He creates access, in himself, to the presence of God. Herein is a fundamental principle of the *Missio Dei* through all ages: too many boundaries stopping you coming to God? God will cross the boundaries and come to you.

The Samaritan woman in John 4 serves as direct contrast in numerous ways to Nicodemus in the previous chapter. He is male, she is female. He is named, she is unnamed. He is elite, she is ordinary. He Jewish, she Samaritan. He is an insider to the temple system, she is marginal. And yet, he fails to believe, while she puts her faith in Christ. His seven-fold dialogue is cut short, while her seven-step journey to the knowledge of Christ is completed. He comes at night-time, while her conversation with Jesus takes place at noon (4:6).

---

89. Kaur, '4 Incredible Christian Women Who Changed India'.

Her story also contains many firsts. Hers is the first of John's complete seven-step dialogues from unbelief to faith. She is the first to hear Jesus say 'I am' (*ego eimai*) (4:26). This is the first of seven absolute 'I am' statements, statements in which Jesus takes God's Exodus self-identifier for himself.[90] For the Samaritans, who only held the first five books of the Old Testament as authoritative, this was a preferred designation for God. Jesus' self-disclosure is contextually resonant.

Searching for a bride

Her story is a key moment in Jesus' dealings with women. There are six times in John when someone is addressed with the vocative 'woman'. This can often sound awkward, or rude, to our ears. But a pattern is building. In 2:4, Jesus says to his mother, 'Woman, what does this have to do with me? My hour has not yet come.' In 4:21, Jesus says to the Samaritan at the well, 'Woman, believe me, the hour is coming when neither on this mountain nor in Jerusalem will you worship the Father.' In 8:10, Jesus says to the accused, 'Woman, where are they? Has no one condemned you?' In 19:26, Jesus says to his mother, from the cross, 'Woman, behold, your son!' In 20:13, Mary Magdalene is asked, 'Woman, why are you weeping?' And in 20:15, Jesus asks Mary again, 'Woman, why are you weeping? Whom are you seeking?' Six times.

John, who loves the number seven, who repeatedly crafts sevens into his narrative, here leaves us hanging, incomplete, off-balance, pointing towards an as-yet-unrealised, eschatological seventh vocative. The final wedding feast of the bride and bridegroom, perhaps?

90. Seven times in the Hebrew of Exodus. Seven times *ego eimai* in the LXX of the Pentateuch. Seven times in Deutero-Isaiah. Seven times absolute (without predicate) in John. Seven times predicated in John.

Do Jesus' encounters with unmarried/single women throughout John all represent aspects of Christ encountering his Church? Of the bridegroom searching for his bride? I think so.

Here in chapter 4, we see a reconstitution of an Old Testament type-scene. In the Pentateuch, whenever we see a man and woman meeting at a well, they are meeting to marry. Abraham's servant finds Rebekkah at a well as wife for Isaac (Genesis 24). Jacob meets Rachel, the love of his life, at a well (Genesis 29). Moses meets his wife Zipporah at a well (Exodus 2). And so on. Normally in this type-scene, or literary trope, a man travels to a foreign land, meets a girl by a well, and one of them draws water. She goes home to tell her family about the stranger, and there is a meal and a betrothal.

This man-meets-woman-at-a-well scene harks back to the garden of Eden. It suggests fruitfulness and the generation of life. Imagine, in semi-arid places, the lush green growth around a well. For Hagar, who does not have a husband, who is a mistreated slave woman, it is God himself who meets her at a well, removing her shame (Genesis 16:7-15). God himself will take responsibility for her. This lowly slave woman responds by being the first person in all Scripture permitted to name God, 'El Roi: the Lord who sees' – a huge honour. This is all in the background to John 4.

This moment between Jesus and the Samaritan woman at a well, a woman who does not currently have a husband, and who is, therefore, in a patriarchal society, without a male interface with the world, recalls these stories. It is a marriage type-scene. The bridegroom has come from heaven to search for his bride. Salvation is through a redeemer taking responsibility, as in the Ruth and Boaz story from Jesus' ancestral line. And yet here, in Jesus' reconstituted scheme of things, this woman does not have to marry to find her place in the world. It is not directly romantic, don't misunderstand. It's all symbolism. Her community meets Jesus' community. She is brought into a new place of shame-removal, the Church. She can now have a place to stand vis-à-vis a patriarchal world, she will have men to represent her; brothers in Christ, uncles in Christ. So when Jesus says to her, 'Everyone who drinks of this water will be thirsty again, but whoever drinks of the water that I will give him will never be thirsty again. The water that I will give him will become in him a spring of water welling up to eternal life' (4:13-14), he could just as well be using the spring-water as a metaphor for marriage. This is a woman who has drunk the waters of marriage several times and yet always been thirsty again. He is offering a different quality of water, a salvation from shame that is superior in its power and permanence even to that which Ruth received from Boaz.

The marital theme of the scene is underscored by a specific reference to the fact that it is Jacob's well, the conversation about marriage, the abundant fecundity of the episode (well, water, vessel, harvest fields), and by its situation in the Cana to Cana section of John 2 to John 4, between the first sign by which Jewish disciples believe and the second sign by which a non-Jew believes.

The Samaritan woman will rush home to tell her community about Jesus, but there won't be a meal. Rather, Jesus declares, 'My food is to do the will of him who sent me'.

Progressive understanding

This Samaritan woman speaks seven times, and progresses from 'How is it that you, a Jew, ask for a drink from me, a woman of Samaria?' (4:9) at the first, to her seventh and final words, 'Come, see a man who told me all that I ever did. Can this be the Christ?' (4:29). Her understanding of who Jesus is develops, therefore, from a Jewish man (v. 9), through someone who can satisfy need (v. 15), to a prophet (v. 19), to eventually the Christ (v. 29).

This process of discipleship happens through dialogue, through interaction around questions and issues that are really important to her. Jesus leads her through a journey of discovery tailored to her situation, all through meaningful, sympathetic conversation. Jesus also speaks seven times in this dialogue. Hers is the most perfect catechism in the whole of John, and perhaps in the whole New Testament. In the process, not only does her insight into who Jesus is develop, but also her grasp of a host of other issues deeply felt and intrinsic to her sense of identity, as we shall see.

The first thing out of her mouth, when she sees Jesus, is: 'How is it that you, a Jew, ask for a drink from me, a woman of Samaria?' We hear in this the bitterness of ethnic pain and gender pain, we sense the polarities within which she lives ('you' ... 'me'), and of a world formed and sustained by otherisation and injustice. It's the first thing she says, the first thing that she notices about Jesus. Her sense of identity which needs articulating as soon as she meets Jesus is that she is a 'woman of Samaria'. In leading her into a fuller view of his personhood, Jesus also guides her out of a life that until now has been violently limited by societal and historical pain into a fuller life, a life where she will 'never be thirsty again,' a life of freedom and of space to be, 'life ... abundantly' (10:10).

This dialogue, then, is a discipleship journey. Throughout John, Jesus will approach different individuals in different ways, with different starting points, responding to different questions and needs. Not only will each of the individual's journey towards a fuller understanding of who Jesus is, but they will also experience the liberative and transformative power of this truth in their daily lived experience. It's never just pure Christology, but a Christology that changes lives. The Word becomes flesh to different individuals in different ways. There is no universal, transferable presentation of the gospel, but a tailored, personalised approach. There is always a deeply personal element, touching the bitter lived experience of the conversation partner.

And so it goes back and forth: question and answer and then more questions. This suggests a very important dimension of how theology is done: questions are raised based on our experience in life in the light of our faith. We do this all the time in our ordinary experience. Some are casual: Why is it raining today in the middle of the dry season? Some are more profound and deal with issues of life and death: Why is there so much suffering, poverty and misery in Africa? Has God forgotten Africa and Africans? Why is my wife barren? Why did my crop fail? What caused the death of my child? These questions cannot be content with simple yes-or-no answers. They touch us deeply. They form part of our ongoing quest as believers for the meaning and purpose of our existence.[91]

All of this is deeply instructive in our quest to learn mission from the Master.

Breaking the binary

The Samaritan woman posits a binary worldview – this mountain or that mountain? Who is right, us or you? So often, in many places, culture wars are framed in terms of irreconcilable opposites, of left or right, of conservative or liberal. Jesus refuses to be drawn. Refuses to choose sides. As a sage, he is able to say, 'both are right,' or, as here, 'both are inadequate'. In the binary-breaking new world that Messiah is ushering in, 'which mountain' becomes a non-question, because we will worship by the Spirit. This creative wisdom strikes the Filipino church as significant.

---

91. Orobator, *Theology*, p. 6.

Often misunderstood as syncretistic, the Filipino predilection for harmonizing opposites cuts sharply against North American 'cognitive simplicity' as the anthropologist Paul Hiebert calls it. 'Twofold judgements seem to be the rule in Western and American life: moral-immoral, legal-illegal, practical-impractical, introvert-extrovert, secular-religious, Christian-pagan.' Such either-or analytical orientation may have something to do with mental conditioning according to the rules of negation in classical logic: 'A is not non-A'. Thus, for instance, 'many North Americans believe that other countries must be on the side of the United States or the Soviet Union. There is no allowance made for politically neutral countries that want to go their own ways and be friends with both.'[92]

Melba Maggay (Philippines) goes on to speak about the 'cognitive alienation' that such binary worldviews create among Eastern Christians, who are 'happily able to live with the engaging perplexities of paradox'.[93] So often, in cross-cultural dialogue, trusting God for a wisdom that breaks the us-them dilemma, that offers an alternative, creative option, that admits the inadequacy of one's own starting point as well as that of the other, is the only way to foster genuine trust and respect.

Better than our ancestors

When the Samaritan woman asks Jesus, 'Are you greater than our father Jacob?' (v. 12), this is a profoundly important question for her. Once, after I had taught on this passage in our local church, one of our Zimbabwean leadership couples stood up to lead the

---

92. Maggay, 'A Religion of Guilt Encounters a Religion of Power', Kindle location 752.
93. Ibid.

congregation in renouncing 'the empty way of life handed down to [us] by [our] ancestors' (1 Peter 1:18, NIV) breaking blood lines and family curses. In this whole passage of Scripture, this was the phrase which stood out to them, and upon which they saw a need to act.

For the 1.5 billion East Asians on the planet, the question of ancestor veneration is a hugely significant one. Asian Christian theology has a long history of wrestling with this cultural reality, and much has been written and taught on both sides of the debate. The answer to her question is that of course Jesus *is* 'greater' than the Samaritan ancestors, but that is no reason to disrespect or dishonour their memory.

Can we as Christians not show that because of Christ, we remember our ancestors *better* and honour them *more* than the unbelievers? Can't we reverence our ancestors as simply the extension of love and respect for distant forebears, foreparts, in obedience to the Fifth Commandment?[94]

David Lim (Philippines), who asks this question in the context of a detailed survey of the historical debate within Chinese Christianity, is really concerned with how to contextualise the gospel among East Asians for whom 'Are you better than our ancestors?' is a make-or-break question that is asked of Jesus and of the Christian gospel. Filial piety (honour for parents), which is the foremost of the eight virtues for a Chinese, is also a distinct moral obligation of Chinese Protestantism.[95] The fifth commandment demands it of us. Also, 'in communalistic cultures, the concepts of being surrounded by "a great crowd of witnesses" (Hebrews 12:1) and "the communion of saints" (in the Apostles'

---

94. Lim, 'Contextualizing the Gospel in Ancestor-Venerating Cultures', Kindle location 7675.
95. Yip, 'Protestant Christianity and Popular Religion in China'. *Ching Feng* 42.3-4 (July-December 1999), pp. 141-142.

Creed) make sense.'[96] It's not possible to provide a simple answer to this deeply personal, powerful and existential question. But the question, asked by the Samaritan woman in this dialogue, really matters, and must not be ignored. Liew (Asian-American) also discusses this:

> When Jesus approaches the woman for water, she raises several descent-related concerns: (1) the long-standing barrier between Jews and Samaritans because of the latter's mixed lineage (4:9); (2) Jesus' status vis-à-vis 'our ancestor Jacob' (4:12); and (3) the different locations of worship according to ancestral traditions (4:19-20). Despite these concerns, her encounter with Jesus ends in her proclamation and the confession by many Samaritans that Jesus is the 'saviour of the world' (4:28-30, 49-42). In other words, by centering on Jesus, John is constructing a community that goes beyond the limits of descent. Its construction is based on faith, confession, or consent.[97]

When the woman later asks, 'Our fathers worshipped on this mountain . . .' (v. 20), Jesus replies talking about *the* Father: '[you will] worship the Father' (v. 21). Adherence to the land and traditions of the fathers is important. But Jesus is introducing her to *the* Father, whose claim on her life and originating of her story ante-dates that of her biological ancestors. His claim on her is older than theirs.

Mission and postcolonialism

The history is important. Jesus is not speaking to her as a decontextualised individual, but as a Samaritan, someone

---

96. Lim, 'Contextualizing the Gospel in Ancestor-Venerating Cultures', p. 8001 to Kindle location 8001.
97. Liew, 'Ambiguous Admittance,' p. 205.

embedded in a community and in a history. The fact that she is unnamed could mean that she is representative. As she appears on the scene, she is three times described as a 'Samaritan woman' (vv. 7-9), underscoring her ethnicity, much in the same way that Ruth is always called 'Ruth the Moabitess'. The important things about her in this story are that she is Samaritan, and that she is a woman.

The famous verse, 'You have had five husbands, and the one you now have is not your husband' (4:18), mirrors exactly the Samaritans' experience of being colonised.[98]

In the 2 Kings account, many of the people living in Samaria were scattered to other nations, and settler colonists from *five* foreign nations were brought into Samaria (2 Kings 17:24). This admixture, both ethnically and also religiously, was the reason that the 'pure' Judeans in the south of the nation would henceforth refuse to have anything to do with this 'mongrel' people. Policies like this, here implemented by the Assyrians, have often been used by colonial powers. Whether the Ulster Scots, given land in Ireland by the British in order to generate a loyal Protestant buffer in the seventeenth century, Stalin's *dekulakizations* in the former Soviet Union, or countless other population transfers and ethnic cleansings, there have often been strategies of unthinkable violence, ethnocidal de-rooting of a people from their land and of a land from its people, a violation of history, often an environmental devastation (incoming peoples lose generations' worth of accrued wisdom vis-à-vis the management of the land), a national trauma so familiar to many across our modern world.

Such en masse dislocations have frequently resulted in intergenerational trauma. Direct survivors often do not want to talk about what they have seen and experienced, even decades

---

98. Chacko, *Intercultural Christology*, p. 130.

later. Often, it is not until the third generation that people begin to question and explore the whys and the hows of such experiences. This was the case with the Holocaust, the Armenian genocide, and Partition between India and Pakistan.

Much of our world today is postcolonial. Many communities carry intergenerational trauma. The twentieth century was one of the most violent centuries we have witnessed, and what was sown in the twentieth is reaped in the twenty-first. Jesus' approach to the Samaritan woman has much to teach us about sensitive gospel witness within such communities in our time.

If Jesus' description of the woman's marital history is personal and individual, then it is filled, not with judgement, but with sympathy. She had either been repeatedly widowed or repeatedly divorced – and divorce was exclusively at the male prerogative. She has been handed, by her family, by her destiny, from husband to husband. If the man she is now with has not married her, again this does not speak to *her* immorality, but to *his*. She is a victim of pain and mess and brokenness, of the sins of others.

But maybe Jesus' description, which so neatly parallels the history of Samaria, is a collective one (couched in indirect, metaphorical language in order to avoid the shame and pain associated with such memories). In this scenario, possibly the current 'man' is the Roman Empire, continuing Samaria's painful history of colonisation. This particular strip of land has been repeatedly occupied throughout its long history, the plaything of mighty empires. Even today, Jacob's well, traditionally located in Balata village on the outskirts of Nablus, is in the Palestinian West Bank, under threat from Israeli settler colonialism. There have very rarely been times when this particular geography has experienced independence, rest, agency. If this reading is accurate, then the woman's retort in verse 17 ('I have no husband') expresses anger and resistance to ongoing domination. So Chacko (India), says, 'I believe it must be an angry and immediate response that came out of frustration because of the continued colonial domination on the land.'[99]

As such, Jesus' conversation with the Samaritan woman, framed as it is by her geography and history, is instructive for all those today who wish to share Christ with those who live under colonial conditions, those with histories of pain, those whose memory and national identity has been violated.

The story begins by speaking of land, in verse 4. Land is so powerful. There are countless moving stories from Partition in which people who were forcibly dislocated from their *zameen* (ancestral land), took with them jars of earth or handfuls of stones which they would then touch every day to continue their spiritual connection to their home soil.[100]

The woman keeps trying to use the language of polarity (vv. 9,20), and Jesus keeps taking away polarities in his responses. Jesus approaches through vulnerability and real need (he needs a drink), thus ennobling her as host – an ennobling so sacred for those who have experienced national trauma in relation to their land. To be approached as host is to be seen as belonging. For a Jew to approach a Samaritan as a host is to validate her claim.

Jesus engages with her theological questions linked to a very precious national narrative: 'Our fathers worshipped on this mountain, but you say that in Jerusalem is the place where people ought to worship' (v. 20). Many commentators either see this as a distraction technique – she is trying to avoid Jesus' direct personal questions by throwing up a smokescreen of theological bluff; or else they see her narrative as plain wrong – the Northern kingdom was wrong to create its own cultic centre in place of Jerusalem; a view constituting a very one-dimensional reading of the Old Testament. In fact, Jesus' response shows both

99. Chacko, *Intercultural Christology*, p. 130.
100. Empire Podcast, 'Partition' 8th November 2022 (Goalhanger Podcasts), https://open.spotify.com/episode/51M9szl5FjBXGyUgAh4BMZ (accessed 7.3.24).

perspectives to be flawed. Jesus seems to take her seriously as a theologian, dignifying her important question with a serious answer. He sees her question as a natural follow-on from his observation about Samaria's history. He takes her (and us) by surprise by affirming neither Samaria-centric nor Jerusalem-centric worship. In a profound, famous, and world-changing statement, Jesus, entrusting breath-taking revelation to this most unexpected of disciples, declares:

> 'Woman, believe me, the hour is coming when neither on this mountain nor in Jerusalem will you worship the Father ... But the hour is coming, and is now here, when the true worshippers will worship the Father in spirit and in truth, for the Father is seeking such people to worship him. God is spirit, and those who worship him must worship in spirit and truth.'
>
> *(John 4:21-24)*

He listens closely, dignifies her with a serious answer, entrusts her with profound revelation, tends to peacebuilding by refusing either historical narrative as absolute, and refuses polarities and otherisation. These are profound skills for mission in colonial or postcolonial contexts. If we could demonstrate even a fraction of Jesus' sensitivity and wisdom in our cross-cultural conversations, we would be doing better than we are at the moment! In this way, Schneiders concludes:

> The entire dialogue between Jesus and the woman is the 'wooing' of Samaria to full covenant fidelity in the New Israel by Jesus, the New Bridegroom. It has nothing to do with the woman's private moral life but with the covenant life of the community.[101]

---

101. Schneiders, 'A Feminist Interpretation', p. 249.

The Indian Church

The Indian Church has long loved this story, as she has long loved John's Gospel as a whole. Sadhu Sundar Singh, India's original contextual theologian and wandering evangelist, loved by European Christian leaders such as C.S. Lewis and Corrie Ten Boom, made famous the saying that what was needed for India was 'the water of life, but not in the European cup'.

This story is seen, in various Indian contexts, as Jesus breaking caste. To drink from the vessel of a woman of a different caste is unthinkable pollution, even as today different drinking vessels are kept distinct from different groups – drinking is direct pollution.

There is a strikingly similar story in Buddhist tradition, where the disciple Ananda accepts a drink of water from a lower-caste woman, an important origin story in Buddhism's emergence from the Hindu milieu as a caste-free Way. Thus, in Indian perspective, along with Jesus' defying of geographic, ethnic and gender boundary norms, the acceptance of a drink also defies caste restrictions.

Jesus, who comes to the Samaritan village and asks a woman for water, corresponds in many ways to Ananda, a famous disciple of Buddha who asked a Matanga Caste woman for water at a well. The social distancing between communities is seen in her question, 'How do you ask water of me, an outcaste who may not touch thee without contamination?' (see John 4:9). Ananda replied, 'My sister, I ask not of thee thy caste, I ask for water to drink' (see John 4:10, 13-14). He breaks the sociocultural and religious barriers in drinking the water.[102]

---

102. Thomaskutty, 'The Gospel of John', pp. 149-150.

Does she call him a prophet because of his supernatural knowledge, or because of his solidarity with the margins, his interest in justice? Even here, 'Sir, I perceive that you are a prophet' (v. 19) encourages us to view the prophetic in postcolonial conversation as having much to do with an understanding of historic pain, intergenerational trauma, and the speaking of words which help this woman to feel seen, known, understood.

Udit Raj – a Dalit, and himself a Buddhist – notes, 'Born as a higher caste Jew, in the ancestral and kingly clan of David, Jesus did not have any hesitation to take water from a Samaritan woman, an outcaste woman – which gives a notion that there is no caste or creed before the might of thirst and hunger.'[103] Indian writer Rekha Chennattu makes her a role model for modern Christians: 'The story of the Samaritan woman could empower Indian women to awaken their dormant spiritual energy, the life-giving force . . . This awakening is needed for women to look at their presence and mission in the Church from a new perspective.'[104]

Michael Amaldoss, in *The Asian Jesus,* reflects on the dialogical approach to teaching as being the way that gurus interact with disciples:

In the story of the encounter of Jesus with the Samaritan woman we have an example of how a guru should handle a disciple, respecting her/his freedom and guiding her/him along to make basic choices in life (Jn 4:1-42). The method used is one of dialogue.[105]

---

103. Raj, 'Cry of Christ'.
104. Chennattu, 'Women in the Mission of the Church'.
105. Amaladoss, *The Asian Jesus*, Kindle location 1471.

The whole community

This woman also proves to be an extremely effective evangelist, inviting her whole community to encounter Christ. We see here, as so often in the New Testament, an experience of communal conversion, where the village turns out initially because of her testimony, but eventually many come to have their own faith. In communalistic cultures, individual conversion often does violence to peoples' natural kinship connections – just as Jesus warned Nicodemus when he said, 'You must be born again.' Many from the village believe at the words of Christ. And they articulate their faith in a unique way, 'We know that this is indeed the Saviour of the world' (4:42). Again, such a profound articulation of the person and work of Christ in the mouths of unlikely, unnamed Samaritans, takes our breath away.

> The proclamation by the townspeople of Sychar that Jesus is the 'Saviour of the world' (John 4:42) was not merely a vindication of the claim of Samaritans to equal participation with Jews in the salvation offered by Jesus but also of the equal participation of women in that salvation. 'World' is a universalist term, and the invisible subgroup of every excluded group is women.[106]

This could only have been articulated by non-Jews. Jewish disciples, from within their tradition, could only have seen Christ as 'Saviour of Israel'. It takes those from outside to understand that salvation is also for those outside. This is like the difference between the 'World Series' baseball tournament, in which only US teams compete, and the 'World Cup' football tournament, in which teams from all over the world compete. A baseball team cannot truly be 'champion of the world' without leaving the

---

106. Schneiders, 'A Feminist Interpretation', p. 241.

borders of the United States. And Christ cannot be seen to be Saviour of the world without leaving the boundaries of Israel, as he does in John 4.

Finally, we reflect on Ephrem the Syrian's words about the woman's progressive understanding of Christ:

> At the beginning of the conversation he [Jesus] did not make himself known to her, but first she caught sight of a thirsty man, then a Jew, then a Rabbi, afterwards a prophet, last of all the Messiah. She tried to get the better of the thirsty man, she showed dislike of the Jew, she heckled the Rabbi, she was swept off her feet by the prophet, and she adores the Christ.[107]

---

107. Ephrem the Syrian quoted in Bailey, *Middle Eastern Eyes*, p. 215.

Chapter Eight

Shepherd

(John Chapters 6 to 10)

The wolf is upset about what he left behind, and the
shepherd is upset about what he took away.

(Armenian proverb)

Ugandan church leader Kefa Sempangi tells the story of meeting
one of brutal dictator Idi Amin's assassins and torturers,
responsible for the deaths of hundreds of people. This man
was converted when he read John 8:44, 'You are of your father
the devil'. He realised in that moment that in working for Idi
Amin, he had been serving Satan, and he repented and gave his
allegiance to Christ.[108]

This section, chapters 6 to 10 of John's Gospel, is held together
by the uniting theme of Jesus as Shepherd, ending with Jesus'
iconic declaration, 'I am the good shepherd. The good shepherd
lays down his life for the sheep' (10:11).

A friend of mine has lived among nomadic peoples in the
deserts of Chad. When I asked her which aspects of the gospel
resonated most with her Chadian friends, she told me, 'Everything
to do with shepherds. That is their world, their whole life. It is
concrete and every day and matter of fact and deeply resonant

---

108. Sempangi, *A Distant Grief*, pp. 129-130.

for them.' The great theologian John Mbiti (Kenya), recalling his childhood tending sheep, reflected, 'As I went about in my youth looking after these animals, little did I realise that the gospel was right there in front of me.'[109]

Yet, lest we get lulled into a false sense of security by the pastoral idyll, let's not forget that Jesus' statement 'I am the good shepherd' is also political. It's a criticism of the failure of the existing shepherds of Israel. I am the *good* shepherd, as opposed to you *evil* shepherds. Underlying this is the prophetic criticism of Ezekiel 34, where the prophet scathingly rebukes Israel's failed shepherds. Many African Christian leaders have used this metaphor to criticise their own corrupt governments. Hannah W. Kinoti (Kenya) wrote an essay on Psalm 23 entitled 'In the Valley of the Shadow of Idi Amin'.[110] Timothy Wangusa (Uganda) wrote a parody of Psalm 23, 'The state is my shepherd', the point, of course, being that the authoritarian state was seeking to replace God. David Gitari (Kenya) often preached from John 10 during Kenya's political crisis of the early 1990s.

> The passage in question is so well known in Africa because it immediately follows the much-quoted verse 10:10, in which Jesus promises his followers life in abundance. Preaching to a gathering that included many politicians, Gitari concluded, 'Go to parliament and be a good shepherd.'[111]

For Jews, God as the Shepherd of Israel who led them out of Egypt, through the desert and finally into the promised land was a core part of their theological understanding. In their national imagination, the image of the tall figure of the pillar of cloud by day and the pillar of fire by night marching before the tiny,

---

109. Mbiti, quoted in Jenkins, *The New Faces of Christianity*, p. 147.
110. Kinoti, 'Well Being in African Society and in the Bible'.
111. Jenkins, *The New Faces of Christianity*, p. 147.

ant-like figures of the people of promise, stretched out across the wide desert plain, was re-envisioned every day as tall, lone shepherds were seen striding out in front of their flocks on the way to pasture.

There are certain things that a shepherd does. Psalm 23, written by Jesus' ancestor the wilderness shepherd David, captures the responsibilities undertaken by the Lord as Shepherd of his people in sublime, ageless poetry. These key shepherd-actions, as God led his people through the wilderness towards the promised land, included the provision of manna/bread/ pasture, water, leadership through the darkness, a sense of journey/pilgrimage towards an ultimate destination, with the whole sequence taking place in the context of danger/enemies.

The October feast of Sukkot (Tabernacles/Booths) was a moment of collective remembrance of these dynamics as both historical and paradigmatic, a real key festival in the nation's self-understanding and God-understanding. For a whole week, the nation would move out of their houses and live in crudely constructed shacks or tents, a festival rich in symbolism that looked back to the wilderness journey, and looked forward in hope to the end-times shepherd, the belief that God would once again come and shepherd his people.

The Sukkot prayer in Nehemiah 9 captures all the key elements of the wilderness journey; 'They kept the feast seven days, and on the eighth day there was a solemn assembly, according to the rule' (Nehemiah 8:18). Here are some highlights of the prayer they offer at this moment:

'And you saw the affliction of our fathers in Egypt and heard their cry...' 9:9

'By a pillar of cloud you led them in the day, and by a pillar of fire in the night to light for them the way in which they should go.' 9:12

'You gave them bread from heaven for their hunger and brought water for them out of the rock for their thirst, and you told them to go in to possess the land that you had sworn to give them.' 9:15

'You gave your good Spirit to instruct them and did not withhold your manna from their mouth and gave them water for their thirst.' 9:20

'Sihon king of Heshbon and ... Og king of Bashan.' 9:22

We see here light (leadership by a pillar of fire), bread from heaven (manna), water from the rock for thirst, the wilderness journey from the deliverance in Egypt towards the promised land, and the presence of enemies (Sihon and Og). All these elements are commemorated at Sukkot, all are mentioned in Nehemiah 9 and Psalm 23, and all are fulfilled by Jesus in John 6 – 10.

This section of John brings to the fore all of these shepherd-actions, the supernatural provision of bread (6:1-59), water for the thirsty (7:37-39), light (8:12), protection (8:1-11), and the good shepherd passage (10:1-18).

Shepherd language in John

Throughout John's Gospel, shepherd language is in evidence. Discipleship is articulated as following ('follow me'), with disciples sometimes successfully following Jesus, and at other times failing to follow. In addition, there is pathway language, 'I am the way.' Speaking of Jesus as the Way has long been especially meaningful to Asian Christians. Michael Amaladoss (India) explains:

The symbol of the way evokes rich resonances in Asia. In the Chinese religio-cultural tradition one would think immediately of the Tao and in the Indian religious tradition one would recall the marga. Buddha also spoke of the eight-fold path. A look at these would enrich our own understanding of the richness of the symbol of the way.[112]

Samuel Escobar (Peru), one of the fathers of Latin-American liberation theology, writes that the idea of road, or journey, is also very important for Latin-American theology: 'As Latin American thinkers we chose to do our theology not contemplating Christ from the comfortable distance of the balcony, a secure and easily received orthodoxy, but from following him on the troubled roads of our Latin American lands.'[113] This distinction between the balcony and the road became paradigmatic for liberation theology, and is very in tune with the themes of John's Gospel, where Word becomes flesh and takes to the road with us, inviting his disciples to follow him out of one reality and into another. The weariness and dust of the road are essential ideas for Latin-American theology with its emphasis on the poor, the illiterate, the unfortunate. Jesus, as shepherd, is the Way.

The leadership of Jesus is articulated as gathering, like the gathering of a flock. John tells us that the high priest spoke like this:

> He did not say this of his own accord, but being high priest that year he prophesied that Jesus would die for the nation, and not for the nation only, but also to gather into one the children of God who are scattered abroad.
>
> *(John 11:51-52)*

The call of Peter to pastoral (shepherding) ministry at the end of the Gospel is replete with shepherding language. Chapter 21 is full of 'following' as well as instructions to 'feed my sheep'.

---

112. Amaladoss, *The Asian Jesus,* Kindle location 901.
113. Escobar, 'Doing Theology on Christ's Road', Kindle location 653.

Chapter 10, the famous 'good shepherd' chapter, is rich in the imagery of sheep and pasture and shepherding, including the famous missional promise, 'And I have other sheep that are not of this fold. I must bring them also, and they will listen to my voice. So there will be one flock, one shepherd' (v. 16), whereby Jesus expands the familiar Old Testament concept of the flock of God beyond ethnic Jews, a profound expression of the *Missio Dei*, the great purpose of God to unite all people under the headship of Christ. Putting all this together, Wright (England) puts it like this: 'When we are watching the story of Jesus unfold, we are also watching the story of Israel's God coming back, as he had long promised, to rescue and "shepherd" his people.'[114]

Let's look at the ways in which Jesus fulfils this symbolic role of shepherd in this section of John.

I am the bread

The feeding of the 5,000, clearly a favourite of the Gospel writers as it is recorded in all four Gospel accounts, happens around Passover, one year before Jesus' death (6:4). Passover, when the people remember deliverance from the Egyptian oppressor, and long for deliverance from the Roman oppressor. Passover, the original shepherd context as God led his sheep out of Egypt. John tells us that 'a large crowd was following him, because they saw the signs that he was doing' (6:2), following being shepherd language and signs being Exodus language (Nehemiah 9:10).

John points out that this event takes place 'the other side of the Sea of Galilee, which is the Sea of Tiberias' (6:1). Biju Chacko (India) proposes that the double naming of the sea reminds us of the Roman Imperialistic context and that renaming the sea after the emperor 'indicates how colonialism operates, a slow

---

114. Wright, *How God Became King*, p. 187.

transference of natural resources under its grip, to the extent of naming it after the colonisers. The mention of "Tiberias" thus indicates the imperial setup of this locale and its sociopolitical reality'.[115] The grain stores are full of food, but the people are starving, because Rome has commandeered the grain. The Sea of Galilee is full of fish, but the fish belongs to Caesar – he has renamed the sea after himself. The context is not just one of poverty and hunger, but of restive malcontent. The nation's shepherds have failed to provide for the people – and the people are hungry.

'Jesus said, "Make the people sit down." Now there was much grass in the place. So the men sat down, about five thousand in number' (6:10). Why would John tell us about the grass, unless he was reflecting Psalm 23:2, 'He makes me lie down in green pastures'?

Jesus' feeding of the crowd with bread and fish is both subversive (bread and fish belonged to Caesar and were taxable – these fish are from the very lake that has been renamed and appropriated by Caesar),[116] but is also the act of a true king. Kings provide food for their people. Jesus, born in the house of bread, Bethlehem, feeds his people with bread. Jesus is also, as Messiah, beginning to undo the curse. Where Adam had been told, 'By the sweat of your face you shall eat bread' (Genesis 3:19), the Second Adam is now providing miracle bread without the people having to sweat for it.

Jesus' dialogue with the crowd throughout chapter 6 matches John's preferred approach, with the crowd speaking seven times. On this occasion, they advance in their understanding through the first five statements, from 'This is indeed the Prophet' (6:14),

---

115. Chacko, *Intercultural Christology*, p. 172.
116. Resistance movements have often politicised the reclaiming of their natural resources as a rallying point; consider Gandhi's call to Indians to make their own salt, when salt production was monopolised by the British.

through 'Rabbi' (6:25), to 'Sir, give us this bread always' (6:34) – just like the Samaritan woman's progressive understanding to the symmetrical request, 'Sir, give me this water, so that I will not be thirsty or have to come here to draw water' (4:15).

Unlike the Samaritan woman, however, the Judaian villagers (John here emphasising their Judaian heritage, drawing a distinction with the outsider Samaritan woman)[117] stop progressing in their understanding, choking on the bread of life, and use their final two moments of direct speech to grumble and doubt (6:41-42, 6:52). They are not yet ready to believe.

Jesus' teaching in this chapter centres on the 'I am' saying, 'I am the bread of life' (v. 48). He expounds this in relation to the manna in the wilderness, and also in relation to his having come 'down from heaven' (vv. 57-58). He also makes a great deal of the connection between bread and life, including eternal life and being raised up 'on the last day' (v. 54). There is also a 'for the world', global element: 'the bread that I will give for the life of the world is my flesh' (v. 51).

Bread is considered sacred in many cultures, not least the cultures of the ancient Middle East. Rihbany (Syria), in his classic *The Syrian Christ,* writes, 'The *'aish* [bread] was something more than mere matter. Inasmuch as it sustained life, it was God's own life made tangible for his child, man, to feed upon.'[118]

'Bread is the head of everything', says an old Russian proverb. 'Better bread with water than cake with trouble', says another. Lenin's revolutionary slogan was 'peace, land and bread' – aimed at the starving masses who were being failed by their shepherds. At Russian weddings, bride and groom share bread together, the foundational symbol of life and sustenance.

The first day ends with 'Perceiving then that they were about to come and take him by force to make him king, Jesus withdrew'

---

117. Kanagaraj, *John*, p. 70.
118. Rihbany, *The Syrian Christ*, p. 139.

(6:15). They desire to make him king because he has fed them, as their current shepherds are failing to do. And the detail of there being 5,000 men? A Roman legion numbered 5,000 men. There was one Roman legion occupying Palestine. Jesus is able to feed his people and able to field an army. Of course they want him as king! Mark makes this even more explicit, with this story positioned close to the story of the Gerasene man, who was delivered of a 'legion' of demons which went into a herd of pigs – a striking use of the Roman military term. The standard of the Tenth Legion, which occupied Judea, was a boar.

How can the importance of 'I am the bread of life' be communicated in places where people do not eat bread? Havea, a Pacific Islander, imagines how Jesus would have taught if he were Word become flesh among the Pacific Islands. Havea insists that Jesus would have added a further identification of himself, 'I am the coconut of life.'

> The coconut is chosen as it is fundamental to the existence of life in the Pacific Islands. Coconut trees are to be found on every island ... In terms of Christology, the coconut is 'life' in two ways. The first is that the coconut supports and sustains the everyday life of the islanders. Coconuts are a life source in the islands. Every part of the coconut tree is used in some way to sustain life on the islands by way of shelter, food, and everyday utensils and utilities. Secondly, the life cycle of the coconut parallels or symbolizes the events of incarnation, death, resurrection, ascension, and Pentecost. The coconut fruit grows at the top of the coconut tree; when it ripens, it falls to the ground below. Given the nature of its shape it will roll to the lowest point of the ground where it will stop. If it is left on the ground, it will undergo a process whereby the coconut dies. In this way the fallen and disregarded coconut produces a new tree, which itself produces fruit to

satisfy people's hunger and thirst . . . The biblical parallels are obvious. Jesus was at first in the presence of the Father, equal with God on high – but he did not remain there. At the right time he came down to earth, descending to the lowest points of human life. In his life journey and ministry he was discarded and left to die. From his death and broken body came new life, a life which has produced 'food and drink' to satisfy the hunger and thirst of the world.[119]

Streams in the desert

From 7:1 through to 10:21, the scene is the feast of Sukkot in Jerusalem. This joyous October festival, which looked back to the wilderness journey, and forward to the last days when the Lord would again come and shepherd his people (Ezekiel 34; Zechariah 9 – 11), also looked to the present as a harvest festival, a prayer for rain at the end of the long summer and for light by which the crops would grow.[120]

On the seventh day of the feast, the priests would fill large golden vessels with water from Siloam, Jerusalem's spring and main water source, and process along the Temple Way leading from Siloam to the temple precinct, followed by the jostling crowds, and pour out the water at the base of the altar.[121] Looking back, a remembrance of water in the wilderness, looking forward, a prayer for the last days river of God (Ezekiel 47), and looking practically, a prayer for rain. It is important not to overlook the prayers for rain, as our brothers and sisters who live closer to and wholly dependent upon the caprices of nature remind us. By October, there would have been no rain in Jerusalem for

---

119. Carroll, 'Coconut Theology', pp. 537-539.
120. Neyrey, *John*, p. 136.
121. *b. Suk.* 4:9.

five or six months, so Sukkot was timed agriculturally as well as spiritually. It is in this context that Jesus stands up and makes his iconic appeal:

> On the last day of the feast, the great day, Jesus stood up and cried out, 'If anyone thirsts, let him come to me and drink. Whoever believes in me, as the Scripture has said, "Out of his heart will flow rivers of living water." Now this he said about the Spirit, whom those who believed in him were to receive, for as yet the Spirit had not been given, because Jesus was not yet glorified.
>
> *(John 7:37-39)*

The observant reader will note that, in the subsequent response to Jesus' claims, allusion is made to his Bethlehemite pedigree; 'Has not the Scripture said that the Christ comes from the offspring of David, and comes from Bethlehem, the village where David was?' (7:42). Indeed, Christ's descending from David, and birth in Bethlehem do, as is implied, not only affirm his Messianic status, but align him with the great sweep of shepherding throughout Scripture, which arcs through Bethlehem, home of shepherds, and of David the shepherd king, through prophecies such as Micah 5:2, to the birth of Jesus, witnessed by shepherds. This rich tradition is discussed in my book *The Bethlehem Story: Mission and Justice in the Margins of the World*.

On the next day, the eighth day of this seven-plus-one festival, we will see the Shepherd protecting a vulnerable woman accused of adultery, a beautiful and tender fulfilment of the 'in the presence of my enemies' (Psalm 23:5) motif, to which we will turn in detail in the next chapter.

And then, still on that final day of Sukkot, he will utter a stunning and dramatic claim to fulfil the light theme of Sukkot, 'I am the light of the world' (8:12).

The Good Shepherd

And so, having fulfilled the responsibilities of the shepherd regarding bread, water, light, protection, and leadership from somewhere to somewhere else, having completely fulfilled the festival of Tabernacles in himself, as he will later fulfil Passover in his own person, Jesus brings this section to summation by describing himself as the Shepherd. He takes the divine identifier for himself, 'I am the good shepherd' (v. 11). He is claiming to be God, come to shepherd his people, as promised.

This Christological image is rich in so many ways. It is concrete, not abstract – much easier to understand than some of the more philosophical ideas of how the Trinity holds together. It is accessible – people from around the world understand what a shepherd does. It resonates with the entire biblical story; sheep and shepherds are a recurring theme which builds throughout Scripture to the perfect fulfilment in Christ. And it has hence proven a strong way in particular for Muslims to engage with Christ. Whilst Pauline Christology has frequently created stumbling blocks for Muslims, John's approach offers easier on-ramps for dialogue, as Bailey writes:

> In the inevitable coming theological interface with Islam, *Christology from the mouth of Jesus* has the potential to bypass centuries-old roadblocks to understanding and authentically communicate afresh, without compromise of meaning, the biblical understanding of who Jesus affirmed himself to be.[122]

The Shepherd speaks of bringing his sheep out – the Greek word is *ekvalei* – to put outside:

---

122. Bailey, *The Good Shepherd*, p. 273, italics mine.

The sheep hear his voice, and he calls his own sheep by name and leads them out. When he has brought out all his own, he goes before them, and the sheep follow him.

(John 10:3-4)

This is significant, because just a few verses earlier, the blind man had been 'cast ... out' [*ekvalei*] of the synagogue (9:34). For the man born blind, while his experience was that the Pharisees were casting him out, in actual fact, the shepherd was leading him out. To be excommunicate in this way was a deeply stigmatising experience, designed as the ultimate humiliation. In honour-based cultures, there is nothing worse than excommunication. Doole (Northern Ireland), wrestling with the unusualness of John's noun *aposynagogos* (9:22, 12:42, 16:2), found only in John, comes up with a translation of an 'out-of-the-synagoger':

They soon learned not to be ashamed of this, but rather adopted it as a badge to be worn with pride. The negative consequences of this social stigma are overcome when they discover that Jesus himself told them that they would be 'Out-of-the-Synagogers.'[123]

The power of excommunication is dishonour, a social pariah status that causes the rest of the community to stay at arm's length, to think twice before conducting business or engaging in a contract with one – similar in many ways to the modern equivalent of being 'cancelled'. And yet Jesus in 16:2 warns his disciples that this *will* happen, and the putting out of the blind man is compared to the leading out of the sheep by the shepherd. In line with Hebrews 12, Jesus is inviting his followers to worldly dishonour.

---

123. Doole, 'To be "An Out-of-the-Synagoguer"', p. 409.

The 'leading out' aspect of the shepherding of Jesus is really important when we are thinking about mission. Israel left Egypt, following the shepherd, without knowing where they were going. And when Jesus calls people out of a system, be it Hinduism or Islam, traditional religion or Communism, or the materialistic atheism of the West, he leads them out into the unknown, into a wide-open space, into a community on the move. We follow the Shepherd and he leads us out – of our structures and parameters and the things that defined our realities and into a desert space, a liminal space. The missional call to discipleship is a call to the unknown. Nicodemus will no longer have his family name, and the Samaritan woman will no longer have her mountain. The things that defined people will define them no longer. We exit Egypt into an expansive desert plain where the wind can blow where it pleases, howling eastwards or northwards. Freedom is a wide-open space, a pilgrimage. And as it took a whole generation to get Egypt out of the affections and spirits of the children of Israel, so we need a long-term view of missional discipleship – some allegiances will take more than a generation to erase, some values more than a generation to cultivate.

Life to the full (10:10)[124]

Both John 10:10 and 10:11 are oft-quoted, much-loved verses around the world. But we must never forget that, in context, they go together. Life to the full occurs when the Good Shepherd is followed. Where earthly shepherds fail, the Good Shepherd succeeds.

One of John's favourite articulations of the mission of Jesus is as his mission to bring life.[125] According to Kostenberger

---

124. The NIV reads, 'I have come that they may have life, and have it to the full.' Popularly, many Christians condense this promise to 'life to the full'.
125. 3:16, 6:57, 10:10, 14:6, 17:2.

(Austria), this is John's 'favourite expression' regarding the redemptive aspect of Jesus' mission.[126] *Zoe* (life) itself occurs thirty-eight times in John, including, significantly, the thematic bookends of 1:4 and 20:31.

'Life' appears to be John's equivalent of 'kingdom' in the Synoptics. In Bauckham's (England) view, 'John tells us, somewhat subtly, that he uses the term "eternal life" (or, often, just "life") as equivalent to the term "kingdom of God" in other Gospels or Gospel traditions.'[127] [128]

John 10:10 is one of the most famous verses in the whole of Scripture, and this is true around the world. Yet, unsurprisingly, different cultures respond to this verse and its promise in very different ways. 'Life to the full' means different things to different people. 'Life is undoubtedly a universal aspiration, yet it stands out as a prime value in indigenous African thought. Therefore African Christologies arise through the confluence of African concepts and biblical affirmations of life, in relation to contemporary realities. Thus a cardinal image of Jesus is life-giver, or the one who fulfils African aspirations for life (John 10:10, 14:6)',[129] writes Diane Stinton (Canada).

Madame Guyon (seventh-century France) is remembered as one of the most influential European Christian women of all time. Her writings were publicly burned, she was denounced as a heretic and imprisoned, and yet her little books continued to spread during her lifetime. Her perspective on John 10:10 was very different from some modern 'prosperity' ideas; for her, 'life to the full' meant the fullness of sharing Christ's sufferings, the fullness of carrying one's cross:

---

126. Kostenberger, *Challenge*, p. 447.
127. Bauckham, *Gospel of Glory*, Kindle location 1553.
128. For example, 'but for the food that endures to eternal life, which the Son of Man will give to you' (John 6:27) is the Johannine equivalent as the Synoptic saying, 'But seek first the kingdom of God and his righteousness, and all these things will be added to you' (Matthew 6:33; see also Luke 12:31).
129. Stinton, 'Jesus Christ', p. 436.

Learn, having done this, to accept equally all His gifts, whether they are light or darkness. Treat fruitfulness and barrenness the same way. Whether it be weakness or strength, sweetness or bitterness, temptation, distraction, pain, weariness, uncertainty or blessing, all should be received as equal from the Lord's hand.[130]

Experiencing the Depths of Jesus Christ went on to have a profound and ongoing effect on subsequent missionary movements. The Quakers were deeply shaped by it. Count Zinzendorf and the extraordinary Moravian movement were influenced by Guyon's writings. John Wesley read it as a young man and was profoundly moved. Hudson Taylor used to recommend it to believers of his day. And Watchman Nee, shaped by this book, had it translated into Chinese and made available to every new convert.

The Middle Eastern Christian minority is beginning to read John 10:10 as a call to resist the minority mindset of ghettoisation, survival and non-engagement, and as an invitation to a fully engaged citizenship. The 2021 ecumenical document, *We Choose Abundant Life-Christians in the Middle East: Towards Renewed Theological, Social, and Political Choices* issued a clarion call to the Church in the Middle East, 'to move from an obsession with existence and survival to taking the risk of presence and witness'.[131] Palestinian Viola Raheb explains: 'For the future of Christians in the Middle East, the document expresses a vision of living together with believers of other religions especially Muslims as brothers and sisters and upholding human dignity and freedom.'[132]

Latin-American Elizabeth Conde-Frazier writes about the everyday struggle of Latina women in the USA, the *luchar*. 'For

---

130. Guyon, *Experiencing the Depths*, p. 43.
131. *We Choose Abundant Life*, p. 42.
132. Raheb, 'Middle Eastern Theologies', p. 432.

evangelicas the power to *luchar*, to fight the good fight, comes from the Jesus who came to give life more abundantly.'[133]

I-Kiribati is one of the tragically disappearing islands, a low-lying atoll that is under grave threat as sea-levels rise due to climate change. Timon and Kaunda are theologians who live on I-Kiribati and seek to articulate a Christian faith in the context of lament as their homeland literally sinks beneath the waves. For them, John 10:10 is a profound challenge to faith; what does life to the full look like when the future of one's homeland is so bleak? 'Here the faith in God the Creator is affirmed and simultaneously questions are raised about how faith in God affects perspectives on climate change.'[134]

Hopefully, this tiny sampling of different takes on this verse shows that 'life to the full' is a really precious promise of Christ, whatever one's context. Jesus, the Good Shepherd who lays down his life for the sheep, the returning end-times shepherd of Israel, is the only one who can bring life, and life to the full. He is gathering his flock. He is fulfilling countless Old Testament themes and expectations. He is critiquing the failed leadership of earthly shepherds around the world. He calls people out of their old realities to follow him. He provides bread and water, light and protection. Israel's God has come back to shepherd his flock, as he promised long ago.

133. Conde-Frazier, 'Latina Evangelicas', p. 66.
134. Carroll, 'Coconut Theology,' p. 542.

Chapter Nine

Accused
(John 8:1-11)

The cockroach cannot be innocent
in a court where the hen is judge.
(African proverb)

We were sitting in a Greek restaurant. It was early evening and the bouzouki players were still tuning up. I had just told Peter that I was writing a book on John. 'John chapter 8 changed my life,' he said simply.

'Tell me?' I asked, leaning back. The others round the table all quietened down too. And Peter, now seventy years old, shared his story.

'Like most Greek Cypriots, I was nominally Orthodox but had no real faith. My entire youth had been misspent in sexual immorality and drug use. I was in my twenties when my closest friend became a Christian. He gave me a copy of John's Gospel to read – I read it in a week, cover to cover. But it was when I got to chapter 8, the woman caught in adultery, that everything changed for me. I realised that the weight of shame I was carrying was exhausting. Like this woman, I felt deeply unclean from my sexual history. It was sapping the life out of me. It's like Jesus stepped out of the pages of the Bible at that moment. He became real. He took away my burden of shame and gave me the power to live differently. When I finished reading through John, I knelt on my own in my room and gave my life to Christ.'

Setting the scene

In the early morning Jesus, having spent the night on the Mount of Olives, returns to the temple courts and sits down to teach the people. In context in John (and we will come in due course to discuss the homelessness of this story and whether or not it truly belongs in John 8), it is the final Sabbath day of the week-long Feast of Tabernacles, or Sukkot. We have seen, in this section of John, so many of the themes of Sukkot being fulfilled in Christ himself. The mighty ideas, arising from Israel's wilderness journey, of God as shepherd going before his people in the pillar of cloud by day and pillar of light by night, are fulfilled in Christ, Israel's true shepherd. As God provided manna, so Christ has fed the 5,000 (chapter 6). As God provided water, so Christ gives the Spirit (chapter 7). As God gave light in the dark wilderness, so Christ is the light of the world (chapter 8). And this section will end with Jesus declaring himself to be the good shepherd (chapter 10).

As the shepherd prepares a table 'in the presence of my enemies' (Psalm 23:5) – protecting vulnerable Israel from the surrounding wolves – so in our verses here, Christ as Shepherd will protect a vulnerable woman from the wolves which surround her. As the shepherd 'lays down his life for the sheep' (10:11), so at the start of the story the crowd is eager to stone the woman, and by the end of chapter 8 they are picking up stones to stone Jesus himself (8:59). Jesus successfully redirects the anger of the crowd away from the woman and onto himself. He interposes himself, so to speak, between the aggressors and their target, diverting their fury and mob violence away from her and towards himself.

At the same time, he redirects the woman's attention away from the crowd and onto himself. In a move which resonates deeply with those surrounded, humiliated, intimidated, threatened, Jesus steps into the circle, confronts the crowd and then turns to the woman. 'Woman, where are they?' he asks (v. 10). And the fearful realise that while they were looking at Jesus, the threat was disbursed.

The final day of Sukkot

This final day of Sukkot stretches from 8:2 through to 10:21. It is Saturday, the Sabbath (9:14). Yes, the Friday was called 'the last day of the feast, the great day' (7:37), when Jesus had made his iconic announcement about the Spirit, the water of life, but Sukkot was a seven-plus-one festival, a week from Saturday to Friday, then an eighth day over the second Sabbath, after which everyone would dismantle their little shacks of sticks and leaves and go back to normal life. This is the context of the account of the accused woman.

In addition, let's recognise the tense atmosphere in Jerusalem during this week. The Roman legion of 5,000 soldiers, ordinarily garrisoned at Caesarea on the coast, would relocate en masse to Jerusalem for each of the three annual pilgrimage festivals, being billeted in the Fortress of Antonia, an imposing imperial building adjoining the temple precinct. Jerusalem's usually small population would be swelled by as much as a factor of ten, as God-fearing people from across the country would gather to their spiritual capital. This teeming mass of humanity, already angry at Roman occupation, taxation and brutality, was like dry kindling only needing a spark to ignite a rebellion. The genteel Jerusalemites, for the most part content with the status quo as collaborators with and beneficiaries of empire, would be massively outnumbered by the rural poor for this week, people who were hungrier, angrier, more nationalistic, more impoverished. Yes, if there was ever going to be a revolt against imperial rule, the pilgrimage festivals, with their narratives of national deliverance and their huge crowds, were the ideal tinderbox.

And so the Roman soldiers sat atop the walls of the Fortress of Antonia watched, eagle-eyed, for any signs of revolt, for any flagrant acts of disobedience and resistance, for any large, unruly gatherings.

And the Jewish religious leaders, having failed in their attempt to arrest Jesus directly the previous day, hatch a cunning plan. They devise a plot to cause Jesus to incriminate himself. 'If we can't arrest him,' they reason, 'we will get the Romans to arrest him for us.'

They bring a woman, allegedly caught *en flagrante* in the middle of an adulterous act, and place her 'in the midst' (8:3). In front of the crowd, in front of the watching Roman soldiers. The trap is simple – will Jesus affirm the law of Moses and decree that the woman should be stoned to death, or will he not? If he opts for community stoning, and everyone takes up stones to throw, this will be in violation of Roman law, which forbade what it saw as lawless lynching, the Roman infantry would flood into the temple courts, disburse the crowd and arrest Jesus for instigating violence. However, if Jesus chooses to let the woman off, then the Pharisees can pin him on disrespect to the law of Moses, and Jesus will lose his popular following. It is a lose-lose situation for Jesus. What is he going to do?

Misuse of the woman, misuse of Scripture

How about the woman? How does she feel? She is not named in the story. She is not spoken to or given a voice by the scribes and Pharisees, only by Jesus after they have all left.

The first thing to notice is that she has been dragged in alone. Where is the man with whom the adulterous act was allegedly committed? It takes two to tango, so where is the tango partner? The law of Moses, which is being used here to test Jesus, is being misapplied. The Torah stated explicitly that both the man and the woman ought to be stoned to death. So where is the man? 'Is his absence a reflection of the perennial double standard associated with women's sexuality?'[135] asks Gench. I think this is a fair question. At the very least, it is clear that the Pharisees are not actually concerned with the law, but rather with trapping Jesus. They are certainly not concerned about the woman, although she is one of the sheep of Israel for whom the shepherds have responsibility. She is powerless, voiceless, a pawn in the games of those more powerful than herself.

This story has been read as good news by women throughout history who have found religious authority oppressive towards their gender. A Saviour who sees, moves towards and protects. Jesus, it seems to me, is angry about two things in this story. He is angry about misuse of Scripture, and he is angry about misuse of the woman.

The (male) mob has dragged this woman into a public space and is prepared physically to stone her. Jesus interrupts the violence. Gender-based violence is a staple of the human condition since the fall. Male strength, God-given for the protection of women, has since the dawn of time been used to harm. The Bible is full of stories of violence against women. The statistics in our world are overwhelming. We miss something important if we miss the gender-based violence in this story. And Jesus interrupts the violence. That's part of what he came to do. That's part of the male incarnation of the Son of God – to show women what male strength is supposed to be for, to show men a different way of

---

135. Gench, *Encounters with Jesus*, p. 52.

being a man. When Jesus crouches to write in the dust, he makes himself small and unthreatening, important body language for a woman who is terrified of violent men.[136]

Jean Kim, reading from a postcolonial South Korean perspective, makes a fascinating observation. She wonders if the man, who has not been dragged into the temple courtyard, was a Roman.

Roman soldiers' marriages were banned for the duration of their service, which for many men began at age eighteen or nineteen and continued for a minimum of twenty-five years. Many soldiers, therefore, cohabited with local women or raped them. Sometimes, local women across the empire would opt for a sexual relationship with the occupiers as a tactic of survival, a strategy today called 'voluntary rape'. Shocking as this idea might be, it is not at all uncommon, even today. Kim continues:

> However, these are not just old stories that happened long ago. Today, similar incidents often occur, especially in military base areas such as Okinawa, Subic Bay in the Philippines, and South Korea . . . [during the Second World War] there would have been about 139,000 'comfort women,' who were forcibly recruited from among young village girls across Asia [by the Japanese army].[137]

Roman soldiers, as so often for military personnel, were immune from prosecution under local law. 'If the adulterer was a Roman soldier (as we might assume), the Pharisees, scribes and even Jesus could not do anything to accuse him.'[138] The same is true today, Kim argues, as she points out the infamous rape by US GIs of a twelve-year-old school girl in Okinawa, which ignited angry

---

136. Hopley, 'Violence Against Women.
137. Kim, 'Adultery or Hybridity?', p. 123.
138. Gench, Encounters with Jesus, p. 58.

protests because the GIs were exempt from being summoned by a Japanese court.[139]

Perhaps it was the case that this woman was in a situation where she was making difficult choices for the sake of survival – there certainly would have been many in Jesus' time, and many throughout history, who have found themselves in similar positions under empire. Western readers can often read biblical stories about sex as being about choice, or consent, while in many parts of the world sex is more about survival. In this scenario, how much more unjust the Pharisees' accusation, the use of the woman's body as bait with which to trap Jesus, the voicelessness of her gender. And how much more remarkable the actions of Jesus which follow!

The other thing which would undoubtedly have aroused Jesus' ire in this story is the misuse of Scripture. The Pharisees are applying only half a verse, they are applying it harshly and without mercy, and they are applying it for the purpose of trapping Jesus, not of honouring God. In the history of Christianity, there have tragically been similar misapplications of Scripture by religious elites for the purpose of protecting the status quo, often at the expense of the vulnerable. Consider the out-of-context verses quoted by the Christian establishment in order to justify slavery, or invoked in the codifying of Apartheid laws, or enjoined in order to proliferate settler colonialism. Jesus' intervention in this passage must also read as a rebuke to religious elites who would misuse Scripture to perpetuate oppression and injustice, as he steps into the circle, with the accused woman, putting his body in harm's way in solidarity with her. Misuse of the vulnerable is one thing, but misuse of the vulnerable in the name of God, backed up by Scripture, is a whole other category of evil.

---

139. Kim, 'Adultery of Hybridity?' p. 125.

The finger of God

Jesus bent down and wrote with his finger on the ground.

(John 8:6)

The gesture functions structurally: Jesus bends down to break the spell of unanimity generated among the crowd of men all of whom stand up, as one, before him ... The point is, he physically distinguishes his position from theirs ... He not only refuses to stand with the accusers, he lowers himself, uncontaminated by the crowd's desire or the very dirt he draws in, a sign of our common origin and end.[140]

Rowan Williams (England), who was in New York when the infamous 9/11 attacks were perpetrated in 2001, and who observed the American public's immediate clamour for military response, wrote afterwards on reflection that Jesus' hesitation, his refusal to be rushed into choosing sides, is a wise response to tragedy: 'He hesitates. He does not draw a line, fix an interpretation ...' Williams exhorts us to 'hold that moment for a little longer, long enough for some of our demons to walk away'.[141]

This intentional hesitation, of slowing everything down, is a key aspect of the decolonising of mission for which we are striving. In a world where decisiveness, efficiency, action, speed are utmost, hesitation seems negative. Slowing down seems counterintuitive. But in a fraught moment where Jesus is being hustled into choosing which side of the line he will stand, he objects to this false binary. He refuses to be pigeonholed as pro-Roman/anti-Moses or pro-Moses/anti-Roman. If part of the *Missio Dei* is the redrawing of boundaries, the worldview change that refuses to accept existing culture wars or battle lines, then

---

140. Joplin, 'Intolerable Language', p. 232.
141. Williams, *Writing in the Dust*, p. 78.

slowing down creates a space for imagination, for a different kind of response. As in the earlier case of the Samaritan woman, Jesus rejects the binary (are you on this side or on that side?) and creates a third space, a different dimension of space, within which he stands and into which he invites the woman to join him. In both John 4 and here, this binary can be seen as ethnic (there, Jews versus Samaritans; here, Jews versus Romans) or as colonial (coloniser versus colonised). Notably, Jesus refuses both sides of the narrative, in John 4 rejecting both mountains and arguing that the Father is to be worshipped in spirit, and here rejecting both judgements and refusing to be pigeonholed as being anti-Torah or anti-Rome.

More than merely a wise response in a colonised space, or profound theological response to narrow human line-drawing, this is something that Jesus is doing today in all of the unreached spaces into which the gospel is penetrating. He creates a third space, a new option, into which he invites people to stand with him.

What did he write in the dust? We will never know. However, one of the permissible Sabbath work-arounds was that, while writing was banned on the Sabbath, writing in dust was permissible, as it could be immediately rubbed out, thus it did not constitute work. Maybe, on this Sabbath day, Jesus is saying to the scribes and the Pharisees, 'See, I know the law just as well as you do, and I can see that your concern is not really for the law.'

Let's not forget, the Law was originally written by the finger of God onto 'tablets of stone' (Exodus 31:18). Words of judgement were written onto the wall of Babylon's banquet hall by the finger of God (Daniel 5:5). And now Christ, who is God made flesh, writes in the dust with *his same finger*.

And where part of the Messianic mandate was to 'take away ... the pointing of the finger' (Isaiah 58:9) in protecting those falsely accused, so Jesus, in his challenge, 'Let him who is without sin ...

be the first to throw a stone at her' (v. 7) removes the accusers from the scene.

The ennobling

After everyone has left the scene, Jesus speaks directly to the woman. He wants to hear her voice, to humanise her, to make sure that her words are recorded for posterity. Everyone has spoken *about* the woman, but Jesus speaks *to* her. Listen to how Howard Thurman, writing as an African-American in 1940s USA, reflects on Jesus' ennobling of this woman:

> This is how Jesus demonstrated his reverence for personality. He met the woman where she was, and he treated her as if she were already where she now willed to be. In dealing with her he 'believed' her into the fulfilment of her possibilities. He stirred her confidence into activity. He placed a crown over her head which for the rest of her life she would keep trying to grow tall enough to wear.[142]

When he speaks, consistent with Johannine convention, he speaks to her in the vocative, 'Woman'. This, as we have seen, occurs six times in John's Gospel, and ties this story into the bigger story John is telling of a bridegroom searching for his bride. Just as later we will have the man and a woman in the garden, early in the morning on the first day of the week, so here we have Jesus and the woman, 'left alone' (v. 9) early in the morning, in the temple courts. The resonances backward to Adam and Eve in the first temple – the garden of Eden – and forward to Jesus and his bride in the last temple – the New Jerusalem – are legion. This woman, who began the story captive, is now free, freed by Jesus. Her story is our story. Jesus has turned wrathful

---

142. Thurman, *Jesus and the Disinherited*, p. 106.

judgement away from us and onto himself. Although guilty, we are given a new beginning, freedom from past habits and from the coercive pressure of the crowd, freedom to make better choices, 'go, and from now on sin no more' (v. 11). The accuser no longer surrounds us, baying for blood, but slinks away with his tail between his legs – the victory not being ours, but Christ's. We stand before him, in the temple courts, grateful, overwhelmed, and frankly stunned at how dramatic a rescue has taken place.

Finding a home

For this reason, for me, this story does indeed fit very nicely within the overall story John is telling. It fits within the section from chapter 6 to chapter 10 of Jesus fulfilling Sukkot. It fits on the final Sabbath day of Sukkot. And it fits with John's wider aims of showing Jesus to be indefatigably obsessed with the marginal and the vulnerable, and in particular, through Christ's use of the vocative 'woman' with the bigger story John is telling about a new Adam searching for a new Eve, about Christ searching for his bride, about temple and garden and new creation.

This story has long been considered homeless. Scholars agree it is authentic and ancient, they just can't agree whether it belongs originally in Luke or John. The earliest manuscripts of John do not include this story. I actually really like the perspective given by Guardiola-Saenz, writing as a Mexican living in the bicultural zone of the Rio Grande Borderlands, who identifies with this homeless story that has won a *situ* for itself within John's Gospel. She feels that, just as Mexican migrants have established themselves within US borders by hard work, almost forcing a home for themselves in a place where they do not always feel welcome, so 'The story has crossed canonical borders and seized a place in the text for more than sixteen centuries'.[143]

---

143. Guardiola-Sanez, 'Border-crossing', p. 138.

Meeting the Judge

Finally, in this story, where one accused is brought to Jesus for judgement, we glimpse for a moment the Judge going about his work. As those who will all one day be likewise dragged before the judgement seat of God, it is good for us to see what kind of judge he is, how he combines justice, mercy and wisdom, how Christ's word carries the true and final authority of the One who will pass sentence on all flesh.

For Ammar al-Basri, the ninth-century Nestorian theologian, this reality was one of the compelling defences for the divine nature of Christ against Muslim arguments to the contrary. In his *Book of the Proof*, he asks, 'If it is the case that all humanity will meet God as Judge, then is it not an act of kindness for the Judge to make himself known to the accused?'[144] As the woman stood face-to-face with her Judge, the One who held the power of life or death in his hands, who with one word could acquit or condemn, could declare her innocent or guilty, so too, one day after her death, this same woman would stand again before the same Judge, look into the same eyes, await the same voice. She has already met the Judge. So with us. Our Judge is not unknown to us, not arbitrary, not impersonal. He has made himself known to us in Christ. We know him before whom we will appear. This same Jesus is the One who holds our fate in his hands.

---

144. Ammar al-Basri, 'The Book of the Proof' *(Kitab al-Burhan)* in Hayek, *Ammar al-Basri,* pp. 19-90.

Chapter Ten

Light
(John Chapters 8 and 9)

It is better to light one small candle
than to curse the darkness.

(Confucius)

Against the backdrop of the final day of the Feast of Tabernacles, Jesus will make another startling claim about himself. Every evening during Tabernacles/Sukkot, great lamps were lit in the temple precinct, and people would dance in the streets with lights. Not dissimilar in feel to India's Divali festival, or the Persian Newruz, these dramatic actions looked back to the pillar of fire leading the people through the wilderness, forward to the hope of eschatological light in darkness, and in the present represented a harvest prayer for the light of the sun for the crops.[145] There is nothing as ancient and spectacular, as universal and hope-giving, as lights shining when the world is dark. The choirs would sing Psalm 27, 'The Lord is my light and my salvation'. At dawn each day, the priests would process to the eastern gate of the temple area, and turn westwards towards the temple, with their backs to the rising sun, proclaiming that, while some of their ancestors

---

145. Neyrey, *John*, p. 136.

worshipped the sun (Ezekiel 8:16), 'our eyes are turned towards the Lord'.[146]

It is in this context that Jesus declares himself to be the light of the world.

> Again Jesus spoke to them, saying, 'I am the light of the world. Whoever follows me will not walk in darkness, but will have the light of life.'
>
> *(John 8:12)*

Where the people were singing, 'The LORD is my light', Jesus says, '*I* am the light.' Where the people were remembering the Lord as the tall pillar of light to be followed through the wilderness, Jesus says, 'Whoever follows *me* will not walk in darkness' (italics mine). The use of the divine claim from Exodus 14, 'I AM', shows that Jesus is claiming himself to be the God of the Exodus. Jesus, undeniably, is claiming to be God. Carson (USA) explains:

> In the context of such powerful ritual, Jesus' declaration must have come with stunning force. He does not let it hang in the air as an abstract dictum. There is an immediate consequence: Whoever follows me (an appropriate thing to do with light if it is the glorious pillar of cloud setting out the way in the wilderness) will never walk in darkness but will have the light of life.[147]

This is the second of seven predicated 'I am' statements (I am the . . .). The first was 'I am the bread of life' (John 6:35), a statement Jesus made having already substantiated the claim with a sign – the miraculous provision of bread to feed the 5,000. Now

---

146. Ford, *John*, p. 164.
147. Carson, *John*, p. 338.

Jesus claims, 'I am the light of the world', and he will *make this word flesh* by healing a blind man. This is not merely a cosmic, theological, conceptual truth about Jesus. It is also a truth that can be personal, individual, experiential. 'I am the light of the world', he says, and then he gives light to an individual in darkness.

The ensuing argument and debate ends with the crowd determined to stone Jesus.

So they picked up stones to throw at him, but Jesus hid himself and went out of the temple.

(John 8:59)

As Jesus, with his disciples, slips away through the narrow backstreets of Jerusalem surrounding the temple (his hour has not yet come), he comes across a man blind from birth. Ever the Good Shepherd, Jesus stops to heal the man. He repeats, 'I am the light of the world' (9:5), our author ensuring that the reader does not lose the connection between the claim and the healing, and then he initiates a powerful and miraculous healing. The man born blind is now able to see.

The man who is the object of the healing will speak seven times, during which he will go from blind, both physically and spiritually, to seeing. Beginning with 'The man called Jesus' (v. 11), through 'He is a prophet' (v. 17), to '"Lord, I believe," and he worshipped him' (v. 38).

Each time he opens his mouth, he takes another step in his journey from darkness towards enlightenment. This happens by dialogue with Jesus, and also by talking to people around him about who Jesus is and what he has done. His physical healing is instantaneous. His spiritual sight is more of a journey, but a journey in which he is actively involved, and in which witnessing to the truth of his changed circumstances before hostile interlocutors is part of his discipleship pathway.

The Pharisees

The other characters in this story are the Pharisees. They also speak seven times, and they go from 'seeing' to 'blind'. They journey in the opposite direction, and their journey is absolute. Their final comment is on their own blindness. 'Some of the Pharisees near him heard these things, and said to him, "Are we also blind?"' (9:40).

This verse represents the climax of the Pharisees' seven times speaking. Until now in this chapter they have been speaking *about* Jesus, and becoming progressively hardened. Now, finally, they speak *to* Jesus himself, confirming their own blindness. And the verse which best summarises what is happening in this story, the key verse, is verse 39:

> Jesus said, 'For judgement I came into this world, that those who do not see may see, and those who see may become blind.'

The man speaks seven times, progressing from blindness to seeing. The Pharisees speak seven times, regressing from sight to blindness.

Jesus describes what the judgement, or justice, of God does, what the life of Jesus achieves, what the great overarching mission of God is aiming to accomplish. The justice of God is a two-sided coin, 'God opposes the proud, but gives grace to the humble' (James 4:6). Hannah sang it like this:

> The bows of the mighty are broken,
> but the feeble bind on strength.
> Those who are full have hired themselves out for bread,
> but those who were hungry have ceased to hunger.

The barren has borne seven,

but she who has many children is forlorn.

(1 Samuel 2:4-5)

The Pharisees in this story have got all the answers, have everything figured out, and sit in judgement on the man born blind. They accuse him of being steeped in sin from birth, and they excommunicate him from the synagogue (9:34). And so Jesus, as well as giving grace to the one who is humble, opposes those who are proud. Those who are too big, he will make smaller. Those who are too small, he will make bigger. In this way, Jesus is making a new world, where equality reigns.

'You were steeped in sin at birth' (v. 34, NIV) is their way of saying, as the disciples had earlier said, that the man must be blind through some sin of his own. This idea, that somehow the man's sin or at least his parents' sin has caused his blindness, is prevalent in religions across the world.

> It is almost taken for granted in many cultures and religions that suffering is a punishment for evil. The theory of karma in Asian religious traditions supposes this. Most penal systems accept the principle. It was common in the Old Testament. We see this in the book of Job. Everyone, including Job, takes it as a matter of course that suffering is a punishment for sin. Only God refuses to accept this principle.[148]

In folk religion, diagnosing the cause of someone's illness or misfortune is extremely important. The 'who sinned?' question asked by the disciples keeps medicine men, wise women, *pirs*,[149]

---

148. Amaladoss, *The Asian Jesus*, Kindle location 1672.
149. A Muslim Sufi holy man or spiritual guide.

hojas,[150] shamans, saddhus and their like in business. Has the patient or a family member broken any taboos? For example, in Egypt and Sudan the *mushahara* customs see sickness as nearly always the result of taboo-breaking. Or has somebody put the evil eye on them? Is sorcery or witchcraft or black magic at work? Is a jinn or evil spirit involved? While Western medicine focuses on the 'how' of sickness, emphasising strictly empirical phenomena, folk religion in many places is more concerned with the 'why' of causality.[151] Thus this question, and Jesus' answer, becomes an important bridge into Scripture for many people.

It is unique to the Christian perspective that 'it was not that this man sinned, or his parents' (9:3). It is rather that sin, entering the world through Adam, has run amok, ruining lives and relationships, causing a disintegration of the moral ecology or the world, a world in which this poor resident of Jerusalem was born blind. If we were to take the analogy of climate change to explain the interconnectedness of things, we would see that individual actions (sins) by every human contribute to carbon in the atmosphere and to the greenhouse effect, but that there is a disproportionate contribution by the Global North, yet a disproportionate impact on the Global South. Sin can be considered to work in the same way. All have sinned, all have contributed to the brokenness of the world and her systems, yet there are some who suffer more than others as a result. Or consider the brown fog of pollution which lies over many of our cities and ruins the health of our children. Everyone contributes to the smoke, yet it is the weak, the poor, the children whose tender lungs suffer the most. Orobator (Nigeria) seeks to explain the pervasive, communal dynamics of sin for his African readers:

---

150. A Muslim wise man or teacher.
151. Musk, *The Unseen Face of Islam*, p. 98.

In a certain sense we can talk of what John the Evangelist refers to as the 'sin of the world' (John 1:29), that pervasive pall of evil that hangs over our world and manifests itself in so many different guises (injustice, oppression, discrimination, violence, marginalization, poverty, idolatry and so on), and whose effects we are all exposed to. It precedes us; oftentimes we participate in and also help to perpetuate it.[152]

Who sinned that this man was born blind? Well, all have sinned, including this man, but while none of those sins resulted in his blindness, his blindness is a consequence of sin. Which is why Jesus speaks of darkness (8:12). Darkness in John is not passive. It is not the absence of light. It is pernicious, active, spreading, choking, like dark smoke from a burning oil refinery, like carbon in the atmosphere, like a monster who we are all feeding. Each one of us contributes, each one of us is impacted and impeded by it, but the impact is not equitable. The darkness discriminates. And the darkness causes us to discriminate. Darkness begets more darkness. Sin creates more sin.

And the darkness is why the temple excludes him, why the Pharisees judge him, why he is considered, far beyond visually impaired, to be someone less than human, someone 'steeped in sin', someone accursed. And the genius of Jesus in this story is not only to save the man from his darkness, but to expose the darkness impairing the vision of the Pharisees. The word *sin/ner* occurs seven times in this chapter – this passage is a meditation on the nature of sin and the nature of sinners. The Pharisees even accuse Jesus of being a sinner, such is their darkness.

The equivalent Synoptic account might be Matthew 12, where Jesus heals a blind man and then is verbally attacked by the

---

152. Orobator, *Theology*, p. 56.

Pharisees. Matthew frames his version spiritually: there was a demon making the man blind, Jesus drives out the demon and then is slandered by the Pharisees and the two are connected. The man's personal oppression is connected to a systemic oppression which, once provoked, lashes out at Jesus through the Pharisees.

John makes the same point, but by talking about light and darkness. These then are more than metaphors, they are metaphysical reality – darkness/blindness is demonic, and light/sight is the powerful gift of God.

There is also, with the emphasis in this story on the man's parents, an ongoing contrast created between family and faith. Where Jesus has already argued with the Jews that inclusion is by faith in him, not by family privilege or descent from Israel, where Jesus' own brothers do not believe in him (7:5), where Nicodemus has been instructed to be born again (3:3), and where, at the cross, Jesus will ask a disciple, not a blood relative, to take responsibility for his mother (19:27), so here the differentiation between faith and family, or between consent and descent (choice and genetics) is continued.

> While the beggar openly confesses Jesus' healing power to the 'Jews,' his parents deny any knowledge of or association with Jesus. Since John gives great emphasis to the congenital nature of the beggar's blindness (9:1, 18-20, 32), one may argue that what this 'sign' reveals is Jesus' ability to overcome the limits of descent, whether it is biological, familial, or ethnic/national.[153]

Inclusion into Christ's new community is by consent, not by descent, by faith not by family. This is of foundational importance to Christianity.

---

153. Liew, 'Ambiguous Admittance,' p. 203.

Light, sight and Christ

John, in due course, will comment on unbelief by reflecting on the words of Isaiah, 'He has blinded their eyes, and hardened their heart' (12:40). Seeing, in John, is connected to faith, as in 12:45-46:

> And whosoever sees me sees him who sent me. I have come into the world as light, so that whoever believes in me may not remain in darkness.

John told us right from the beginning that Jesus is light. Couched in the opening verses of John, rich with resonances of Genesis 1, in which God said, 'Let there be light,' we are told: 'The light shines in the darkness, and the darkness has not overcome it' (1:5).

Darkness, in John, is not neutral. It is not merely the absence of light. It is evil. And so two things need to happen – the light needs to shine, and the darkness needs to be pushed back.

> People loved the darkness rather than the light because their works were evil. For everyone who does wicked things hates the light ...
>
> *(3:19-20)*

When Judas goes out from the Last Supper to betray Jesus, we are told, 'And it was night' (13:30). This is redundant, except for the fact that John is building more and more of the themes of darkness and night-time into the final week leading up to the cross.

Mission and the darkness

Mission always involves these dynamics of spiritual warfare. The darkness in individuals, communities and systems is more than ignorance, deeper than an absence of the knowledge of God in Christ. Islam speaks of the 'times of ignorance' *(jahiliyya)*[154] before prophetic revelation, but the Christian perspective is much more pernicious than this, and the Christian solution is much more powerful than enlightenment, or its modern equivalents of education or development.

Where darkness is systemic, it is also individual, and where it is individual, it is always systemic. Darkness is encountered *in individuals*, in flesh, even where it is an embodiment of territorial or institutional evil. Surely that is one key learning of the murder of African-American George Floyd by white police officers. In this individual evil is a microcosm, a snapshot of a wider, systemic, global evil of racism, of white kneeling on the neck of black, of black saying, 'I can't breathe.'

So our battle is not against flesh and blood, but against the darkness,[155] but it takes place in the flesh and blood of individuals. It was not enough for Christ to declare, 'I am the light of the world'; there also needed to be an individual encounter with him of a blind man needing healing. This word, too, needed to be made flesh. The efficiencies of the internet and media for spreading the gospel are precious, like Jesus' public proclamation in the temple, but there are millions sitting in the backstreets, like this man, who never heard the proclamation. Who will go to them? Who will drive out their darkness? Who will introduce them to the light?

So often, as in this story, the darkness is expressed in oppressive relationships between the powerful and powerless. So often, as in this story, light coming to an individual in the margins provokes a reaction of the darkness in the systemic sense. From here to the crucifixion, the darkness will grow in

---

154. Qu'ran 3:154.
155. See Ephesians 6:12.

John, along with accusation and attack against the light. We see this often in the Scripture – Acts 16 is a famous example. The apostles drive out a demon from a slave girl in Philippi, which upsets so many elements of dark injustice in that city; economic: owners and owned; gender: male oppressing female; racial: they use the apostles' Jewishness as a reason to attack them. Paul and Silas are attacked, stripped, beaten and imprisoned. They have confronted the darkness of the city in this one young woman, and the darkness closes ranks and strikes back at them.

And so it is in Christian mission. We expect the cosmic struggle between darkness and light to be worked out in individuals. And we expect the light to triumph. Personally, systemically and cosmically, the light shines in the darkness, and the darkness cannot overcome it.

Chapter Eleven

Friendship
(John 11:1-54)

Do not walk behind me; I may not lead.
Do not walk in front of me; I may not follow.
Just walk beside me and be my friend.

(Arab proverb)

I grew up in a small town called Larnaka on a Mediterranean island called Cyprus. Larnaka boasts the beautiful church of St Lazarus where, it is claimed, Lazarus was buried when he died the second time. According to tradition, Lazarus, who was raised from the dead by Jesus, was forced to flee Judea due to plots on his life, coming to Cyprus where he was appointed Bishop of Kition by Paul and Barnabas. He is said to have lived a further thirty years, eventually dying of old age. I remember thinking as a young child, cycling past the church on my way to the beach, how strange it must have been for Lazarus to have died once, been brought back to life by Jesus, only to eventually die again. The inevitability of death catches up even with those who have been miraculously delivered from it once!

The Lazarus narrative is a significant turning point in John. It is another instance of 'Word made flesh' whereby Jesus makes a universal, cosmic 'I am' statement; 'I am the resurrection and the life. Whoever believes in me, though he die, yet shall he live, and everyone who lives and believes in me shall never die' (11:25-26), but then makes this word flesh in a real person's story at a real moment in history. In fact, the dialogue between Jesus and Martha emphasises this point:

> Jesus said to her, 'Your brother will rise again.' Martha said to him, 'I know that he will rise again in the resurrection on the last day.' Jesus said to her, 'I am the resurrection and the life. Whoever believes in me, though he die, yet shall he live, and everyone who lives and believes in me shall never die. Do you believe this?' She said to him, 'Yes, Lord; I believe that you are the Christ, the Son of God, who is coming into the world.'
>
> *(John 11:23-27)*

Again, Jesus grants a private self-revelation to a woman, as he did to the Samaritan woman in chapter 4, and as he will to Mary in chapter 20. And again, the clearest Messianic articulation is on the lips of a woman, as Martha declares him Christ, Son of God, he who comes into the world. In the Synoptic Gospels, this pinnacle declaration is put in the mouth of Peter, but here in John, consistent with his emphasis on the margins, it is a woman – in many ways a cipher for marginality and powerlessness in a patriarchal society – who utters this key declaration. Keener (USA) comments in this way:

> [In John's Gospel], Jesus offers private revelation of his identity to the Samaritan Woman (in chapter 4)...to Martha (here in chapter 11), and later reveals himself to Mary Magdalene (20:15-17) after Peter and the beloved disciple departed...He seems to have favoured women and/or those marginalized from centers of structural power...[Martha's] confession [here], [which is] the climactic confession preceding

Jesus' passion, suggests a relatively high role for women's faith [in contrast with] the majority views of John's culture.[156]

The resurrection of Lazarus is one of the seven signs in John, pointing towards the cross. It follows one of the seven predicated 'I am' sayings of Jesus, powerful Exodus-like moments of the self-revelation and self-proclamation of God. But it is also an intensely personal, emotional account, full of weeping and grief. In John there is no Gethsemane agony, but this story provides the agony. We see Jesus raw, laid open, human.

> When Jesus saw her weeping, and the Jews who had come with her also weeping, he was deeply moved in his spirit and greatly troubled. And he said, 'Where have you laid him?' They said to him, 'Lord, come and see.' Jesus wept. So the Jews said, 'See how he loved him!' But some of them said, 'Could not he who opened the eyes of the blind man also have kept this man from dying?' Then Jesus, deeply moved again, came to the tomb.
>
> *(John 11:33-38)*

Jesus stood at the tomb of his friend and wept. God stood at the tomb of all humankind since Adam, the inevitability of mortality, and wept. God is not unmoved, not above grief, not hardened against loss through millennia of conditioning. To weep is not weak, it is God-like. Jesus shows us what God is like, and God weeps. As Moltmann (Germany) said, 'God weeps with us that we may one day laugh with him.'[157] Bauckham (England) reflects, 'If we took this element out of John's story, we would have a Jesus who, obedient to his Father, carried out the destiny decreed for

---

156. Keener, *John*, pp. 844-845.
157. Source unfound.

him, the divine plan for the world, but we could not believe that he did so in love for the world.'[158]

Friendship

Friend(s) is another word that John causes to appear six times in his gospel.[159] Jesus is on a mission to make friends. He teaches about friendship with God in 15:13-15, and he demonstrates it in Lazarus. There are six occurrences because John is creating eschatological longing – we wait for the final consummation of divine friendship. One day number seven, the perfect, sin-free, forever expression of friendship will be established. God is populating heaven with his friends.

Mission, then, as banal as it sounds, is about making friends. We are not called merely to proclaim impersonal truths – 'Christ is the resurrection and the life' – we are also called to be friendly, to love deeply,[160] to 'mourn with those who mourn' (Romans 12:15, NIV). Friendship means pain, betrayal, loss, it means limiting one's sphere of activity – how many people can you meaningfully be friends with? Friendship is inefficient, slow. It rescues us from task-driven, activity-focused Christianity. It delivers us from the tyranny of scale and numbers as the only measure of success.

Cross-culturally, crafting friendships takes even longer. Without the shared experiences and preferences of someone with a similar background to you, even discovering common ground, let alone navigating emotion in the weaker language of one (or both) parties, making good friends in another culture can take years. Many missionaries have local 'contacts' or 'partners'

---

158. Bauckham, *Gospel of Glory,* p. 69.
159. 3:29; 11:11; 15:13; 15:14; 15:15; 19:12.
160. See 1 Peter 1:22; 1 Peter 4:8.

but their friends are people who look like them, people from back home, people with whom relaxing is easier. Many multicultural churches might look diverse on a Sunday, but friendship outside of the meeting is still worked out with people who look like each other, enjoy the same pastimes, eat the same food.

This is not just a white problem. I've met many Nigerian diaspora missionaries who hold a strict distinction between the people with whom they relax and the people who they are seeking to reach. Similarly, I've spent time with Korean missionaries in various places whose children are lonely because they have struggled to integrate with local children. Anecdotally, I reckon the 'friendliest missionaries' award could go to Brazilians, whose warmth, playfulness, humour and often intuitive cross-cultural grace (along with a passion for the universal language – football!) wins them friends everywhere.

If we are to announce to people that God has come to befriend them in Jesus Christ, surely we can't do this without offering our own imperfect selves to those same people in friendship.

V.S. Azariah (India), one of only nineteen majority world Christians among the 1,215 delegates at the 1910 world missionary conference in Edinburgh, famously declared in his speech to all the seasoned white missionaries gathered at the conference, 'You have given your goods to feed the poor. You have given your bodies to be burned. We also ask for love. Give us *friends*.'[161]

Thomaskutty (India), writing about the preciousness of the Gospel of John in Asian contexts, stresses the friendship aspect: 'Asians value friendship at multiple levels, so Jesus' friendship with Lazarus and his family energizes readers, and they can identify with Jesus, who mourns at the tomb of Lazarus.'[162]

---

161. Stanley, *The World Missionary Conference*, Kindle location 1662.
162. Thomaskutty, 'The Gospel of John', p. 135.

Ethiopian American Mekdes Haddis emphasises the importance of friendship in her book *A Just Mission*:

> Relationships are the key to community, and if the mission given by our Lord is to go to the nations and make disciples, we need to do it through deep human relationships that are long-suffering and honouring to God and one another. Think about it – that's exactly the reason Jesus left his glory to become one of us: to see us as we truly are in all our complexities and to understand the depth of our humanity. He chose to experience life through our perspective and take on himself God's judgement that was to come on us. The outcome of his life on earth gave him an unbiased, well-informed, and real relationship with humankind that moved him to deadly obedience on the cross.[163]

Our glimpse into Jesus' friendship with Lazarus is a microcosm of what Haddis is urging on us.

In light of this, the friendlessness and loneliness that dogs so many cross-cultural Christian workers is a symptom of how far we have drifted from 'As the Father has sent me, even so I am sending you' (John 20:21).

The Lazarus story occupies a key place in John's narrative. Jesus has withdrawn with his disciples to the far side of the Jordan River, escaping an arrest warrant (10:39-40). His decision to come back into Judea when he hears that his friend Lazarus is sick is a risky one:

> Then after this he said to the disciples, 'Let us go to Judea again.' The disciples said to him, 'Rabbi, the Jews were just now seeking to stone you, and are you going there again?'
> *(John 11:7-8)*

---

163. Haddis, *A Just Mission*, pp. 63-64.

But for the love of his friend, he is prepared to take this risk, to come out of hiding, to go into the lions' den. Love compels action. Risk taken for reputation is folly, but risk derived from friendship has a logic of its own, an ancient and irrefutable logic. Jesus goes into Judea to raise his friend resulting, ultimately, in his own death, because in John, Lazarus' resurrection is the single key event that triggers Jesus' own arrest and death. At the end of chapter 11, the high priest Caiaphas proclaims, 'It is better for you that one man should die for the people, not that the whole nation should perish' (11:50) and 'From that day on they made plans to put him to death' (11:53).

What was it about this miracle that made the high priest's inner circle so determined to capture and execute Jesus?

There are two reasons. The first reason that presents itself is envy. Both Matthew and Mark explicitly tell us that it was due to envy that Jesus was put to death (Matthew 27:18; Mark 15:10). John is less explicit, but makes the same point. If honour is a limited good, a zero-sum issue, then an increase in Jesus' popularity and reputation means a decrease in the popularity and reputation of the chief priests. The chief priests and the high priestly family, perched precariously between Roman rule and a dissatisfied people close to revolt, predicated their position on their ability to negotiate, to broker a peace, to represent the people to the Roman governor. Losing popular support, they feel, could have dire consequences.

Father Jerome Neyrey (USA) explains this implicit dynamic in terms those less familiar with honour and envy can understand:

The raising of Lazarus causes Jesus' fame to skyrocket . . . As Jesus increases in fame and respect, they proportionately decrease. Moreover, people who think themselves thus injured by another's success are likely to engage in envy. Their actions plotted in 11:45-52 are calculated to cause

Jesus shame, cause the scattering of his followers, and cause the restoration of their honor. But, ironically, they will only increase Jesus' fame and benefit even more peoples.[164]

So the chief priests and the Pharisees gathered the Council and said, 'What are we to do? For this man performs many signs. If we let him go on like this, everyone will believe in him, and the Romans will come and take away both our place and our nation.'

(John 11:47-48)

Such catastrophising could represent their pragmatic political outlook. It also represents one of envy's great tricks: the emotional spiralling of paranoia that quickly pushes one into a narrow alley from which there is only one way forward – the destruction of the other. We see this in King Saul's envying of David, which quickly (and, we are told, demonically) escalates into irrational fear and then harm (1 Samuel 18:9-11). Envy, the devil's oldest device, causes Caiaphas to see Jesus as a threat, one high priest against the other. We must beware envy, its consequences are only ever toxic.

The second reason is slightly less mainstream, but I find it compelling. In this scenario, Caiaphas is brought even more directly into relationship with Lazarus. The Roman leader Valerius Gratus, in an attempt to limit the power of the high priestly office, removed Annas from power and limited the period of presidency for each subsequent high priest. The family of Annas found a way of preserving power by 'keeping it in the family'. Annas, his five sons, his son-in-law Caiaphas and his grandson Matthias all had a turn at this sacred role – at least eight members of the family in total. We know that one of Annas' sons was called Eleazar. The Greek pronunciation of the name Eleazar is Lazarus.

---

164. Neyrey, *John*, p. 206.

Is it possible that our Lazarus, who lived in one of the priestly villages close to Jerusalem, whose family were clearly well-known (11:18-19), were seemingly wealthy (Mary bought an extremely expensive perfume, 12:3-5), could have been this Eleazar, son of Annas, brother-in-law to Caiaphas?

Is it possible that, in Luke's parable about another Lazarus in Luke 16, the only character in any of Jesus' parables to be named, a story in which a rich man dies and wants to come back to warn his five brothers, Jesus is telling an oblique story about his friend Lazarus, who did come back from the dead to warn his five brothers, who refused to listen?

Is it possible that this Lazarus was Caiaphas' brother-in-law? If so, we can see why Caiaphas' response to Lazarus' resurrection was so venomous, so extreme. Envy is always more lethal within families. Lazarus would represent a viable threat to Caiaphas' presidency because he had family legitimacy as well as a resurrection experience, and for this reason, Lazarus, too, needed to be eliminated.

When the large crowd of the Jews learned that Jesus was there, they came, not only on account of him but also to see Lazarus, whom he had raised from the dead. So the chief priests made plans to put Lazarus to death as well.

(John 12:9-10)

If this is such a pivotal story in Jesus' life, why is it absent from the other three Gospels? Surely, a well-known, named individual, close to Jerusalem, resurrected from the dead, would have been front-page news enough that any of the Gospel writers would need to have recorded it? The answer to this puzzle, it seems, is 'protective anonymity'. Mark's Gospel, for example, was written so early that many of the people with whom Jesus had interacted were still alive, and still in danger for their faith. Several of those whom Mark leaves anonymous, John (who is writing decades later when all the key players have passed away and the coast is clear) is able to name. Mark's woman who anoints Jesus, John names as Mary. Mark's disciple with a sword, John names as Peter. And the high priest's servant whose ear is cut off, John names as Malchus.

Why, then, following this convention, could Mark not have told the Lazarus story without naming him? Presumably because it was such a well-known incident in the Jerusalem district, that even to leave Lazarus anonymous would not have been sufficient. But by the time John published his Gospel, the coast was clear and in John's narrative the resurrection of Lazarus is critical to the logic of the story.

Looking forward, looking backward

The final way that John's account of the Lazarus story proves its vital significance, is the similarity between John 11 and other parts of the Gospel.

Looking back from chapter 11, we see that Jesus, who speaks often about life, made some very bold statements in chapter 5:

For as the Father raises the dead and gives them life, so also the Son gives life to whom he will.

(John 5:21)

Truly, truly, I say to you, an hour is coming, and is now here, when the dead will hear the voice of the Son of God, and those who hear will live.

(John 5:25)

Do not marvel at this, for an hour is coming when all who are in the tombs will hear his voice and come out, those who have done good to the resurrection of life, and those who have done evil to the resurrection of judgement.

(John 5:28-29)

As we have repeatedly seen in Jesus' ministry, these are not idle claims of theoretical life-giving. He makes this Word flesh in the real story of a real grieving family, such that all other grieving families at all other times in history might have concrete hope.

Chapter 11 also adds an eschatological dimension to Jesus' claim in chapter 10:

To him the gatekeeper opens. The sheep hear his voice, and he calls his own sheep by name and leads them out. When he has brought out all his own, he goes before them, and the sheep follow him, for they know his voice.

(John 10:3-4)

Lazarus hears Jesus' voice, even from a distance of four days dead. Jesus brings out his own, through the authority of his voice, and his own follow him: 'the dead will hear the voice of the Son of God, and those who hear will live' (5:25). Our following of Jesus started while we were dead in our sins. His first call to each of us by name pierced the silence of our spiritual death and raised our expired spirits to life. We came forth, like Lazarus, were unbound from our grave clothes, and began to follow the Shepherd.

Equally, yet even more wonderfully, when our bodies finally lie in the grave, and the Good Shepherd comes at the end of all things to raise us, as he promised in 5:28, he will call his sheep each by name, and from within our death each one of us will hear his voice, will hear our own name called, will rise, and follow him into a glorious immortal future.

John hereby connects the resurrection of Lazarus with all of our resurrections, with the human story, and with discipleship as the following of the shepherd.

Looking ahead from chapter 11, there are immediate connections between chapters 11 and 12, the burial of Lazarus and the anointing of Jesus for his own burial. The expensive perfume that Mary used to anoint Jesus came from India. She had likely bought it to anoint Lazarus' body, no longer needed it, and instead used it for Christ's. In all of this, Jesus will die because Lazarus does not. The resurrection of Lazarus results in the death sentence of Jesus. Lazarus lives, Jesus dies. There is a substitutionary connection between Lazarus being delivered *from* death and Jesus being delivered *to* death.

This becomes finally clear in chapter 20. John crafts profound textual connections between John 11 (Lazarus' resurrection) and John 20 (Jesus' own resurrection).

Lazarus' resurrection (chapter 11)	Jesus' resurrection (chapter 20)
Linen (11:44)	Linen (19:40; 20:5,6,7)
Face cloth (11:44)	Face cloth (20:7)
Where have you laid him? (11:34)	Where have you laid him? (20:2,13,15)
Jesus wept at the tomb (11:35)	Mary wept at the tomb (20:11)
Take away the stone (11:39)	The stone had been taken away (20:1)
Saw and believed (11:40,45)	Saw and believed (20:8,25,27)

John, the artist, the careful prose-crafter, the theological-symbolism master, the layerer of truth upon truth, who takes 'life' as a major theme throughout his Gospel, centres this theme on a very real moment for a real grieving family. Lazarus comes back from the dead by the voice of Christ, as must we all spiritually at conversion (regeneration), and as shall we all physically at the end of all things. This sign seals the death-warrant of Jesus as the Gospel moves towards its climax, and yet Lazarus' empty tomb is a foreshadowing of Jesus' own empty tomb just a short while later.

Our resurrection is predicated on Jesus' own resurrection. Our rising follows the pattern of his rising. We weep at his tomb because he wept at our tombs. His death is our life.

Greater love has no one than this, that someone lay down his life for his friends.

(John 15:13)

Chapter Twelve

Donkey
(John 12:12-15)

May you never be able to forget.
May you go to your grave still remembering.
(Cypriot curse)

I was born and grew up in Cyprus, in the eastern Mediterranean. Cyprus is not just postcolonial, it has spent almost its entire history being conquered by foreign armies and ruled from distant capitals. Hittites, Egyptians, Phoenicians, Assyrians, Greeks, Persians, Macedonians, Romans, Byzantines, Arabs, Crusaders, Genoese, Venetians, Ottomans, Turks, British and others too, have used the island for its greatest natural resource – its strategic location on the corner of three continents. The sovereign is always distant – seated in Rome or Istanbul or London – and Cyprus is always a chess piece, a distant place, used for its strategic location but rarely valued for itself, for its people, for its own sake.

In this sense, Cyprus has a great deal in common with its close neighbour Palestine. Palestine, throughout its long history, has rarely been independent. It has been the site of proxy wars between mighty empires, the Assyrians, the Egyptians, the Babylonians, the Greeks, the Romans, the Byzantines, the Ottomans, the British; a buffer zone, a battlefield, a corridor, important only for the costal road linking Asia to Africa, for the Mediterranean ports.

> Throughout Palestinian history empires have occupied the land for a certain number of years but were then forced to leave. Most of the time an empire departed only to make space for another empire.[165]

At the time of Jesus, Palestine was yet again under empire – this time the Romans. It is impossible to understand Jesus without understanding what the Roman occupation meant. 'The Roman killing or enslavement of tens of thousands of Galileans and Judeans around the time Jesus was born must have left mass trauma among the people in its wake', writes Horsley (USA).[166] Ordinary people were desperate for a liberating Messiah.

Contemporary postcolonial readings of the Bible highlight perspectives from the underside, the tensions and angers of a people under imperial rule. British and American scholarship may not have been able to see and feel this perspective, having no personal experience of these dynamics. Yet these are sentiments that certainly are present in the text, and are significant in the context.

Under empire

Thurman, writing as an African-American in 1940s USA, argues that the prevailing sentiment among Jews in the time of Christ would have been one of powerlessness and frustration:

> It was this kind of atmosphere that characterized the life of the Jewish community when Jesus was a youth in Palestine.

---

165. Raheb, *Faith in the Face of Empire*, p. 12.
166. Horsley, *Jesus and Empire*, p. 30.

The urgent question was what must be the attitude toward Rome. Was any attitude possible that would be morally tolerable and at the same time preserve a basic self-esteem, without which life could not possibly have any meaning? The question was not academic. It was the most crucial of questions. In essence, Rome was the enemy: Rome symbolised total frustration; Rome was the great barrier to peace of mind. And Rome was everywhere. No Jewish person of the period could deal with the question of his practical life, his vocation, his place in society, until first he had settled deep within himself this critical issue.

This is the position of the disinherited in every age. What must be the attitude toward the rulers, the controllers of political, social and economic life? This is the question of the Negro in American life. Until he has faced and settled that question, he cannot inform his environment with reference to his own life, whatever may be his preparation or his pretensions.[167]

All of this bubbling, seething malcontent was, as we have seen, very much present as the nation made the annual trek up to Jerusalem for Passover. Passover at any rate is a festival of independence, a remembrance of national liberation, a time when nationalistic as well as religious fervour ran high. God smote Egypt in the distant past, and many hoped that he would similarly smite Rome in the present day.

John writes of Jesus' entry into Jerusalem thus:

The next day the large crowd that had come to the feast heard that Jesus was coming to Jerusalem. So they took branches of palm trees and went out to meet him, crying out,

---

167. Thurman, *Jesus and the Disinherited*, p. 12.

'Hosanna! Blessed is he who comes in the name of the Lord, even the King of Israel!' And Jesus found a young donkey and sat on it, just as it is written,

'Fear not, daughter of Zion;
behold, your king is coming,
sitting on a donkey's colt!'
(John 12:12-15)

Palm branches had been a symbol of resistance for more than a century. When Simon the Maccabee rode victoriously into a liberated Jerusalem in 141 BC, the people waved palm branches. The subversive, alternative coins that Jewish zealots printed because they despised the imprint of Rome on the imperial currency used for taxation as idolatrous and unclean replaced the head of Caesar with symbols of palm fronds. For anti-colonial symbolism, think Gandhi wearing a homespun *dhoti*, or the Mau Mau wearing dreadlocks. Such symbols have always been a rallying-point for self-determination, uniting people against oppressive empires.

Thus, as we enter the climactic week, the tension heightens. The crowds become increasingly persuaded that Jesus is Messiah, and therefore that he will lead a popular uprising and throw out the Romans. They throw caution to the wind and, gathering in large numbers, explicitly and publicly acclaim Jesus as 'King of Israel', a treasonous and dangerous claim. The Roman soldiers, billeted en masse in Jerusalem for the festival period, are on edge, expecting that at any moment the smallest spark could set the whole city ablaze.

There is a question about this verse – palm trees do not grow in large numbers in and around Jerusalem, it's too cold in the winters. Date palms are present in great numbers down in

Jericho, seventeen miles away in the sweltering Jordan valley. I wonder if some key zealot agitators had come prepared, bringing large numbers of palm leaves with them from Jericho, hoping to catalyse a mob response and escalate things, rather than the oft-imagined spontaneous garnering of leaves from (non-existent) nearby trees. Mass resistance movements have always utilised symbolism and key PR opportunities, and the ancient world was no different.

Jesus, refusing to allow the situation to get out of hand, refusing to be the figurehead of a violent revolution, refusing to be a military Messiah, de-escalates the moment by choosing, instead of a horse, to ride a donkey. All four Gospels agree on this, but only John calls the animal an *onarion*, which is a diminutive that could mean young donkey, or even little donkey. As Ford (Ireland) explains, 'Having emphasised the messianic power politics of the crowd, John at once undermines it with this little donkey.'[168]

Where most conquerors enter a city on a horse, Jesus chooses to enter Jerusalem for the final time on a donkey. Simon the Macabee ('the Hammer'), a century earlier, had ridden into Jerusalem amid waving palm branches at the head of his army on a horse. He was come as a warrior/conqueror to destroy the enemies of Israel.

But Jesus chose a little donkey instead.

John's account tells us that this happened to fulfil the prophecy of Zechariah. Here are Zechariah's words:

> Rejoice greatly, O daughter of Zion! Shout aloud, O daughter of Jerusalem! Behold, your king is coming to you; righteous and having salvation is he, humble and mounted on a donkey, on a colt, the foal of a donkey. I will cut off the chariot from Ephraim and the war horse from Jerusalem; and the battle

---

168. Ford, *John*, p. 237.

bow shall be cut off, and he shall speak peace to the nations; his rule shall be from sea to sea, and from the River to the ends of the earth.

(Zechariah 9:9-10)

Zechariah's prophecy is anti-war horse and pro-donkey. Because in times of war, kings ride horses, but in times of peace, kings ride donkeys. And Jesus is not coming to start a war, he is coming to inaugurate a peace. Jesus is not coming to shed the blood of his enemies, he is coming to shed his own blood on behalf of his enemies. The Jewish nationalists were hoping that Jesus would overthrow the Gentile Roman oppressors, but Zechariah says that 'he shall speak *peace* to the [Gentiles]'[169] (including the Romans). Jesus' triumphal entry does not divide communities, as with all other conquerors. Jesus has come to create peace, to unite, to bring together. Jesus is not a horse-king, he is a donkey-king!

> Jesus refuses to reinforce their political and nationalist aspirations by riding on a war horse or by stirring up insurrection against the Romans. Rather, he takes steps to enter Jerusalem on a donkey, fulfilling rather different Old Testament promises.[170]

Writing in Cyprus, an island home to Greek-Cypriot and Turkish-Cypriot communities, here are some perspectives on this moment in the story. I have shared some of these thoughts with both Greek Cypriots and Turkish Cypriots, and have found warm acceptance, resonance, even tears.

---

169. Italics mine.
170. Carson, *John*, p. 434.

Jesus is a near king, not a distant king

'Behold, your king is coming to you', declared Zechariah. Where Cyprus has, throughout her history, had distant, disinterested rulers, Jesus is a *near* king, a ruler whose decisions take into account the local, the personal, a Lord who is among the people. 'Behold' renders him visible. 'Your king' renders him personal. 'To you' renders him close.

Too many empires have taken advantage of Cyprus for its strategic location. The danger is sometimes I hear mission agencies or church planters talking in the same way – that Cyprus is valuable for its strategic proximity to the Middle East. They treat Cyprus as an aircraft carrier, not as a place with its own story, pain, aspirations and fears. What about loving Cyprus and Cypriots for their own sake?

'Your king is coming to you' is good news for colonised places which have been governed from afar, impersonally, uncaringly. This nearness, this dignifying visitation, is a key element of the incarnation, which is why Zechariah prophesies rejoicing. To have a near king, a present king, after centuries of foreign rule, is indeed good news.

Jesus honours the local, not the foreign

In Judea, donkeys were indigenous, horses were foreign. The big empires around about, Egypt, Assyria, Persia, Rome, were equipped with horses and chariots, massed cavalry, and were powerful in great rumbling charges over flat ground. Sometimes, kings of Israel aspired to imitate them – Solomon had '40,000 stalls for horses, and 12,000 horsemen' (1 Kings 4:26). Solomon was trying to be like Pharoah in Egypt. He was trying to be something that he was not.

Judea, as a rocky, mountainous place, was the natural home of the sure-footed donkey. Is there something in Jesus' choice of the donkey as a statement pro-local, a criticism of those who were trying to emulate foreign armies, who were not satisfied with who God had made them to be?

In common with neighbouring Israel, Cyprus too is a small, mountainous place which is the natural home of indigenous donkeys, not horses. The Cyprus donkey is a well-loved local beast of burden. Tourists to Cyprus buy donkey postcards, visit donkey sanctuaries, try donkey-milk products. The Cyprus donkey is indigenous, steady, all-enduring, strong, sure-footed. It bears the heat of the sun and the hardships of life with true grit. It is uniquely suited to the temperament of the island.

In many ways, the Cyprus donkey is like the Cypriot people; long-suffering, faithful, resilient, strong.

There is a tendency, there has always been a tendency, for small places to despise their own indigenous identities in favour of more attractive, more powerful foreign examples. Solomon longed to build an Egyptian-style cavalry, but it was useless in mountainous Judea. Jesus' choice of the indigenous donkey is a striking affirmation of the local.

Jesus champions the faithful, not the flashy

Contextual Christianity must honour local strengths. The Church in Cyprus is faithful, not flashy. It's been 2,000 years since Sergius Paulus came to faith (Acts 13), and the Cypriot Church has endured empire changes, conquests, persecutions, the ravages of time. She and her leaders need to continue to be humble, long-suffering, steady, sure-footed, patient. For Mitri Raheb (Palestinian), a *longue durée* perspective on history helps us to understand Jesus' promise that 'the meek ... shall inherit the earth' (Matthew 5:5):

Jesus wanted to tell his people that the empire would not last, that empires come and go. When empires collapse and depart, it is the poor and the meek who remain. The 'haves' from the people of the land emigrate; they seek to grow richer within the centres of empire. Those who are well educated are 'brain drained' and vacuumed up by the empire. Who remains in the land? The meek, that is, the powerless! Empires come and go, while the meek inherit the land. Jesus' wisdom is staggering.[171]

A rider on a horse looks magnificent; tall, poised, straight-backed, noble. It is impossible to ride a donkey and look dignified. Impossible! Donkey-riders look awkward, uncomfortable, inelegant. The posture of Christians should be like that of their Lord – donkey-riding, unprepossessing, unimposing, meek.

Jesus is a peace-king, not a war-king

In times of war, kings ride horses. In times of peace, kings ride donkeys. Zechariah promised a peace-king who would 'cut off' weapons and military installations, who would 'speak peace' to the nations (not just to Israel, but also to their enemies). As the Japanese proverb states, 'A good sword is the one left in its scabbard.'

The Messiah who has to judge history ... has become present within it as a victim, as the slaughtered Lamb, who has gathered together the peoples, races, nations and languages through his victimal blood and not his conquering power. It is the intrahistorical challenge to imperial power, but it does not oppose it as another empire, at least within history, but

171. Raheb, *Faith in the Face of Empire*, p. 99.

as its counterpart, as the voice of its victims, through the Lamb, himself a victim, who nevertheless is the true and just criterion of history.[172]

Cyprus remains divided since 1974, with the Green Line festering like an unhealed wound etched across her chest from East to West. Lefkosia-Lefkoşa-Nicosia is the only divided capital city in the world. The UN-patrolled buffer zone is lined with barbed wire, military hardware, pointed weapons. Zechariah promises a peace-king who will remove military presence, who will rule from sea to sea. There are many Cypriots, on both sides of the divide, who long for the removal of military hardware, the end of enmity, and a true and lasting peace.

In the history of conquests, Fatih Sultan Mehmet riding into Constantinople in 1453 on a white charger at the head of the Ottoman army is a classic example – and one with deep resonances on both sides of the Greek-Turkish divide. This king on a white horse meant, for the Muslim Turkish conquerors, victory and, for the Christian Greek defenders, defeat. The history of Cyprus has always borne this out. Conquered either by Christian or Muslim armies, when one community has celebrated, the other has barricaded itself in and expected the worst. When the Christian Venetians conquered Cyprus in 1489, the Turkish Cypriot minority were terrified. And when the Muslim Ottomans took the island in 1571, the Greek Cypriots were scared. Cyprus has never been conquered by a king who treated both communities with parity.

The Filipino experience of receiving the gospel via a colonising power is not dissimilar to that of many places. Jesus was introduced to the Philippines as a horse-king at the head of an army, rather than as a donkey-king who will suffer at the hands of Rome.

---

172. Miguez et al., *Beyond the Spirit of Empire,* Kindle location 4200.

Unfortunately, the religion that carried the name of the one who was crucified by the imperial power of his time played a crucial part, wittingly or unwittingly, in the subjugation and colonization and continuing suffering of the Filipino people. The cross came along with the swords and cannons of the *conquistadores* as the bible came along with the guns of modern imperializing nations. Mission and colonization were inseparable: to colonize was to missionize, and to missionize was to colonize.[173]

Jesus loves humility and hates pride

Zechariah tells us that the donkey-king is humble. Rather than the proud war horse, he rides the lowly colt. And it's not even *his* colt – our penniless Saviour had to borrow someone else's! Cypriots, having seen many proud empires come and go throughout history, sit in their coffee shops with a *longue durée* circumspection – proud kings come and go and we are still here. But a humble king! One who comes 'not to be served but to serve, and to give his life as a ransom for many' (Matthew 20:28). That is an unheard-of idea!

'Donkey' is an insult in most languages and cultures, and Jesus rode into a Jerusalem full of insults, of scorn, of mockery and beatings, of betrayal and death. The crowds lining the streets would have had their worldviews upended and their perspectives on power overturned as they watched this peasant-teacher riding his little donkey. You can see why Judas betrayed him. You can see why the mob turned against him. No one wanted a donkey-king. Jesus did not live up to their expectations of violent revolution.

For the Church in Cyprus – indeed, for the Church in any postcolonial communities in small places – it is good to reflect

---

173. Fernandez, 'Filipino Theology', p. 320.

on these truths. 'God opposes the proud, but gives grace to the humble' (James 4:6). He does not perpetuate the us-and-them divisions, but forges a new world where we and they become one as weapons and barriers are dismantled. Charismatic 'horse' leadership is overrated, while faithful 'donkey' perseverance is underrated. Local strengths must be acknowledged, and imported foreign ideas are not always best.

The donkey-king has much to say to us today.

Chapter Thirteen

Feet

(John 13:1-17)

Those who eat together never eat one another.

(African proverb)

In the seventeenth and eighteenth centuries, during the late Ming and Qing dynasties, Christianity flourished in China; 1692 was a climax of the Church's prosperity, when the emperor, Kangxi, published an edict of complete toleration of Christian teachings.[174] Yet all this fruitfulness was despite the lack of a full Chinese Bible – indeed, the Chinese Catholic Bible was not translated in full until the 1960s. Instead, select stories from the Gospels were spread through evangelistic tracts, devotional books, meditation guides, and so on. And the most widespread, the most popular story of all was the story of Jesus washing his disciples' feet from John 13.

Dr Yanrong Chen, following her extensive research on the classical Chinese publications of the seventeenth and eighteenth centuries, concluded that this particular story's popularity and power, even though it is only recorded in John's Gospel and not in the Synoptics, was due to its resonance with the Chinese culture of the time at various levels.

---

174. Moffett, *A History of Christianity in Asia*, p. 125.

To Chinese audiences in the late sixteenth century, the footwashing story of Jesus and his disciples was unique and intriguing. First of all, there would not be confusion because the footwashing story and the particular occasion associated with washing feet did not exist in any non-Christian Chinese tradition. Confucius and Buddha were not portrayed as washing their students' feet before they suffered or were captured. There were no other anecdotes of washing feet in Chinese literature overlapping with the role of Jesus in the biblical story. Chinese incorporation of the Christian biblical footwashing account should be bereft of intercultural hermeneutics and accommodation to non-Christian concepts. Meanwhile, Chinese audiences would face fewer obstacles in understanding this story than in understanding other theological subjects. Washing feet is a daily activity, after all, and the episode is purely human in its scope. Besides, its storyline in the Bible pericope is straightforward enough that no prior knowledge or sophisticated reasoning is required to comprehend it. Therefore, the clear narration of the footwashing event and its uniqueness make the story a good theme for tracking down Chinese expressions of the biblical story.[175]

Squeezed into an upper room off a narrow street in the old city, Jesus and his disciples sit down to the Passover meal. You eat Passover with family, but Jesus and his disciples are family now. They sit on the floor around a shared bowl, reclining on cushions, because, as the Passover *Seder* goes, 'Once we were slaves in Egypt, but now we are free!' Jesus rises, undresses, and wraps a towel around his waist. Then he begins, one by one, to wash the feet of his friends. Judas is there too, betrayal already festering in

---

175. Chen, *The Diffused Story*, pp. 27-28.

his heart and in his plans. His feet are not exempt. As he washes, Jesus dialogues with Peter, explaining, teaching, instructing. In due course Judas will step outside into the darkness, the darkness having already overwhelmed his soul. And Jesus will remain with his disciples for this long final night, all the way through to chapter 18.

The purpose of the footwashing

Why this dramatic teaching moment on Jesus' final evening? What is being communicated? This story is both a symbolic demonstration of Jesus' mission, and also of our mission. Jesus is acting out his redemptive story. And also, he is setting an example for his apostles to emulate. He is performing a dramatic prefigurement of his cleansing sacrifice at Calvary, in which we clearly see the three movements of Jesus' mission on display; taking off the garments (*kenosis*/emptying), taking the position of a slave (incarnation), washing feet (atonement). Yet, this passage also speaks to our mission as sent ones. In 13:14-15 Jesus says, 'I have given you an example.' In verse 34 he says, 'Just as I have loved you, you also are to love one another.' So from this story we learn soteriology (the doctrine of salvation), and also missiology. Jesus' story is enacted, and is cast as paradigmatic for our stories. 'The juxtaposition of the uniqueness and the exemplariness of Jesus' self-giving service is not at all incongruous', adjures Richard Bauckham (England).[176]

The Chinese book *Guxin Shengjing*, from the eighteenth century, was written in colloquial Chinese, the everyday language used by commoners, telling Bible stories and then explaining them with commentary. This book explains this story to its contemporary Chinese audience in this way:

---

176. Bauckham, *The Testimony of The Beloved Disciple*, p. 196.

This is an analogy. As for people's body having filth, [they] enter into water and take a bath. [They] wash clean, get out of the water, [and] put on clothes. [But their] feet get dirty and need to wash again. Taking a bath is like to remove major sin; washing feet is like to remove minor sin. Even though you have no major sins, no need to take a bath, but [you] have minor sins, [then you] should wash feet. Taking a bath means to receive baptism and to confess. Washing feet means to do meditation, to recite prayers, to whip body, to cry hard, and so good work, [in order to] eliminate minor sins.[177]

Equivalent scriptures, associating the humility of the incarnation with the humility expected of Christ's disciples in their subsequent mission, can be found in both Mark 10:43-45 and Philippians 2:3-7. All three of these passages take Christ's missional humility as the example for our missional humility. All three use the word *doulos* (slave). All three apply the relative dynamics of dishonouring oneself to bring honour to others, of becoming lesser in order to make others greater.

The tone and atmosphere of the footwashing

Verse 1 speaks of love, and the atmosphere in this chapter is intimate, proximate, tender. We see that humility is not just a technical positioning of oneself, but an attitude of the heart that fills the room. They are eating food together – a sign of sacred friendship. You can't preach to people unless you eat with them. It is a highly relational scene. Not mission *to* but mission *with*. There is equality, horizontality; dipping their bread in the common bowl together. This is a Palestinian meal sitting on

---

177. Chen, *The Diffused Story*, p. 94.

the floor around shared food. See how far the Son of God has condescended to now be sharing a common bowl with deniers and betrayers!

Verse 2 says that the devil was present in the heart of the betrayer. We are in the final week of Jesus, in the shadow of the cross, and it is night. The other aspect to the atmosphere here is danger, risk, vulnerability, and the presence of evil.

Authentic mission must hold both of these together in tension. Love begets humility. And danger begets humility.

It is in order, as we paint the picture of the disciples sitting together around shared bowls of food, to listen to Rihbany's (Syria) reflection on Jesus' handing a 'morsel' or 'sop' to Judas:

> To one familiar with the customs of the East, Jesus' handing the 'sop' to his betrayer was an act of surpassing beauty and significance ... those morsels are exchanged by friends. Choice bits of food are handed to friends by one another, as signs of close intimacy. It is never expected that any person would hand such a sop to one for whom he cherishes no friendship ... To the one who carried in his mind and heart a murderous plot against the loving Master, Jesus handed the sop of friendship.[178]

Undressing like Jesus: cross-cultural divestment of power, privilege and preference

[Jesus] rose from supper. He laid aside his outer garments, and taking a towel, tied it round his waist.

(John 13:4)

---

178. Rihbany, *The Syrian Christ*, pp. 48-49.

The Undressing of Christ is his symbolic enactment of what Paul calls in Philippians 2:7 his *kenosis*, or emptying. 'The incarnation meant the deliberate self-limiting of a divine being in order to be truly and fully human',[179] said Witherington (USA). The same cluster of verbs is found in 10:18, when Jesus, instead of laying down his garments, speaks of laying down his life: 'No one takes it from me, but I lay it down of my own accord. I have authority to lay it down, and I have authority to take it up again' (see John 13:12).

Garments speak of identity in Scripture; you can identify people because of what they wear. That's the force of the parable of the Good Samaritan in Luke 10 – the robbers strip the man naked so the priest does not know who he is, and whether or not he has responsibility for him. From his clothes, the priest would have known whether this was an Israelite, or an Egyptian, or an Idumean up from the desert. But naked men all look the same, so the priest cannot discern whether or not he has a duty of care to this individual. Jesus is born naked and dies naked, stripped by the soldiers who gamble for his clothes. He is an everyman. Nakedness, denoting humiliation, vulnerability and a loss of self, is a powerful metaphor for Christ's condescension. He strips himself of all authority and privilege, empties himself of his divine prerogatives, and stoops to enter the world.

This mode of mission, while uniquely Christ's own, is also exemplary for those who seek to emulate him. What, then, should *our* undressing look like? When we cross cultures for the sake of Christ, in what ways do we need to 'undress'?

Cross-cultural divestment of power

Hudson Taylor's famous undressing from Western clothes and putting on of Chinese dress signified a refusal to rely on the

---

179. Witherington, *The New Testament Story*, Kindle location 2693.

political power of the West, the gunboat diplomacy backing up British citizens. Mission that relies on power is colonialism.

When American pastor Andrew Brunson was eventually released from prison in Turkey and was photographed at the White House with President Trump, this reinforced the idea that Christianity is American, that missionaries are agents of the State, and therefore that the gospel is somehow foreign or undermining of national identity. For the Turkish Church, this photograph was problematic.

Language acquisition shifts us away from relying on cultural power. Language is power, and where the gospel is shared in English (or other 'powerful' colonial languages), this can disempower non-English speakers. Many argue that globalisation is a powerful cultural current that can be harnessed for the gospel, while in fact cross-cultural witnesses ought to resist the temptation to present a Western culture-packaged gospel.

It is also unsustainable to rely on financial power. On their first mission trip, Jesus sent the Twelve out with no money, so that they had to rely on the hospitality of those to whom they were going. There is no coincidence that this method led, just a few verses later, to spiritual power in healing and deliverance.[180] In many cases, the financial power of missionaries is inversely proportional to their spiritual power.

In the West, power is an idol. We think we need it and we can't imagine succeeding without it. There is a profound danger that without cross-cultural divestment of power, whether political, cultural or financial, Western missionaries merely export their idolatry along with the gospel.

Sri Lankan theologian D.T. Niles was very taken with the need for Western missionaries to follow Christ's example in the divestment of power.

---

180. See Mark 6:7-13.

He was a true servant because He was at the mercy of those whom He came to serve ... To serve from a position of power is not true service but beneficence ... The only way to build love between two people or two groups of people is to be so related to each other as to stand in need of each other. The Christian community must serve. It must also be in a position where it needs to be served.[181]

We must break the cycle of pride in the Giver and humiliation in the Receiver.

Nanthachai Mejudhon (Thailand) advocates 'meekness' as an important contextual approach for reaching Thai Buddhists. Thai people, argues Mejudhon, do not respond to pushy, argumentative evangelism. They do not respond to arrogant Westerners. Christians need to develop long-term, genuine, sincere relationships with Buddhists. Only in authentic meekness will the gospel bear fruit among Thai communities.[182]

Cross-cultural divestment of privilege

The great sin of the privileged is judgementalism. To serve from a position a privilege is merely to patronise. White privilege is indubitably embedded in modern missiology, just as it is inextricably embedded in the world view of modern missionaries from Europe and North America.

The unlearning required is more than just a symbolic removal of garments. Decolonisation must be not just of practices and processes, not just of biases and prejudices, but of the mind, and of the spirit.

In practice, such undressing can happen if sufficient time and intentionality is allowed at the point of entering a new culture.

---

181. Niles, *This Jesus*, pp. 23-27.
182. Mejudhon, *Meekness: A New Approach to Christian Witness to the Thai People*.

To allow several years to unlearn old habits and ways of seeing the world, as well as learning a new language, new customs and perspectives, is an essential step. It is like being born naked, stripped of previous competencies, titles and claims. Your previous academic, professional or ministry successes mean nothing as you seek, toddler-like, to express basic needs and make friends in a new language.

One profound antidote to privilege is pain, which is perhaps one reason that most famous missionary stories are so full of suffering and tears and loss. Pain without hope of recourse begets empathy, it levels the playing field, it strips away difference and distance between rich and poor.

Cross-cultural divestment of preference

As well as power and privilege, the cross-cultural witness must learn also not to idolise one's preference. Preference is soft power which imports unnecessary and unprofitable foreign flavours into what ought to become an indigenous Christianity. Those planting churches in other cultures must reflect, for example, on how much of their view of church practice is preference, rather than scripturally mandated.

We are well aware that nineteenth-century English missionaries brought to Africa the gospel plus European cultural righteousness, from church organs and archdeacons to clothing and manners, much of which was not only inappropriate and unhelpful, but actually otherising, exacerbating the gulf between Westerners and 'natives' and couching this gulf in religious and moral terms.

However, cross-cultural church planters today continue to export a Christianity dressed in Western clothes, whether certain ideas about what leadership needs to look like, or expected corporate worship styles, or even cultural expectations of what good exegesis or preaching looks like. Where money is involved, there can be an expectation of budgeting or reporting that plays to Western strengths and exacerbates differences between 'us' and 'them'.

In all of this, the undressing Christ speaks to us. This *kenosis*, or emptying, is a necessary first step to the crossing of any cultural boundary. As always, Jesus is showing us how to proceed.

Becoming slaves like Jesus (vv. 4-5)

[Jesus] rose from supper. He laid aside his outer garments, and taking a towel, tied it round his waist. Then he poured water into a basin and began to wash the disciples' feet and to wipe them with the towel that was wrapped round him.

(John 13:4-5)

Jesus became a slave. *Doulos* really means slave, and the costume and role that Jesus here takes upon himself was reserved for the lowest of slaves. The role of washing feet was such a shameful job that within wealthy Jewish households, even Jewish slaves were not given this role, only Gentile slaves. The Talmud taught that students of a rabbi could be his servants, and could do anything for him, except anything to do with his feet. In the Middle East today, feet or shoes are considered so unclean that one ought to apologise before speaking about them, 'Please excuse me for using this four-letter word.' When Saddam Hussein's great statue in Bagdad was brought down at the fall of his regime, television footage showed Iraqi citizens beating the statue with their shoes.

In the equivalent passages in Philippians and Matthew,[183] *doulos* is also used; 13:16 puts slave and apostle together in the

---

183. Philippians 2:4-8; Matthew 10:24.

same verse. The emphasis in all this is less the common idea of serving others, or 'ministry', and more profoundly linked to the shame and subalternality of slavery. If God has joined 'slave' and 'apostle' together, let not man separate them! Jesus will be betrayed for a slave's price and die a slave's death in crucifixion. The Free One will offer himself as a slave that the enslaved ones might be freed. On this Passover night, as the disciples eat the traditional meal whereby the bitter herbs remind them of the bitter tears of slavery, and the reclining on cushions signifies 'once we were slaves in Egypt, but now we are free', the whole *Seder* drenched in the symbolism of slavery, the actions of Jesus must have been profoundly disturbing to the disciples. We, on the other side of the cross, equipped with Paul's supplementary reflections on slavery to sin and freedom in Christ, are able to recognise John's art in all of these weighty references. What, then, is the significance for us of Jesus' emptying himself, taking the very form of a slave, 'being born in the likeness of men' (Philippians 2:7)?

Firstly, slave is the opposite of empire. Where empire demanded of the world, 'become like us', slaves had no choice but to become like the household to which they were enslaved. Imagine two planets, each with their own gravitational pull. Empire seeks to suck everyone and everything into its own orbit. Slavery is the opposite. Slaves are pulled into the orbit of those more powerful than themselves. There has always been an underclass diaspora in the world, an alternate globalisation. There has always been a forced migration of slaves, of refugees, of economic migrants. Christian mission does not enter new cultures as empire, but as slave. It does not seek to dominate, to coerce. It allows itself to be shaped, to be dominated by context. It comes, like Christ himself, 'not to be served but to serve' (Matthew 20:28). It demonstrates a subversive influence. It operates from below, not from above.

Scripture shows that the disciples proclaimed the gospel through humility, persecution, and years of service using culturally subversive methods. Nowhere in Scripture do we find Jesus using force to get people to follow him; quite the contrary – he lets people choose between him and their comfortable lives, and if they choose the latter, he leaves them alone.[184]

Secondly, humiliating oneself elevates the other. The dynamics of honour are relative, not absolute. If the pie has ten slices, and I only take two, I leave eight slices for you. For Christ to crouch down and wash his disciples' feet is to elevate his disciples. 'You stoop down to make me great' (Psalm 18:24, NIV 1984). To take a lower seat is to vacate the higher seats for others. This stark, visceral image of Christ kneeling before the feet of his disciples has dominated the Christian imagination for centuries, and must continue to do so.

Thirdly, slave as influence through entering another's world is a theme throughout the Bible. All the way through Scripture, slaves enter the world of another (often a pagan king) and exercise godly influence from below, from within, through maintaining godly witness in the midst of untold suffering. Rulers show their fears and vulnerability to a trusted slave in a way that they never would to a peer, because the slave is not a threat, not a rival. Slaves reach the soft underbelly rather than the hard outer shell. So Joseph influences Pharoah. And Daniel influences Nebuchadnezzar and Darius. And Esther influences Ahasuerus. And Naaman's wife's slave girl influences Naaman. Isaiah famously articulates the 'servant songs', depicting Israel as standing within this great tradition of influential slaves, of impact through suffering, of invisibility to the world but chosenness in

---

184. Haddis, *A Just Mission*, p. 48.

the sight of God. David Devenish (England) reflects on the vital importance of this theme in Scripture:

> The biblical word 'servant' is wonderfully rich in its meaning. It embraces both the dignity of the Anointed One ('chosen one'), but is also the appropriate attitude for a Christian leader, who should genuinely regard himself as a 'slave' to people, rather than standing presumptuously on that dignity. The idea of dignity attached to servanthood is something that cannot be understood outside of the example of Christ. However, being sent as Jesus was sent means that we take this attitude. In the book of Isaiah there is a collection of what are often called 'Servant Songs', in which the term 'servant' sometimes refers prophetically to Christ and sometimes to the people of God. We are now the corporate anointed servant, with the dignity of God's commissioning and the power of the Holy Spirit upon us. Our mission, like him, is to bring justice to the nations.[185]

Lamin Sanneh (Gambia) agrees:

> The mission of the church is to be a servant to the world in the name of Christ, and to hear the cry of the poor, the wounded, the outcast, the hungry and thirsty, the sick, the orphan, the cry of mothers for their children. The mission of the church is to hear these cries with the ears and compassion of Christ and to respond with his grace and example.[186]

Paul, referring not to contextualisation of the message but rather to contextualisation of the messenger, speaks of himself in these terms in 1 Corinthians 9.

---

185. Devenish, *What on Earth is the Church For?*, pp. 29-30.
186. Sanneh in an unpublished conversation with Hill, quoted in *Salt, Light and a City*, p. 56.

For though I am free from all, I have made myself a servant [slave] to all, that I might win more of them. To the Jews I became as a Jew, in order to win Jews. To those under the law I became as one under the law (though not being myself under the law) that I might win those under the law. To those outside the law I became as one outside the law (not being outside the law of God but under the law of Christ) that I might win those outside the law. To the weak I became weak, that I might win the weak. I have become all things to all people, that by all means I might save some. I do it all for the sake of the gospel, that I may share with them in its blessings.

(1 Corinthians 9:19-23)

Washing feet like Jesus: Touching the shame of a culture

Jesus answered him, 'If I do not wash you, you have no share with me.'

(John 13:8)

Share (*meros*) speaks of becoming part of the body of Christ: a mystical communion. If you accept such service from the hand of Christ, there is a fusion that happens, a joining. Being touched and healed at the point of one's greatest shame creates an attachment of love and trust that cannot come from any other source. Consider the stories in Scripture whereby those who have experienced deliverance end up following the deliverer around. The very experience of being touched by Christ invites a joining, a bond.

There must be teaching, correction, confrontation, healing enacted cross-culturally. The purpose of Christian mission is of course to bring change. However, footwashing as an image of the change that is wrought by the gospel into the cultures of the world is remarkable. It is intimate, proximate, humble, compassionate. It speaks of years spent together, trust earned, mutual love and respect.

The need to touch the shame of a culture

The only way to touch people's lowest place is to get even lower. Do you want to touch their feet? Get below their feet! Feet in the Bible are more than gross, or distasteful. They represent deep shame and uncleanness. Jesus is touching the disciples in the place of their deepest untouchability.

Many cultures are too proud to show their darkest secrets to outsiders (particularly to Westerners) – 'You don't hang your dirty laundry where everyone can see it.' It takes a long time, a very long time, to earn cross-cultural trust. Just as we often joke that, for royalty, the smell of fresh paint is normal, because wherever they visit in the world, their hosts do their utmost to spruce themselves up to present their best face to their Majesties, so often with foreigners, it can take years to get past the well-presented face of a culture into its darker secrets. This is natural. Here, it has taken the disciples until John 13 before they allow Jesus anywhere near their feet.

Feet as the opposite of head

Again, this is a challenge to the power-narrative. Where some Western evangelicals have spoken about 'upstream influence' and the desire to impact culture through people of power, Christ's approach is to the margins, to the outcast, to the feet. We should be seeking to wash the feet of our cities, not the head. The aspiration of the Church should not be to 'take the city' but rather to 'serve the city'. Could urban church planting, rather than being targeted at the corridors of power, rather be aimed at the cul de sacs and ghettos? Which part of your city is the most feet-like; dirtiest, toughest, perhaps most concealed? Is not the attention of the stooping Christ fully focused on the feet, not the head?

Washing as correction and healing

Washing feet is such a great metaphor for humble, cross-cultural evangelism and service. The Word of Christ has cleansing power.

> That he might sanctify her, having cleansed her by the washing of water with the word.
>
> *(Ephesians 5:26)*

> You are clean because of the word that I have spoken to you.
>
> *(John 15:3)*

Washing is certainly a New Testament metaphor for the action of the Word. The feet of humankind, although originally beautiful in the image of God, have accumulated the grime and filth of a 1,000 generations, as we have walked through history. And so we say to our sisters and brothers, 'Your culture, like mine, has acquired some dust and dirt along the road of history, maybe a few scratches. Come, let me serve you with the washing of water of the Word, as you serve me, and let us see what beauty is revealed within.'

Washing as uncovering what's already there

As feet are washed with water through the Word, what emerges are beautiful feet, feet exhibiting the common grace given to all people, scattered liberally through the cultures of the world. We see, emerging from the filth and grime, latent genius, the contribution of the recipient cultures to the beauty of the Global Church.

Rowan Williams (England), on the bicentenary of the British and Foreign Bible Society in 2004, said, 'Every language and culture [have in them] a sort of "homing instinct" for God – deeply buried by the sin and corruption that affects all cultures, yet still there, a sleeping beauty to be revived by the word of Christ.'[187]

Kosuke Koyama, reflecting on his own Japaneseness, which was so important to him, wrote;

The name of Jesus Christ does not stand for demolition or 'scorched land bombing'. He did not destroy everything of my former education and formation when I came to him. After I became a Christian I still lived in the cultural world of Japan. I worship Christ with the emotion and thought which derives from the culture of Japan. I am led to believe that Jesus Christ inspires me to find out ways in which I can make use of my Japanese heritage. I, who was born in the Japanese culture, who wear Japanese-ness with my skin, am re-receiving my own culture. It is not experience of demolition but of resurrection.[188]

And lest we think this is only for the *beneficiaries* of our mission, the washing of our own feet by Christ is in some way the revealing, throughout our lives, of the destiny and purpose which God had already bestowed. The disciples' feet, oftentimes a biblical symbol for obedience in movement ('How beautiful ... are the feet of him who brings good news', Isaiah 52:7; 'feet fitted with the readiness [of] ... the gospel of peace', Ephesians 6:15, NIV) are here washed and blessed by Christ for their missional readiness. He washes their feet as a prelude to sending them. And, as anyone engaged in mission will testify, the disclosing of

187. Williams, *Sowing the Word*, p. x.
188. Koyama, *Three Mile an Hour God*, p. 67.

our missional usefulness feels like an ongoing, lifelong washing away of our own prejudices and blindnesses to reveal what God had designed for us from the start.

Jesus' mission was humble mission. He sends us in the same spirit and to the same end. Every time we approach a cultural boundary, consider: we undress like Jesus, we come as slaves, like Jesus, and we wash feet, like Jesus. As Hudson Taylor wrote, 'Pray that this principle of becoming one with the people, of willingly taking the lowest place, may be deeply inwrought in our souls and expressed in our deportment.'[189]

---

189. Taylor, *The Spiritual Secret,* p. 295.

Chapter Fourteen

Paraclete
(John Chapters 14 to 16)

With *guanxi* nothing matters.
Without *guanxi* everything matters.
(Chinese proverb)

Jesus has spent three years gathering a community of misfits, outsiders and marginal people. He has been to them an influential friend, a broker, a mediator. He has used language like, 'I will ask the Father' (John 14:16) or 'I am going to the Father ... I will come to you' (John 14:28). This going and coming, this asking, reads as the role of mediator, or intercessor. One of the things the disciples have gained, in Christ, is what we could call *an influential friend*.

In many communalistic cultures, such influential friends, well-connected contacts, people who know people who can get things done, are an absolutely essential part of life. Where the structure of society is that of patron-client relationships, brokers are the glue that arrange connection, repair relationships, make introductions. A well-connected friend is one's greatest resource.

In Turkey, the word for this role is *torpil*. Before beginning any endeavour, one first finds out if one has a *torpil* in that area – an old school friend, perhaps, or a family member. In Arabic, people speak of *wasta* – a word derived from 'the middle', technically meaning 'a go-between' but used more generally for influence.

'Do you have any *wasta* in such and such a department?' In Chinese culture, *guanxi* means the social network, connections and mutual obligations within which one is embedded and through which one gets anything done. An outsider, with no *guanxi*, cannot expect anyone to trust them or to achieve anything. My Russian friends look for *po blat*, someone with the influence without which it is impossible to get anything done in Russia.

While Jesus is only rarely explicitly called a broker in Scripture (Hebrews 9:15; 12:24, 1 Timothy 2:5; 1 John 2:1), his acting as a go-between connecting the Father and the disciples goes without being said in the New Testament.[190]

> The New Testament writers talk about the ways Jesus acts as broker and expect us to see it. This only became a challenge when we individualists who are not familiar with the system of brokerage began to read the New Testament. In John's Gospel, Jesus frequently speaks about being sent by the Father into the world (Jn 4:34; 5:30; 6:38). Jesus also speaks about going back to the Father (Jn 13:1; 16:5). This is classic brokerage. Jesus is the Father's broker, sent to the other party, us.[191]

And now, on the final night before his crucifixion, Jesus seeks to comfort the disciples that, although he will be leaving them, they as a fledgling community will not be left as 'orphans' – i.e. without an *influential friend*. No, he will ask the Father to send them *another Paraclete* – the Holy Spirit.

Jesus does not leave them lots of rules. Or a manual. He never wrote a book. He doesn't even really leave them leaders: 'I'm

---

190.   Neyrey, "'I am the Door" (John 10:7,9): Jesus the Broker in the Fourth Gospel'.
191.   Richards and James, *Misreading Scripture with Individualist Eyes*, p. 267.

going but I entrust you to Peter . . .' No. He is not saying, 'When I go, do this and do that . . .' In fact, moral exhortation is pretty much absent from these chapters of John, apart from 'A new commandment . . . love one another' (John 13:34).

Instead, he spends several chapters – a long last supper! – talking about someone who is going to come who will be with them. There are five places in chapters 14 to 16 where the *Paraclete* is mentioned. It's clear that English Bible translators have struggled with this word, translating it variously as comforter, counsellor, helper, just to name a few. On translation, I agree with Chacko (India), who states, 'No one term covers all the functions; therefore instead of settling with any one English term, it would be good to translate this word as Paraclete.'[192] Because, in the English-speaking world with its assumption of equality, well-connected friends smack of cronyism or nepotism, it's been difficult for those in an individualist, merit-based society to appreciate the value or the virtue of the Paraclete, we need to look to communalistic cultures with their dependence on social capital and reciprocal obligations to help us understand this term. Jerome Neyrey (USA), who is consistently insightful into the cultural world of the New Testament, explains it like this:

> Although 'advocates' appear in a court, they more readily appear in other venues, such as palaces, temples, and forums. Even in a court, an advocate does not function in a forensic role but rather as a partisan supporter. In Philo, an 'advocate' may give advice about a difficult decision or provide support for someone making a claim or settling a dispute. But Advocate/Paraclete did not mean an advocate in the sense of a lawyer. It meant rather a man who would appear in court to lend the weight of his influence and

---

192. Chacko, *Intercultural Christology*, p. 180.

prestige to the case of his friend, to convince the judges of his probity, and to seek a favourable verdict.[193]

In their excellent book, *Misreading Scripture with Individualist Eyes*, Richards and James (USA and England)[194] are at pains to explain how, in communalistic cultures, the role of mediator, broker, influential friend, a well-connected third party is absolutely essential in all areas of life. This complex web of inter-connected dependencies is a fact of life in group-orientated cultures. Other inflections of this kind of role might be that of an intercessor, an advocate, a middleman, a fixer.[195] Presenting evidence from Greek writings prior to the Gospel of John, Richards and James agree with Neyrey that the role of Paraclete seems to have been a 'partisan supporter'.

Tricia Gates Brown's (USA) thorough book, *Spirit in John*, extends the idea:

The *paracletes* are not portrayed as advocates in the court but as persons striving to use their connections and 'influence' to sway those involved in the formal court proceedings . . . *paracletes* denote powerful individuals among the crowd striving to persuade the jurors to decide in favour of their client before the trial has even commenced . . . The word *Paraclete* would best be translated 'mediator' or 'broker.'[196]

Richard James, writing in his Middle Eastern context, reflects on what this means for his Middle Eastern friends and their understanding of the Holy Spirit.

---

193. Neyrey, *John*, pp. 267-268.
194. Richards having lived in Indonesia, and James in the Middle East.
195. Richards and James, *Misreading Scripture with Individualist Eyes*, p. 271.
196. Brown, *Spirit in the Writings of John*, p. 181.

My collectivist friends find John's passage far more comforting than I ever did. The disciples have been following Jesus, who multiplies bread, heals the sick, deflects trouble from the authorities. He has provided protection and provision, and now he says he's leaving them – but he is providing another broker, who comes from the father, the Spirit of truth. Jesus doesn't explain it; the disciples don't need someone to explain what a broker does. What comforts them is that they are getting an amazing broker: one who will be with them forever. This passage has been cold comfort for me because I didn't really understand what a broker did . . . Now that we understand better what John meant, we can be comforted.[197]

There is certainly a correlation, in the missions space today, between lack of material resource and experience of the resource of the Holy Spirit. The fast-growing Pentecostal and charismatic forms of Christianity in the Global South are among the poor, the marginal, the illiterate. The wealthy Global North Church knows less of the life of the Spirit. Cross-cultural workers who are well-funded see less of the power of the Spirit in their ministries, those who have less material backing seem to see more miracles.

Latin Americans have long insisted that traditional European and North American theologies of the Spirit were too static and disconnected from the suffering and economic hardships of the peoples of Latin America. Furthermore, Pentecostals have felt that many of the mainstream North American theologies were overly preoccupied with theoretical issues within theological discourse and have lost the evangelistic urgency needed to evangelize the world.[198]

---

197. Richards and James, *Misreading Scripture with Individualist Eyes*, pp. 271-272.
198. Tennent, *Theology in the Context of World Christianity*, p. 168.

A community of the Holy Spirit is not a community reliant on material resource and merely sprinkled with a supplementary seasoning of the Holy Spirit. No, these are Jesus' followers, shortly to be bereft of his presence, terrified and abandoned, being promised another Paraclete who will take responsibility, arrange and initiate, provide and lead, as Jesus has been doing for three years. I've had the privilege of worshipping in churches in cities where life is hard, work hours are long and demanding, and the opportunity for corporate worship on a Sunday is a source of strength. The experience of the Paraclete in such spaces is one of drawing down grace and endurance from the Father at the beginning of a new week. I think of the various Filipino diaspora fellowships across the Middle East, where domestic workers who are often treated as no better than slaves spend the entirety of their one day off in church.

There are five mentions of the Paraclete in chapters 14 to 16. Let's consider these one at a time, remembering two things. Firstly, John, of all the Gospel authors, writes about the Spirit the most personally, the most like a knowable person. He has had decades of personal relationship with and knowledge of the Holy Spirit. He is writing, in a sense, about his friend. All the promises made by Jesus here, John has experienced to be true. Secondly, all the things that are here spoken of as the work of the Spirit, have also been spoken of, in John's Gospel, as the work of Christ, hence 'another Paraclete', one who will continue the ministry of Christ in the same vein, an unbroken continuity between the work of Christ *for* the community, and the work of the Spirit *through* the community.

The Holy Spirit has been anticipated throughout John. He was seen to be abiding on Jesus (1:32-33), Nicodemus needed to be born of the Spirit, who cannot be seen but discerned (3:1-10), the Spirit will be given 'without measure' (3:34), 'God is spirit' who should be worshipped 'in spirit and truth' (4:23-24), the words of Jesus as 'spirit and life' (6:63), the Spirit as 'rivers of living water', not yet given (7:37-39), and Jesus 'troubled in . . . spirit' (11:33; 13:21).

1. Presence: The Spirit brings the presence of God (14:16-18)

And I will ask the Father, and he will give you another [Paraclete], to be with you for ever, even the Spirit of truth, whom the world cannot receive, because it neither sees him nor knows him. You know him, for he dwells with you and will be in you. I will not leave you as orphans; I will come to you.

(John 14:16-18)

Orphans are vulnerable. They are often exploited, mistreated, alone. Jesus speaks of his own presence ('I will come') in virtually the same breath as he speaks of the Spirit's presence. These verses are profoundly Trinitarian; the Father, Spirit and Son are involved.

In many countries, the legal system dictates that a vulnerable adult or someone who is underage be accompanied by an appropriate adult. This role is not the role of the lawyer, rather it involves relationship and trust. The appropriate adult, or chaperone, protects, supports, explains, represents. Jesus tells us that he is not leaving us as orphans, because we will have the Paraclete, the Holy Spirit, accompanying us.

'He dwells with you . . .' Dwelling (sometimes translated 'abiding' or 'remaining') is a big word in John (forty times). 'The Word became flesh' and made his dwelling among us (John 1:14). The Spirit descended as a dove and rested on/remained on Jesus (John 1:32). Jesus encouraged his disciples 'abide in me'/remain in the vine (John 15:4) In the same way, the Spirit will rest-abide-remain-dwell with you (plural) and in you (plural). Jesus is promising a community of the Spirit, a people among whom and within whom the Holy Spirit dwells.

2. Instruction: The Spirit brings the instruction of Jesus (14:26-27)

But the [Paraclete], the Holy Spirit, whom the Father will send in my name, he will teach you all things and bring to your remembrance all that I have said to you. Peace I leave with you; my peace I give to you. Not as the world gives do I give to you. Let not your hearts be troubled, neither let them be afraid.

(John 14:26-27)

Remember our vulnerable person – the one who needs an appropriate adult? There is also a sense in which this advocate explains things, interprets things, helps them understand what is happening. It is said that one of the adult daughters of the Sheikh of Sharjah has Down's syndrome. Wherever she goes she is accompanied by her chaperone, who explains, instructs and no doubt gives her father a peace of mind and confidence, knowing that she is well looked-after.

In the first instance, Jesus is talking about the role that the Holy Spirit will play in the writing down of the New Testament as Holy Scripture. Jesus has spent three years teaching, telling parables, doing miracles and wonderful things, and his disciples have witnessed it all. When the time comes, in due course, for the teachings and actions of Jesus to be committed to written form in the Gospels, the Holy Spirit will be intimately involved in this process, both in the remembering and in the understanding of what Jesus had said and done.

In a predominantly oral or semi-literate culture, like that of first-century Judea, people have formidable memories. And memory is communal. One person recites a parable that Jesus told, or an event from his life, and the others correct them in the recital. In this way the community preserves accurately, word-for-word, the tradition. Communal recitation is intrinsically conservative, because the community is able to pass on the tradition precisely. When literate people doubt this, it is because they have never sat round a campfire with storytellers from non-literate societies and listened to hour upon hour, even day after day, of word-perfect recitation. For example, there have always been storytellers who can recite, word-for-word, the Persian classic the *Shahname*, 'The Book of Kings', which is an epic poem 50,000 rhyming couplets long.

> For most of the time *Homo sapiens* has been around, most of us were unable to read or write, but we were able to commit to memory long poems, huge amounts of information, and extensive, multi-layered narratives. Even the lodestones of Western literature such as the *Iliad* and the *Odyssey* were consigned to memory centuries before they were written down.[199]

Jesus adds to this natural confidence in oral tradition an additional safeguard – the indwelling Spirit, himself the Eternal Author, will be involved in the process. Jesus promises that the Holy Spirit will remind and explain, instruct and expound. So the Scriptures, we believe, are 'God-breathed' (2 Timothy 3:16, NIV): inspired by the Holy Spirit, the very words of God! Reliable, holy, without error, life-giving!

There is a secondary sense of this verse for us: for us also the Holy Spirit takes the Bible and illuminates it, helps us understand it, brings it to our remembrance. Samuel Ngewa (Kenya), ever

---

199. Sattin, *Nomads*, p. 20.

the pastor, says what we are all thinking in his commentary at this point:

> Some people have used this verse as the basis for claiming that the Holy Spirit has taught them all kinds of things. Thus we have to consider whether there are any limitations on what is likely to be taught. The first point to remember is that the Holy Spirit will be sent in Jesus' name (14:26), which means that his will and that of Jesus are one. Thus he will never contradict what Jesus has said. Instead, he will continue where Jesus left off. The Trinity are interested in teaching a particular curriculum. Jesus had been the disciples' teacher for three years, and has spoken what the Father gave him to say (see 7:16, 8:26, 40, 47). But three years was too little for the disciples to learn everything they would need to know . . . This is the context in which Jesus promises the teaching of the Holy Spirit.[200]

The result? Peace. We are not afraid or anxious or troubled because the Holy Spirit takes the words of Jesus, works them into our lives, and puts peace in our hearts. Let us not miss that 'Let not your hearts be troubled, neither let them be afraid' (John 14:27) is about *hearts* – so the instruction of the Holy Spirit is not just brain-instruction but heart-instruction.

3. Witness: The Spirit bears witness, and so do we (15:26-27)

> But when the Helper comes, whom I will send to you from the Father, the Spirit of truth, who proceeds from the Father, he will bear witness about me. And you also will bear witness, because you have been with me from the beginning.
>
> *(John 15:26-27)*

---

200. Ngewa, *John*, 1310.

'Witness' has been a big word in John. The Samaritan woman bore witness about Jesus. Some have wondered, and I'm tempted to agree, whether 'witness' is not a better word in the twenty-first century than 'mission;' more directly scriptural, less loaded with colonial overtones, more personal and less organisational. There is a simplicity to the idea of witness; a witness in a court of law simply says what they have seen. It's not their job to persuade or argue or dispute, simply to recount the testimony of their experience.

Let's not forget, also, that the word translated *witness* here is from the Greek root *martyr.* And that this conversation is happening during the dark week before Jesus' own martyrdom. That there is an atmosphere of fear and betrayal, of plots and violence. So while witness is simple, it is also risky. It demands courage. The dominant theme of chapter 15 is how much the world hates the disciples. Witness intimidation, the scaring of a witness so that they will not testify, is at work.

Don't fear, says the Lord, the Spirit 'will bear witness about me. And you also will bear witness' . . . verse 26 is beautifully Trinitarian, where Jesus sends the Spirit from the Father, and the Spirit bears witness about Jesus. Newbigin (England) wrote concerning these verses:

> Mission is not simply the self-propagation of the church by putting forth of the power that inheres in its life. To accept that picture would be to sanction an appalling distortion of mission. On the contrary, the active agent of mission is a power that rules, guides, and goes before the church: the free, sovereign, living power of the Spirit of God. Mission is not just something that the church does; it is something that is done by the Spirit, who is himself the witness, who changes both the world and the church, who always goes before the church in its missionary journey.[201]

---

201. Newbigin, *Open Secret*, p. 56.

4. Conviction: The conviction of the Holy Spirit (16:7-8)

Nevertheless, I tell you the truth: it is to your advantage that I go away, for if I do not go away, the [Paraclete] will not come to you. But if I go, I will send him to you. And when he comes, he will convict the world concerning sin and righteousness and judgement.

(John 16:7-8)

The conviction of the Holy Spirit brings a deep sense of what is right and what is wrong. Sometimes, in the hyper-individualistic societies of the modern West, this idea easily becomes twisted into 'I feel this is right', 'I don't feel there is anything wrong in what I am doing', 'If it feels good to you', 'As long as it doesn't hurt anyone'. I have been a pastor long enough to hear people say unbelievably stupid things in the name of the leading of the Holy Spirit.

Jesus is definitely saying, 'I'm leaving you the Holy Spirit who will work in your consciences, who will guide you into what is right and wrong . . .' but we often miss this as thinking it is a deeply individualistic, subjective thing, a feeling, rather than a community exercising Spirit-informed, Scripture-based discernment. Communal conscience is more resilient and more conservative than individual conscience. The positive power of shame can unite a community around a conviction. But this is more than just a generation-on-generation maintenance of the status quo. The Spirit is dynamically involved in initiating conviction about certain issues. Jesus is speaking of an ongoing process, an active engagement of the Church with the Person of God the Holy Spirit.

For Kangaraj, in the multi-religious environment of India, the word *convict* here has 'a forensic tone, meaning to expose, to prove someone guilty, to persuade a wrongdoer to change their mind'.[202] It is very clear that to convict the world of sin is the role of the Holy Spirit, not of the missionary. In cross-cultural mission, this is extremely important. Cross-cultural Christians can be so quick to call out sin, to judge, and can so often be mistaken. In my book *Global Humility* I wrote an extensive section on 'Moral Humility'. For so many reasons, moral judgement cross-culturally falls down; often because one's view of Christian morality is deeply embedded within one's received cultural world view. Thus, in a trite example, jumping a lunchtime queue at an international pastors' conference is an abomination to an Englishman, while for others the concept of queueing may be completely alien! This is not a moral issue, it is a cultural one.

Adeney explains that the guest cannot criticise the host, as it robs them of their status as host.[203] Who are you to come into my country and tell me that the traditions we inherited from our fathers are wrong?

When Christ affirms that it is the Spirit who will convict the world, we need to take him at his word. We trust that God the Holy Spirit, whose mission this is and whom we are following, will take responsibility for the conviction, repentance and salvation of the nations into which we are ministering the gospel.

In John Taylor's account of the beginnings of Christianity in Uganda, it is the Holy Spirit, not the missionaries, who is the hero of the story. The missionaries were emphasising that if these young Ugandan men wanted to be baptised, they needed immediately to abandon polygamy. But the Spirit at work in the consciences of the converts, as they heard the stories of Jesus, drew them to his example in humility (which they did not see in the missionaries), proximity to the poor (which they also did not

---

202. Kanagaraj, *John*, p. 160.
203. Adeney, *Strange Virtues*, p. 132.

see in the missionaries), and that slavery was incompatible with allegiance to Christ.[204]

Newbigin's reflection on this and similar stories is lengthy, but absolute gold for our understanding of the Holy Spirit as the One who convicts in mission:

> Who has the right to decide the ethical content of conversion at any time or place – the evangelist or the convert? The place where the virus of legalism gets into the work of evangelism is the place where the evangelist presumes that he or she knows in advance and can tell the potential convert *what the ethical content of conversion will be*. This is what has happened over and over again. The missionary has had the power and has believed that he or she had the right to lay down the ethical preconditions for baptism – that he or she was ruler over the gospel instead of being its servant.[205]

All of the tree is in the seed. We sow the seed of the gospel and trust that, as it grows in the conscience of a community, so the conviction of the Holy Spirit will also become clear. What is striking, in Taylor's account above, was that the Spirit helped the new Ugandan converts to discern sin in the white missionaries, who owned slaves, were not among the poor, and did not demonstrate humility. The Paraclete, no respecter of persons, desires holiness in all God's children.

5. The Voice of God: The Spirit speaks

> When the Spirit of truth comes, he will guide you into all the truth, for he will not speak on his own authority, but whatever he hears he will speak, and he will declare to you

---

204. Taylor, *The Growth of the Church in Buganda*, pp. 45-49.
205. Newbigin, *Open Secret*, p. 136, italics mine.

the things that are to come. He will glorify me, for he will take what is mine and declare it to you.

(John 16:13-14)

Fundamentally, Christian life and mission is about following the voice of the Holy Spirit. If Acts teaches us anything, it is about the supernatural leading of the Spirit. Philip, Peter, Ananias, Barnabas, Paul, the elders and apostles, all are directed by the Spirit. There are some clear verbs associated with the Holy Spirit in these verses: guide, speak, declare.

The voice of God is communal. The Church is to be a community of the voice of God. God's voice is not the sole privilege of leaders or prophets. The 'you' in these verses is plural.

The voice of God is truth-aligned. Any leading of the Spirit will measure up to the Bible, will not contradict the life and teachings of Jesus, who said 'I am the truth.'[206] The Sharjan princess' chaperone guides and instructs her on behalf of the sheikh. The Spirit is the 'Spirit of truth' because he is consubstantial with the truth, because he *is* the truth.

The voice of God is authoritative. 'He will not speak on his own authority ...' the promptings of the Holy Spirit are not just a suggestion. God is speaking.

The voice of God is predictive. He will 'declare ... the things that are to come'. God knows the future and can speak about the future. In fact, he loves to do this.

The voice of God is Jesus-rich. 'He will glorify me'. Churches that are full of the Holy Spirit talk about Jesus a great deal. Our songs are songs about Jesus. Our personal witness is all about Jesus. Spiritual gifts shine light on Jesus. Teaching and writing magnify Jesus. Lives of obedience, submitted to the Spirit, glorify Jesus.

---

206. See John 14:6.

In these five mentions of the Paraclete across these chapters, Jesus is describing a community of the Spirit, a people who will experience his presence, obey his instruction, sustain his witness, discern his conviction and hear his voice.

Chapter Fifteen

Garden
(John 18:1-27)

Calamity will come to you from those you love.
(Han Fei Tzu)

After the last supper, Jesus and the disciples exit the walled city, cross the Kidron Valley in the dark, and go to the garden, on the slopes of the Mount of Olives, called in the other Gospels Gethsemane. Gethsemane means *oil-press* in Aramaic, and this is the place where the Anointed One will be squeezed, that his oil may flow. Humanity betrayed God in the garden of Eden, now humanity will betray God in the garden of Gethsemane.

> When Jesus had spoken these words, he went out with his disciples across the Kidron Valley, where there was a garden, which he and his disciples entered. Now Judas, who betrayed him, also knew the place, for Jesus often met there with his disciples. So Judas, having procured a band of soldiers and some officers from the chief priests and the Pharisees, went there with lanterns and torches and weapons.
>
> *(John 18:1-3)*

The gardens around the city were not empty. This is Passover, the biggest festival of the year, when, as far as possible, Jews from across the nation and even from the diaspora[207] would gather into the tiny city. Jerusalem's small population would be boosted by as much as a factor of ten, from 100,000 to 1 or even 2 million. The Passover feast was supposed to be celebrated within the city walls, but it's impossible to get such a large crowd of humanity into such a small city. Hence, the religious authorities created a workaround. A decree was issued that artificially extended the city limits to include the gardens that surrounded Jerusalem, just for Passover. In this way, those camping in the market gardens around the outside of the city walls, having travelled many days to be there, could also partake in the feast while camped in the gardens.

Those who travelled from the north, taking the route along the river Jordan rather than the direct route through Samaria, would climb upwards from the Jordan Valley towards the city and would camp on the Mount of Olives. This garden, then, that Jesus and the disciples come to after celebrating their meal in a city house, is not empty. There are 40-50,000 Galileans camping here. We think Jesus is alone in the garden. Jesus isn't alone in the garden. If Judas had wanted to get Jesus arrested secretly, he would have brought the soldiers to the house, earlier in the evening, when there were only a handful of men who could have offered no resistance. Why, then, does Judas bring the soldiers to arrest Jesus in a place in which there are so many Galileans? I think he is trying to trigger the revolution. He is disappointed that Jesus has ridden into the city on a donkey, not a horse. He is disillusioned that the Messiah who he thought would overthrow the Romans, would start the revolution, has done no such thing. 'Perhaps,' he reckons to himself, 'if I get him arrested among a bunch of hot-headed Galileans who have been feasting and drinking all night, perhaps they will all lose control, attack the soldiers, and the

---

207. Acts 2:5.

revolution will kick off, and once it's started, no one will be able to stop it!'

Maybe that's why he kisses Jesus. 'I'm doing this for you, Jesus! I'm helping you! I'm doing this for us!' When we try to get Jesus to do what we want, we are acting like Judas! In Eden, God kissed man with life (Genesis 2:7). In Gethsemane, man kissed God with death.

In the verses that follow, John will so craft the narrative that we see Jesus saying three times, 'I am (*ego eimai*).' As we have seen, Jesus seven times will make an 'I am' statement with a predicate (e.g. 'I am the bread of life'). But he will also make seven absolute 'I am' statements, with no predicate, often lost in translation in English. The final three of these seven, the climax of this sequence, are spoken in this moment (vv. 5, 6, 8).

'I AM' is the Exodus name of God (Exodus 3:14), God's self-disclosure at a moment of national salvation. It is a name unique to God. And John has taken the self-disclosure of God and put it into the mouth of Jesus. Just as it would have taken huge courage and absolute conviction for John, under the inspiration of the Holy Spirit, to rework the opening lines of Genesis, 'In the beginning, God' to portray the Son as eternally pre-existent with the Father, 'In the beginning was the Word' (1:1), so it would have taken equal conviction to place God's unique name from Exodus into the mouth of Jesus.

These kinds of approaches have long been significant in Christian witness to the other great Abrahamic monotheistic faiths, Judaism and Islam. While adherents of both religions resist direct, confrontational, polemical approaches to arguing the divinity of Christ – they find such approaches vulgar, crass, blasphemous – John's subtle, artistic, compelling repositing of the tenets of monotheism in the very words of Jesus have proved fruitful in bypassing stubborn, sometimes banal evangelism that argues and insults and horrifies. John's delicate, indirect, beautiful argument that Jesus is God enables the reader to believe without losing face, without losing an argument. Where low-context cultures which value directness and 'saying it like it is' might appreciate the Gospel of Mark, those high-context cultures which respect subtlety, metaphor and multiple layers of meaning have delighted in the Gospel of John. If you are witnessing to Muslims, trust these texts. Trust their power, their artistry, their subtlety. The verses before us are a prime example of John's high Christology communicated through narrative rather than through proposition, employing symbolic language, symbolic numbers, suggesting and implying profound truth while leaving it up to the reader to draw their own conclusions.

> Then Jesus, knowing all that would happen to him, came forward and said to them, 'Whom do you seek?' They answered him, 'Jesus of Nazareth.' Jesus said to them, '*I am* ...' Judas, who betrayed him, was standing with them. When Jesus said to them, '*I am* ...' they drew back and fell to the ground. So he asked them again, 'Whom do you seek?' And they said, 'Jesus of Nazareth.' Jesus answered, 'I told you that *I am* ... So, if you seek me, let these men go.' This was to fulfil the word that he had spoken: 'Of those whom you gave me I have lost not one.'
>
> *(John 18:4-9, my italics)*

Oh, the drama of this scene, the thrice-repeated refrain, 'I am', the drawing back and falling to the ground of the soldiers! The soldiers are seeking Jesus of Nazareth, yet they encounter the 'I am'. So is it with readers of these words through the generations, that those who seek Jesus of Nazareth meet, in him, the 'I AM' of Exodus. Jesus, ever the Good Shepherd, tells the soldiers to arrest him and not his disciples, the Good Shepherd laying down his life for the sheep. And oh, the irony of the true Light of the world being arrested in darkness by those who come with artificial lights in their hands.

> Then Simon Peter, having a sword, drew it and struck the high priest's servant and cut off his right ear. (The servant's name was Malchus.) So Jesus said to Peter, 'Put your sword into its sheath; shall I not drink the cup that the Father has given me?'
>
> *(John 18:10-11)*

Judas' plan nearly works – trust a hot-headed Galilean to draw his sword and attack! Peter, a fisherman and probably not a very good swordsman, swings his sword around and hacks off Malchus' ear. Jesus is quick to rebuke him, quick to get him to sheath his sword, quick to suggest that Christ-followers do not draw the sword. Jesus is bound and led to the house of Annas, father-in-law of Caiaphas, whose house is traditionally identified in the south of the city, the large house of a wealthy family.

Denial

> Simon Peter followed Jesus, and so did another disciple. Since that disciple was known to the high priest, he entered with Jesus into the court of the high priest, but Peter stood outside at the door.
>
> *(John 18:15-16)*

Jesus is taken, and Peter follows. Following is sheep language. Peter is doing what he has been invited to do; Jesus had called him by saying, 'Follow me' (Matthew 4:19). But when he gets to the door into Annas' courtyard, he stops following. He is afraid. He freezes.

So the other disciple, who was known to the high priest, went out and spoke to the servant girl who kept watch at the door, and brought Peter in. The servant girl at the door said to Peter, 'You also are not one of this man's disciples, are you?' He said, 'I am not.'

(John 18:16-17)

Jesus has three times said, 'I am.' Now Peter will three times say, 'I am not.' That says it all, doesn't it? The difference between Jesus and us; he is the 'I am'. We are the 'I am nots'. Everything that he is, I am not. I am not faithful. He is. I am not perfect. He is. I am not loyal. He is. He's the Good Shepherd. I am not a good sheep. That is the great mystery of the gospel, that the 'I am' should lay down his life for the 'I am nots'. Lay down your life for good sheep, by all means, but not for treacherous sheep!

Now the servants and officers had made a charcoal fire, because it was cold, and they were standing and warming themselves. Peter also was with them, standing and warming himself.

(John 18:18)

The charcoal fire is an unusual detail. Peter will deny his Lord next to a charcoal fire. And, after the resurrection of Jesus, Peter's restoration will take place next to another charcoal fire. This detail ties this scene to the scene on the beach in chapter 21.

Now Simon Peter was standing and warming himself. So they said to him, 'You also are not one of his disciples, are you?' He denied it and said, 'I am not.' One of the servants of the high priest, a relative of the man whose ear Peter had cut off, asked, 'Did I not see you in the garden with him?' Peter again denied it, and at once a cock crowed.

(John 18:25-27)

In the emotional cultures of the Middle East, to speak or deny once is pardonable. It is put down to being caught up in the moment, to passion or anger or a brief loss of self-control – all perfectly acceptable. Once is forgivable. But three times? Three is decisive. It is considered. It is vehement and categorical. It's not just a blip, it's a lasting act of the will, a choice. So Peter's three-time denial is extremely significant. He has stopped following Jesus. He has chosen to betray. He has chosen to abandon. This is apostasy. This is denial in the strongest possible terms.

Several hours earlier, Jesus had prophesied Peter's denial.

> Simon Peter said to him, 'Lord, where are you going?' Jesus answered him, 'Where I am going you cannot follow me now, but you will follow afterwards.' Peter said to him, 'Lord, why can I not follow you now? I will lay down my life for you.' Jesus answered, 'Will you lay down your life for me? Truly, truly, I say to you, the cock will not crow till you have denied me three times.'
>
> *(John 13:36-38)*

Peter is saying to Jesus, 'You called me to follow you. I left everything to follow you. You are my Shepherd and I am your sheep. And now you're telling me that I cannot follow you where you are going tonight?' Jesus, who is about to go into the hornet's nest, into the enemy's camp, right into death and out the other side, who will according to the Apostles' Creed, 'descend into hell',[208] tells Peter, 'You cannot follow me now, but you will follow afterwards.'

And Peter, full of bombast, declares, 'I will lay down my life for you.' Like many bold followers, like too many young missionary candidates, Peter is willing to die for his Lord.

---

208. See https://www.catholic.org/prayers/prayer.php?p=220 (accessed 12.4.24).

I once carried out a comparative exercise on risk with a group of young English theology students and a group of Middle Eastern pastors. The English students, like Peter, saw themselves as willing to risk all, willing to die for the cause, unafraid. The Middle Eastern pastors generally preferred to keep their heads down, to care for their families and flocks and not to rock the boat unnecessarily. They had less bombast and more wisdom. A fascinating distinction, where risk for one group was purely theoretical, while for the other it was part of the warp and woof of life. Peter, who makes such great claims, a few hours later is eating his words.

Oh, Peter, sheep don't lay down their lives for the shepherd! No, the shepherd lays down his life for the sheep! You don't die for Jesus, he dies for you. And, until he has died for you, you can't follow him into the difficult places. Peter cannot follow Jesus until Jesus has died for him. Without the empowering grace that issues from the death and resurrection of Jesus, Peter cannot follow him where he is going. Following is never by our own willpower, but by the Spirit's power, and the Spirit is not given until Jesus dies.

Rihbany, recalling his childhood in rural Syria, explains that the cock crow served in the night as a way of tracking time:

We always believed that the cock crew three times in the night, and thus marked the night watches. The first crowing is at about nine o'clock, the second at midnight, and the third about three in the morning ... And how often, while enjoying a sociable evening with our friends at one of those humble but joyous homes, we were startled by the crowing of the cock, and said, 'Whew! It is *nissleil* (midnight).' The hospitable host would try to trick us into staying longer by assuring us that it was the evening and not the midnight crow.[209]

---

209. Rihbany, *The Syrian Christ*, p. 279.

In this way, the third cock crow in verse 27 signals the dawn. Peter's long night of betrayal gives way to the dawn of realisation. Certainly, verse 28 confirms that 'then they led Jesus from the house of Caiaphas to the governor's headquarters. It was early morning', the Roman governor traditionally starting work at dawn. So it is time for the Priestly party to hand Jesus over to the Roman governor, Pilate.

Peter later *will* follow Jesus in his manner of death. Like his Lord, he will be executed for his testimony, crucified for his belief. Like many who follow the crucified Lord, he himself will face crucifixion in due course.

And so we consider. Jesus is three times the 'I am'. Peter (and us with him) is three times the 'I am not'. Three times a denier of Christ by actually denying himself as a disciple. And, when it is time for restorative grace in chapter 21, Jesus will reveal himself to his disciples three times, and on the third time, in the presence of a charcoal fire, he will speak words of restoration to Peter three times. Where Peter denies his Lord three times, he is forgiven three times. He is decisively, formally, conclusively readmitted into the fellowship of faith.

But for now, Jesus is led away to be crucified.

Chapter Sixteen

Exchange
(John 19:1-37)

Who eats it won't know the bitterness of the onion,
but he who chops it does.
(Turkish proverb)

For the gospel meaningfully to impact the varied cultures of the world, the significance of the death of Jesus, the crux and centre of the good news, must be reflected upon from a rich range of global perspectives, examined like a diamond from all sides in order truly to appreciate its beauty.

To reduce the gospel to forgiveness of sins, a Billy Graham-type, individual response to the cross, requires the responder to think in terms of internal conscience, in terms of forensic guilt and forgiveness, in terms of courtroom and judge. However, not all societies in the world think in categories of guilt-innocence. For some societies, the pressing moral questions are more about honour-dishonour, or fear-power. In other words, the deepest question being asked may not be 'How can I have my guilt forgiven?' but rather, 'How can we show our faces before God?' Not all societies make decisions, or even view identity as individuals, but rather as communities. The individual is part of an embedded whole, and cannot or should not or could not even conceive of changing religious allegiance as an individual. Some communities care so strongly about justice, and the damage that sin has wrought horizontally between people, that a message of vertical reconciliation with God is inadequate – the more pressing need is societal transformation.

When we draw near to the cross in the company of the Global Church, we see that all these aspects are present, even in the way that John tells the story. We see a gospel big enough to heal all the wounds of the world, a cross powerful enough to answer all of humanity's deepest heart cries. We see a cosmic, global salvation. We see, as the Samaritans saw, that Jesus truly is 'the Saviour of the world' (John 4:42).

John's telling of the cross, as with his whole book, is considered, rich, symbolic, theological and relevant to a wide variety of cultures and people. Compared with Matthew and Luke, which are far starker, darker, bleaker, John is writing with more hope. He is writing both historically/factually as an eyewitness but also, as one writing decades later, having seen the global fruit of the gospel, having read the letters of Paul, he is writing with theological insight unparalleled, often coded symbolically. These dynamics will become clear as we read about Jesus' final hours.

Under empire

In a postcolonial world, conscious of the violence of empire, it is important to understand crucifixion as a tool, in the hands of the unblinkingly brutal Romans, designed to terrorise local populations into submission.

> The Romans deliberately used *crucifixion* as an excruciatingly painful form of execution by torture (basically suffocation), to be used primarily on upstart slaves and rebellious provincials . . . Many of the victims were never buried but

simply left on the crosses as carrion for wild beasts and birds of prey. As with other forms of terrorism, crucifixions were displayed in prominent places for their 'demonstration effect' on the rest of the population ... Seeing their relatives, friends and other fellow villagers suffering such agonising death would presumably intimidate the surviving populace into acquiescence in the reestablished Roman imperial order.[210]

Many suffering under multiple modern forms of oppression have seen Jesus as a powerful example of non-violent resistance. He was executed with the usual Roman punishment for rebellious provincials (crucifixion). Two *lystai* (insurrectionists, freedom fighters) were crucified along with Jesus. All of this expresses that the Romans viewed Jesus as a seditionist, a revolutionary, a fact of great comfort to those whose daily experience is the crushingly hopeless claustrophobia of unjust regimes.[211]

Behold the Man!

Barabbas was an insurrectionist fighting against Roman occupation, and for the liberation of his people. So were the other two men crucified on the right and left of Jesus. Today's scheduled crucifixion, on the high day of Passover, is calculated as a warning to all those zealots and freedom fighters hoping to use the festival as a chance to rebel against Rome. Negatively, you could call him a guerrilla or terrorist; positively, a freedom fighter. It always depends which side you are on. His real name wasn't Barabbas. Bar-abbas means son (*bar*) of a father (*abbas*). No doubt, when he was arrested, he refused to give his real name to the Roman

---

210. Horsley, *Jesus and Empire*, p. 28.
211. Bermejo-Rubio, 'Jesus and the Anti-Roman Resistance', p. 15.

authorities, in order not to endanger his family. It is a cheeky answer, but also a claim to represent all sons of all fathers. He feels he is representing his people. He is fighting on behalf of all sons and all fathers. And yet, when his life is exchanged for Christ's, all sons of all fathers are freed by *the* Son of *the* Father.

The guilty one is freed and the innocent one condemned, a profound picture of substitution. But also, the rebellious one is freed as the obedient one is condemned. The violent one is freed as the non-violent one is condemned. The one who took history into his own hands is freed while the One who trusted God's perfect plan, even under empire, is condemned. Liberation is not earned by Barabbas' military strategy, but is gifted by the punishment of Christ. Barabbas is 'released' (see 18:39), Jesus is 'taken' (see 19:1).

The betrayal, trial, crucifixion and death of Jesus all happen on Friday, the sixth day of the week, days being counted from sunset to sunset. The sixth day of the week is *our* day, humankind's day. It is the day we were created. Six is our number, the number of not-quite-seven, of striving and falling short, of never quite achieving rest, never quite attaining holiness, inability to grasp eternal life. Six is humankind's number, and it can never become seven.

The crucifixion of Jesus on the sixth hour (12 p.m.) of the sixth day of the week (Friday) has immense symbolic value. He is representing humankind. The Son of Man dies at humanity's hour on humanity's day. He is absorbing all of our futility and mortality, our woeful inadequacy, and standing trial as the representative of us all. When Pilate announces, 'Behold the man!' (19:5), John is portraying Christ as humankind, as representative of all humanity.

Here's the man! Here is the true image of the true God. Here is the one who has brought God's wisdom into the world.

Here is the living embodiment of God, the one who has made the invisible God visible. Here is the king.[212]

Christ is sarcastically given a crown of thorns and a purple robe. Kings were crowned with that over which they ruled. The king of a nation which produced bronze was crowned with bronze. Caesar had a crown of leaves, as he ruled over productivity and fruitfulness. Jesus was crowned with thorns, representing the curse, Adam's punishment (Genesis 3:17-18). The purple robe, a colour reserved for royalty, was ironic, because Jesus is punished for claiming to be king, yet actually he *is* King.

Jesus is tried as the representative of all humankind. This trial is the long-awaited trial of all humankind. It is Adam's trial and the trial of all in Adam. It is our trial. The charge of treason (sedition, rebellion) against God? Guilty! We all have sought our own independence and tried to throw off the authority of God. We are all *lystai* against the rightful king, deserving the execution reserved for *lystai*. The charge of claiming to be king? Guilty! We all have claimed kingship over our own lives, rather than submission to the rule of God. Punishment? Shameful, painful, repellent crucifixion.

This, the long-awaited trial of humankind, takes place on humankind's day, with Jesus as our proxy and representative. We guilty ones (like Barabbas) are freed and the Christ is sentenced for us, found guilty for us, and is condemned to death for us.

The politically shrewd chief priests, who are supposed to claim no king but Yahweh, have totally lost their way, as they claim, 'We have no king but Caesar' (19:15). What was, for the chief priests, political expediency, a survivor-pragmatism, a collaboration with empire, is unmasked as blasphemy. As part of the Passover

---

212. Wright, *John for Everyone*, p. 118.

tradition, they would sing, that very day, the *Nismat,* a hymn sung at the conclusion of the greater Hallel. These are the words:

> From everlasting to everlasting, thou art God:
> Besides thee we have no king, redeemer or saviour,
> No liberator, deliverer, provider,
> None who takes pity in every time of distress and trouble
> We have no king but thee.[213]

The exact words in this final line are replaced with 'We have no king but Caesar'. The death of Jesus exposes political collusion for what it is, blatant blasphemous rejection of God as king.

John's narration of the crucifixion scene is rich in detail and symbolism. What follows is not exhaustive commentary, but some ideas to help us see how the death of Christ is indeed good news for all nations, and for all people. This will be considered in terms of various kinds of exchange.

Verdict exchange (vv. 16-22): His submission for our treachery

For what crime was Jesus sentenced? Insurrection-treason-sedition – he 'claimed to be king' (John 19:21, NIV). Criminals would have their crime-identity written on a sign and hung on them, 'rapist', 'murderer', 'runaway slave'. The inscription on Jesus' cross was 'King of the Jews', written in Aramaic, Latin and Greek (19:19-20). This is treason because there is no king but Caesar. The crime for which Jesus is found guilty is actually our crime – we claimed to be king over our own lives. Humankind claimed kingship over creation, and lordship over our own destiny. The three languages suggest the universality of Jesus'

---

213. Neyrey, *John,* p. 305.

reign, 'symbolising that Jesus was exalted on the cross as the King of the people of all languages'.[214]

In verse 30, we read, 'He bowed his head and gave up his spirit'. We, who would never bow our heads, never give up, never submit, see his perfect submission, behold his surrender! 'Hey, sisters and brothers,' he is saying, 'this is what it looks like to trust God completely.'

Irenaeus, in the second century, wrote, 'By his obedience unto death the Word annulled the ancient disobedience committed at the tree.' Man for man, tree for tree, son for son.

When we come to the cross, we lay down our claim to be king, and we receive a spirit of surrender. Jesus takes our rebellion and gives us obedience. He takes our treachery, and gifts us his perfect submission.

Garment exchange (vv. 23-24): His clothed-ness (honour) for our nakedness (shame)

> When the soldiers had crucified Jesus, they took his garments and divided them into four parts, one part for each soldier; also his tunic.
>
> *(John 19:23)*

Four soldiers each take one item of clothing: robe, head cloth, belt, sandals. It was not unusual for soldiers to take the garments of those whom they were crucifying. It was also not unusual for those crucified to be naked. This was part of the shame associated with this public form of execution, intended as a deterrent. Many of those watching would not have minded being killed fighting for their nation – an honourable death with a sword in one's hand and

---

214. Kanagaraj, *John*, p. 186.

a cry of 'freedom' on one's lips. But the dishonour of the painful, slow, unmanning of death by crucifixion, the superstitious dread of the curse of hanging unclaimed and unburied in the public space, and the spectre of public nakedness, so utterly abhorrent and distasteful for a Jewish male were deemed by Rome to be a powerful deterrent for this stubborn, intractable people. It was the *shame* of the cross that was feared (Hebrews 12:2).

> What hurts worse, pain or shame? The process of crucifixion at every step entailed progressive humiliation of the victim and total loss of honour. Beatings were generally publicly administered to shame the offender and to warn others who would see it inflicted. Such gruesome spectacles were also for the entertainment of the crowds. So all eyes watched as the sentenced person was stripped naked. One third of the blows were given to the front of the body and the rest to the back, suggesting that the person being flogged was beaten on the tenderest parts of the body. In an honour-shame world, the insults, humiliations and mockery would crush the soul as no whip could. Being stripped before all and fixed naked to a cross bring shock to the soul long before the body fails. Shame kills.[215]

John is clear in narrating that Jesus' undergarment was also taken by the soldiers, and that Jesus was left without a shred of covering.

> But the tunic was seamless, woven in one piece from top to bottom, so they said to one another, 'Let us not tear it, but cast lots for it to see whose it shall be.' This was to fulfil the

---

215. Neyrey, *John*, p. 302.

Scripture which says, 'They divided my garments among them, and for my clothing they cast lots.'

(John 19:23-24)

All four Gospels quote from Psalm 22 at this moment, but only John mentions the dividing of the garments.

The Clothed One became naked that the naked ones might be clothed. Since Eden, nakedness has been associated with shame. God provided for Adam and Eve's covering with animal skins, perhaps involving the first sacrifice. Throughout Scripture, being 'exposed' or 'uncovered' or 'naked' symbolises public humiliation, while covering and garments represent the removal of shame. The Old Testament word for atonement derives from a root meaning covering (*k-p-r*). Jesus, the supremely Noble One, the One of greatest and untarnished reputation, allows himself to be stripped in order that we might be clothed. We are the soldiers, taking his clothing for ourselves. Yes, he lets us take them from him, but in reality he is gifting them to us. 'Dressed in beauty not my own'[216] says the hymn. Thus, the supremely Honourable One was dishonoured, that the shame-filled ones might have their shame covered.

If you are from a culture that does not think or speak much about moral emotions like honour, the chances are that this scene and its explanation does not appeal to you in a deep way. You may understand the ideas, without them moving you to worship or bringing you to tears. If, however, you are from a culture where shame is not an emotion, but a demotion, and where death is more desirable than dishonour (including, by the way, the ancient Near Eastern culture in which John was writing), this facet of the death of Christ carries sublime power to transform lives.

---

216. Robert Murray McCheyne (1813-43), 'When This Passing World is Done', https://www.hymnal.net/en/hymn/h/545b (accessed 21.2.24).

Kingdom exchange (vv. 23-25): First-last: last-first

But standing by the cross of Jesus were his mother and his mother's sister, Mary the wife of Clopas, and Mary Magdalene.
(John 19:25)

Verses 24 and 25 constitute something of a formal juxtaposition. There are four soldiers, and four women. As John has previously juxtaposed Nicodemus (male, Jewish, centre, named) with the Samaritan woman (female, Samaritan, marginal, unnamed), or the blind man with the Pharisees (9:39), so now there are four soldiers and four women standing by the cross.

The soldiers take something from him, the women have something (someone) taken from them. The soldiers are men, the women are women. The soldiers represent power, weapons, force, while the women are vulnerable. The soldiers are the oppressor, they serve the Empire; the women are the unfortunate, the colonised, those born on the wrong side of the world. Yet the soldiers are serving the wrong king, while the women are serving the wronged King (who is the right King). The soldiers are unnamed, but the women are named, seen, specific, identified, celebrated, valued. Even in his agony, Jesus notices and speaks to one of the women – his mother.

At the cross, the important are rendered unimportant, and the insignificant ones are rendered significant. Jesus, through his death, is turning the world upside down. He is resisting the proud and embracing the humble. He is making a new world where justice will reign. The cross is a judgement on the world, a changing of the status quo, an intervention into our unequal societies where Romans oppress Jews, soldiers rule civilians, and men lord it over women. Jesus, a week earlier, on his final entry into Jerusalem, had predicted this:

'Now is the judgement of this world; now will the ruler of this world be cast out. And I, when I am lifted up from the earth, will draw all people to myself.' He said this to show by what kind of death he was going to die.

(John 12:31-33)

There are no individual exorcisms in the Gospel of John, just the one great casting out of the 'ruler of this world' in the death of Christ. The ruler of this world:

Represents powers beyond the human individual, dynamics of evil, falsehood and death that are, so to speak, systemic and can take hold of and shape human lives, communities, values, and powerful global forces (religious and secular, economic, political, military, judicial, racial, sexual, scientific, ideological) in devastating, hate-filled, malicious, horrifying and destructive ways.[217]

Jesus' lifting up on the cross is his enthronement, the beginning of his kingdom, the transformation of society. For us who, like the women at the cross, live in a world dominated by injustice, inequality, segregation and systemic evil, this understanding of the death of Christ as the overthrow of Satan and the inauguration of the kingdom of God is good news. This perspective, known as Christus Victor,[218] which sees the crucifixion as the decisive victory over evil, the judgement of the world with its sin-soaked systems, and the beginning of Christ's powerful and just reign, to be consummated on his return, is especially celebrated in communities where injustice and evil are an everyday experience.

---

217. Ford, *John*, p. 245.
218. Aulen, *Christus Victor.*

Melba Maggay (Philippines) articulates why and how the Christus Victor understanding of the death of Christ is so essential in her nation:

> To us, what counts most is access to the center of power that rules our lives and the universe. Religious activity is focused on ways of opening oneself to the strength and curative potency of beneficial powers, whether they be in nature or in the spirit world. Prayers, devotions, sacrifices, and ascetic practices such as denial of physical pleasure, fasting or self-mortification, are mostly meant to increase potency . . . The Protestant emphasis on Christus Victor, Christ as a victorious power . . . like the image in Colossians of a Roman conqueror in triumphal march, exhibiting to all and sundry his military booty of defeated and distraught powers (Colossians 2:15), needs to be stressed as a counterpoint to the feeling of helplessness and powerlessness fostered by images of God as either dead or dying. The Gospel may need to be re-centered on Jesus as 'Lord of the spirits,' and on His redemptive work as the regaining of creation, the buying back of a wretched earth once under the clutches of evil powers.[219]

In his death, Jesus disarms the mighty and champions the vulnerable. The first become last, and the last become first.[220] There is a powerful inversion of the status quo, an overhaul of the kingdom of darkness and an inauguration of the kingdom of light, where justice reigns.

---

219. Maggay, 'A Religion of Guilt Encounters a Religion of Power', Kindle location 573.
220. See Matthew 19:30.

Family exchange (vv. 25-27): His new family for our old families

Ever since Eden, the human family has been broken. It is notable how sin, once it has entered the world, works its way through the human family, destroying the relationship between Cain and Abel, then between siblings, cousins, tribes and ultimately nations. The Big Human Family is broken. Our smaller nuclear families, messy. So many of the horizontal, family sins that ruin relationships have been absorbed by Jesus on his way to the cross: betrayal, slander, envy, abandonment, violence. He feels grief at the death of Lazarus. He sees his mother being abandoned and his heart is broken – he feels that pain that we have all felt at some point for a family member, longing, regret, wistfulness, anguish. He is betrayed by a friend. He is abandoned by his other friends in his hour of need. He is sold and killed by brother humans. He experiences violence at their hands. In all of these ways, he heals the dysfunction of the family of Adam, at the same time inaugurating and inviting us into his beautiful, loving, not-perfect-but-precious family, the Church.

> When Jesus saw his mother and the disciple whom he loved standing nearby, he said to his mother, 'Woman, behold, your son!' Then he said to the disciple, 'Behold, your mother!' And from that hour the disciple took her to his own home.
>
> *(John 19:26-27)*

Mary had other sons after Jesus. But at this point they do not believe. In 2:12 Jesus' brothers are described separately from the disciples. In 7:5 we are told that his brothers do not believe in him. Later, after he has risen from the dead, Jesus will appear to his brother James,[221] and James will believe, and become a

---

221. See 1 Corinthians 15:7.

significant leader in the Church. But for now, Jesus entrusts his mother to John (the disciple whom he loved). Mary at this point has no husband, and her eldest son is dying, so who will take responsibility for her? In a society where women had very little by way of rights, every woman needed a man who would take responsibility for her to represent her in the public arena. Jesus, in entrusting her to his disciple John, who is not a blood relative, is making a huge statement. The family of faith, Jesus is suggesting, trumps natural family. Here, at the foot of the cross and in the death of Christ, the Church is born. When Jesus rises from the dead, he calls his disciples his 'brothers' (20:17-18).

This is of enormous significance in family orientated cultures, where individual identity is subsumed within and predicated upon family identity, where belonging is belonging within family.

Turkish society is entirely family based. When a Turkish individual encounters Christ, they very often lose their natural family. Disowned by parents, renounced by brothers, thrown out of the family home, disinherited, these are not unusual reactions. A Muslim Turk choosing Jesus brings shame on their family, and very often loses everything accruing to them from the family name. This is not dissimilar to the Nicodemus story. The Turkish Church, aware of this reality, very often offers hospitality, care and a network of support to those who have left everything to follow Jesus. They understand that the family of faith replaces blood family. They understand that the offer of church family is part of the offer of the gospel. They understand that just as a new-born baby needs parents, so new-born Christians need community.

In 1994, a landmark Catholic gathering, the African Synod, met together to pose the question, 'Church of Africa, what must you now become so that your message may be relevant and credible?' The synod's decision was 'a fundamental option of the Church as family'. In other words, the African understanding of family is the best way of building and representing church communities.

> This model of church is deeply rooted in the way many Africans understand themselves. To take one obvious example, an African can hardly define himself or herself without reference to his or her immediate and/or extended family. My favourite illustration of this typically African value comes from obituary announcements in newspapers. Each announcement begins by stating the name of the deceased and then goes on to describe this person by listing the names of all relatives and family members: He was the husband of ..., the father of ..., the grandfather of ..., the son of ..., the cousin of ..., the uncle of ..., the son-in-law of ..., step-brother of ..., the nephew of ...[222]

This is also an essential truth in countering racism. The apostle Paul makes this connection between the death of Christ and the Church as family in Ephesians:

> For He Himself is our peace, who has made both one, and has broken down the middle wall of separation, having abolished in His flesh the enmity, that is, the law of commandments contained in ordinances, so as to create in Himself one new man from the two, thus making peace, and that He might reconcile them both to God in one body through the cross, thereby putting to death the enmity.
>
> *(Ephesians 2:14-16, NKJV)*

Yusufu Turaki, a Nigerian scholar, writes of the family dynamic on display in Ephesians 2, 'In him all human differences, hostility

---

222. Orobator, *Theology*, pp. 86-87.

and barriers are resolved. Jesus Christ has a cure for the evils of racism, tribalism and divided humanity.'[223] Ruth Padilla DeBorst (Ecuador-Costa Rica) speaks of the purpose of the cross as 'to tear down all humanly-constructed walls and spiritually-bolstered exclusions so that unity becomes visible, to remind them that we were all once dead, and now we are alive in Christ'.[224]

And John Stott (England) brings all these ideas together in an important paragraph:

> He died and rose again not only to save sinners like me (though he did), but also to create a single new humanity; not only to redeem us from sin but also to adopt us into God's family; not only to reconcile us to God but also to reconcile us to one another. The church is an integral part of the gospel. The gospel is good news of a new society as well as of a new life.[225]

Blood is family language (1:13), and a shared experience of the blood of Christ bonds us as brothers and sisters, whatever our background. In the words of Ponca Chief Standing Bear, 'The blood that will flow from mine will be of the same colour as yours ... The same god made us both.'[226] Blood, unlike skin, is the same colour for everyone. The Church is forged at the foot of the cross, in the death of Christ. Christ's parting bequest to his mother and to his beloved disciple was one of mutual responsibility and care, one for another. The exchange is between the sin-infested family of physical descent from Adam, and the new family inaugurated by the sinless new symbolic head of the human race, Jesus Christ. This is what Jesus is getting at in his lengthy discussion with the

---

223. Turaki, 'Ephesians', p. 1456.
224. Padilla DeBorst, 'A New And Glorious Life'.
225. Stott, *Ephesians*, p. 129.
226. Haddis, *A Just Mission*, p. 46.

crowd in John 8:39ff. Though they claim genetic descent from Abraham, Jesus argues that their real father is the devil, because their actions are sinful, not faithful. Paul says it more succinctly, 'Not all who are descended from Israel belong to Israel, and not all are children of Abraham ... it is not the children of the flesh who are the children of God, but the children of the promise ...' (Romans 9:7-8).

In November 1983, Welbeck Street Baptist Church in Ashton-under-Lyne, UK, hosted a fast in support of Vinod Chauhan, a Hindu migrant of Indian origin who was under threat of deportation. During the weekend, retired white working-class church member, Hilda Carr, felt prompted by the Spirit to her own personal act of solidarity. She recounted it to a BBC Radio Manchester reporter in her own words:

> I remembered a part of the Bible that said we are of the same blood. Something . . . a little voice behind me said, 'Prove it.' I just got up ... I didn't get up myself, I'm sure I didn't. I was guided or I was led, and I went straight and got a needle out of the needle case, switched the kettle on, sterilised the needle, wrapped it up, and put me coat on and went straight across to the church. I live quite near ... I asked Paul [the minister] if he thought it would be right that I should ask Vinod that if I drew my blood, just pricked the thumb that was all, if he would agree to draw his blood and we would put it on the blotter; and then asked Paul if he could tell the difference, and he couldn't.[227]

This powerful personal act by an ordinary church member, placing two drops of blood side by side, signifies what Chief Standing Bear had declared, that the blood of all humans is the

---

227. Weller, 'Coming Full Circle', p. 177.

same colour. The blood of Christ symbolises and constitutes his new family, the Church.

Thirst exchange (vv. 28-30): I thirst: You shall never thirst again

> After this, Jesus, knowing that all was now finished, said (to fulfil the Scripture), 'I thirst.' A jar full of sour wine stood there, so they put a sponge full of the sour wine on a hyssop branch and held it to his mouth. When Jesus had received the sour wine, he said, 'It is finished', and he bowed his head and gave up his spirit.
>
> *(John 19:28-30)*

Humankind is thirsty. Thirsty for love, for hope, for meaning. We are dying of thirst in this desert world. Jesus is the eternally quenched one. His is an eternal satisfaction. In his incarnation, although he was susceptible to bodily thirst (4:6-7), he was also in a position to quench the spiritual thirst of others. He offers 'living water' to the Samaritan woman (4:10). He invites all who are thirsty to come to him and drink (7:37). He announces that his blood is 'true drink', that gives eternal life (6:54-56). All the way through John, Jesus has been trying to give people drinks. At Cana in Galilee, he gave the best wine, and in generous abundance.

'I thirst' is our ancient cry, and he cries it for us! He takes our thirst, and gives us his will-never-thirst-again quenchedness. The cheap, sour wine on a sponge that we offer to him does not compare with the fine, abundant wine that he offers us.

This subterranean watercourse throughout John, which surfaces in chapter 4 by a real well talking about spiritual thirst (Jesus was thirsty at the sixth hour in Samaria, and now again he is thirsty at the sixth hour at Calvary), in chapter 7:38-39 when Jesus announces that "'Out of his heart will flow rivers of living water." Now this he said about the Spirit' now resurfaces in the body of Jesus, as water and blood will pour from his side. Literal and figurative waters intermingle. Stephen Moore (Ireland) writes beautifully about this journey:

> At the Samaritan well literal earthly water was declared superseded by figurative living water (4:13-14), which was later interpreted as the Holy Spirit (7:39), which has now become available through Jesus' death as symbolised both by his giving up the *pneuma* as he expires (19:30) and by the fresh flow of water from his side (19:34). But this water is neither simply material and literal, since it is symbolic, nor fully spiritual and figurative, since it is physical . . . Literality and figurality intermingle in the flow from Jesus' side, each contaminating the other, which is to say that we cannot keep the literal clearly separate from the figurative in the end.[228]

Indeed, we reflect, Jesus is Word made flesh, he is both divine and human, both spirit and flesh, both God and man, from heaven and from earth. He makes the invisible visible, the distant near, the incomprehensible accessible. In Jesus, the distance between heaven and earth is dissolved. It is no surprise, then, that in Jesus physical and spiritual realities intermingle, as they have throughout John. It is no surprise that beyond every literal layer of meaning lies a figurative layer. The body of Christ is a paradox, a vessel for both literal and spiritual water, a portal between heaven and earth.

Enoch Wan (China) proposes that Jesus Christ is the *tien-ren-he-yi-di-tao* (heaven-man-unite-one-tao). Because Chinese

---

228. Moore, 'Impurities in the Living Water', p. 290.

thought is 'holistic' and 'integrative', this expression for Christ can hold together the both-and of divinity and humanity, of heavenly and earthly in the one person of Jesus.[229]

The Satisfied One became thirsty that the thirsty ones might be satisfied.

Passover exchange (vv. 31-37): His Sonship for our slavery

Jesus dies at exactly the time that the Passover lambs are being sacrificed in the temple, lambs born in Bethlehem to be slaughtered in Jerusalem at Passover. And here we see 'the Lamb of God, who takes away the sins of the world' (1:29), born in Bethlehem to be sacrificed in the temple in Jerusalem at Passover.

Jesus has deliberately delayed being captured until the Passover. His followers assumed that this was because he could have maximum impact in a coup attempt at Passover, when millions were gathered and sentiments were running high.

Passover is about liberation of slaves. The people had been in slavery for generations in Egypt. One perfect, unblemished lamb was slain for each father's house, 'a lamb for each household' (Exodus 12:3), and none of its bones could be broken. Its blood was placed on the doorposts, using hyssop branches (Exodus 12:21-22). The Lord brought his double-edged sword of judgement to Egypt; the firstborn sons of the oppressors were killed, the firstborn sons of those protected by the blood of the lambs were delivered. And in the morning the people came out of Egypt. They had once been slaves, but now they were free.

In John's Gospel, 'everyone who commits sin is a slave to sin ... So if the Son sets you free, you will be free indeed' (8:34-36). The contrast of slavery and freedom is Passover language. Passover

---

229. Wan, 'Jesus Christ for the Chinese', p. 5.

was a time when God led the people out, and Jesus has affirmed that 'The sheep hear his voice, and he calls his own sheep by name and leads them out' (10:3). One lamb was sacrificed for each household, and Jesus has taught that his death as the firstborn of the Father is for the whole household of those who will believe (3:16). Here, a hyssop branch is mentioned (19:29), he died before a soldier was needed to break his legs to speed up death, meaning that 'Not one of his bones [were] broken' (19:36), and in the morning (20:1), his people will be free.

'Blood' is the language of sacrifice. A soldier pierces his side with a spear, and blood rushes out all over the one who pierces him. So with us – it is we who are responsible for his death, yet his blood washes over us. 'They will look on him whom they have pierced' (John 19:37), John's quotation from Zechariah, also refers to 'a fountain will be opened' (Zechariah 13:1, NIV). The blood and water that gush out of his side is often spoken of scientifically, as eyewitness proof of his death (the plasma separates after death), but in the early Christian centuries it was taken as miraculous and symbolic – blood and water rushing out like a fountain and falling on the very ones who pierced him, cleansing the earth!

Early tradition names the soldier who pierced him as Longinus, who was subsequently converted, went to Anatolia as a missionary, and was martyred there. Matthew Henry (England) writes:

The blood and water that flowed out of him were significant. They signified the two great benefits which all believers partake of through Christ – blood for atonement, water for purification. Guilt contracted must be expiated by blood; stains contracted must be done away by the water of purification. These two must always go together . . . they signified the two great ordinances of baptism and the Lord's supper.[230]

---

230. Henry, *Commentary,* p. 1622.

Tradition also sees Jesus' body here as the temple. The temple was always associated with the flow of blood – sacrifice – particularly on Passover. It was also associated with the flow of water, as we saw in John 7 and as was prophesied in Ezekiel 47, when a mighty river of life would flow from the temple. Jesus' body has already been introduced to us as a new temple ('he was speaking about the temple of his body', 2:21) on Passover, in the temple, two years previously. Mary Coloe (Australia) summarises, 'The personalising of the temple, begun in the transfer of temple imagery to Jesus, then continued with the promise of the divine indwelling in the community of believers constituting them as "my Father's household," is completed in this scene.'[231] Blood and water flow from his body, the Temple, to the world.

And so the Son forsook his freedom and died the death of a slave, so that we slaves might gain freedom and be made sons. Passover is our freedom. We who have long been slaves walk out under the blood and are freed! Jesus' death does not liberate Israel from slavery to Rome, but frees the human family from a greater tyranny, the oppressive lordship of sin.

In all this, Son of God became Son of Man, that we sons of men might become sons of God. The Living One dies, that we dead ones might live.

---

231. Coloe, 'The Nazarene King', p. 847.

Chapter Seventeen

Commission
(John Chapters 20 and 21)

If you think you are too small to make a difference,
try sleeping with a mosquito.
(Dalai Lama)

Jesus was executed on a Friday. Friday is the sixth day of the week, the day on which we were created – our day! And so the Son of Man dies representing all sons of men. And it is not just any Friday. It is also Passover. At the very time that the Passover lambs were being sacrificed in the temple, so the Lamb of God (who is also the Temple) dies for the sins of the world.

We have just had a week of de-creation, of darkness and defeat and death. The old world has been judged and found guilty, humankind has been judged and found guilty. Easter Friday is the end of the old world, the unravelling of everything. His friends bury him before sunset, as the Sabbath begins at sunset. They bury him quickly, and nearby:

Now in the place where he was crucified there was a garden, and in the garden a new tomb in which no one had yet been laid.

(John 19:41)

On Saturday, the seventh day, everybody rests. Everybody waits. As on the original first week, God rested on the Sabbath, 'because on it God rested from all his work that he had done in creation' (Genesis 2:3), so now God in Christ has completed the work of new creation, and he rests. Before resting, the work of creation was 'finished' on day six (Genesis 2:1). And in the words of Jesus, the work of new creation is 'finished' on the cross, on the sixth day of the week, with a cry of 'It is finished' (19:30).

> Wait, John says to us. Watch with me through this sabbath, this quiet, sad rest. Wait for this, the final day, the seventh day, to pass. God rested on the seventh day. So must Jesus. But this whole book has been about new creation. Wait for the eighth day.[232]

Sabbath was such an important Old Covenant law. It was one of the Ten Commandments. It carried the death penalty. Throughout John, Jesus has been repeatedly accused of Sabbath-breaking. And yet, for Christians under the New Covenant, Saturday is no longer a holy day of rest. There is, however, a different kind of Sabbath-rest for us to enter, as the writer to the Hebrews exhorts:

> So then, there remains a Sabbath rest for the people of God, for whoever has entered God's rest has also rested from his works as God did from his. Let us therefore strive to enter that rest.
>
> *(Hebrews 4:9-11)*

Our Sabbath-keeping or Sabbath-breaking has to do with entering into the finished work of Jesus. Between Christ's death in chapter 19 and resurrection in chapter 20 there is a pause,

232. Wright, *John for Everyone*, Kindle location 2457.

a space in which Jesus rests. He has, after all, declared, 'It is finished' (19:30). He will not speak again until 20:15. And the only way for humankind to exit our endless cycle of weeks, our consistent incapacity to advance from day six to day seven, is to rest in the death of Jesus Christ. There is no striving, no work, no attainment able to carry us through to the Sunday of new creation. Only the rest of faith in the finished work of Christ can save. It's important, in this book about mission, to remember the Sabbath-keeping of faith. Mission people are hard-working people, not always good at resting. Rest, friends, in his finished work. Victory, salvation, new creation, the ingathering of every nation, the dismantling of the old and the inaugurating of the new all belong to him.

And Sunday becomes the Christian day of worship. Consider Justice as getting what is deserved, Mercy as *not* getting what is deserved, and Grace as getting what is *not* deserved. Among the Abrahamic religions, Islam holds as sacred Friday, Judaism holds Saturday and Christianity, Sunday. Friday is the day of Justice, payment of the price, which is Islam's most prized divine attribute. Saturday is the day of Mercy, of forgiveness and rest, and is Judaism's favoured insight into God. The resurrection takes us beyond Mercy to Grace, beyond the removal of sin to the bestowal of righteousness, beyond the forgiveness of debt to the crediting of surplus, beyond Saturday to Sunday, beyond an end-of-the-week of darkness and into the beginning of the new week of light.

Christianity's most treasured divine attribute is grace, and our holy day is Sunday. So comes Sunday.

Now on the first day of the week Mary Magdalene came to the tomb early, while it was still dark, and saw that the stone had been taken away from the tomb.

(John 20:1)

In the chill pre-dawn, in the silence, at the time when demons and wild beasts are still a-prowl, Mary Magdalene approaches the tomb, which is in a garden. It's early morning on the first day of the week, in a garden. The birth of God's new week, of God's new world. Adam went from the garden to the grave. Now Jesus steps from the grave into the garden.

Mary notices that the stone is no longer in place, and she runs to tell Peter and John, who then engage in their famous early morning foot race, running towards the tomb, as are all human beings since Adam. 'The other disciple,' presumably our author, '... went in, and he saw and believed; for as yet they did not understand from the Scripture, that he must rise from the dead' (20:8-9).

Now this is an important verse in mission. It is possible to see and believe without yet (and note the yet!) understanding from the Scripture. Our thinking is often dominated by Paul's assertion that 'faith comes by hearing, and hearing by the word of God' (Romans 10:17, NKJV), a cognitive, educational approach to evangelism, whereby we somehow think that people need information in order to have faith, whereas sometimes, as here, it is the other way around. For example, a large proportion of people from Muslim backgrounds who today are encountering Christ, do so in a vision, or dream, or miraculous experience of some sort, and then as a result seek out understanding from the Scripture. The 'yet' is important, however, because Scripture must still be part of the journey, but sometimes 'seeing' and 'believing' can pre-date 'understanding from the Scripture'.

Also, for many disciples on the frontlines of mission, there will be experiences and encounters for which they might not (yet) have a theology, but that they still embrace with faith, and subsequently diligently search the Scriptures to seek fresh understanding. Famously in this regard, John Wimber is reported to have said 'experience changes theology'. At times missionaries without much theology or experience of spiritual warfare find themselves in situations where the demonic is very real. They then search the Scriptures for answers, and find that there are plenty – they had just never asked the question before. Peter and John had no theology for the resurrection until they experienced it, and then went back to the Scripture to discover that it was there all along. Peter, later, had no theology for Roman soldiers being filled with the Spirit, until he saw it happen first in Acts 10, and later reflected theologically in Acts 15.

Mary's commissioning

The men having returned home, Mary remained by the tomb, weeping. As Christ wept at the tomb of his friend Lazarus, so Mary weeps at the tomb of her friend Jesus.

> Having said this, she turned around and saw Jesus standing, but she did not know that it was Jesus. Jesus said to her, 'Woman, why are you weeping? Whom are you seeking?' Supposing him to be the gardener, she said to him, 'Sir, if you have carried him away, tell me where you have laid him, and I will take him away.' Jesus said to her, 'Mary.' She turned and said to him in Aramaic, 'Rabboni!' (which means Teacher).
>
> *(John 20:14-16)*

For Palestinian scholar and pastor Katanacho, Mary's tears represent the grief felt by his people;

> Perhaps Mary is similar to Palestinians. Palestinians are grieving because they have lost their young men and women. They continually experience political and religious oppression. They frequent graveyards carrying with them

the burden of sorrow and despair. Although they live in a circle of hopelessness and death, the one who released Mary from her circle of death can also empower them with his life. Christ can raise Palestine and end all forms of enslavement. He is the way, the truth and the life.[233]

If we are looking for stories as bridges between Scripture and universal human experience, we need look no further than Mary's grief. Women weeping are to be found on every corner of the planet, in every eon of history. Jesus' tender question, 'Woman, why are you weeping?' is infinitely translatable, infinitely comprehensible, supremely personal.

The first word of Christ after his death and resurrection is 'Woman'. The Church, after all, is the reason for his passion. It's only natural that, on awaking from the sleep of death, his first thought should be for her. As Adam's first recorded words were for his bride (Genesis 2:23), so too Christ's.

Mary is looking for Jesus, but actually Jesus is looking for Mary! She supposes him to be the gardener . . . actually he *is* the gardener! He is the gardener of God's new creation. As Adam was placed within the first creation to 'work it and keep it' (Genesis 2:15), so the Second Adam in the new creation. Margaret Daly-Denton's (New Zealand) commentary on John in the Earth Bible Commentary series, which gives attention specifically to nature and ecology in the Bible, is called 'Supposing Him to Be the Gardener'. She writes:

> As the gardener, he is the son who has learnt to do gardening work from his gardener-Father, who planted the first Garden of Eden (Gen 2:8) . . . In fact, this evocative scene where a

---

233. Katanacho, *John Through Palestinian Eyes*, p. 123.

man and a woman meet in a garden abounds in the Edenic references that have been audible throughout the gospel.[234]

He calls her by name, 'Mary' (v. 16). We know that the Good Shepherd calls his 'sheep by name and leads them out' (10:3), and that Jesus raised Lazarus by calling him by name and commanding him to 'come out' (11:43). Jesus, who himself has come out of the grave, is calling Mary out of her grief and hopelessness. The resurrection of Jesus makes a way for the resurrection of Mary.

And now we see the man and the woman in the garden. The idea that Jesus and Mary in the garden somehow represent a re-take on the man and the woman in the garden in Genesis 2 has ancient pedigree – the Church has always seen lots of Genesis in John. Adam calls his wife 'Woman' and also names her (Genesis 2:15, 23; 3:20). That somehow Jesus is a bridegroom seeking a bride, that Mary represents the Church – us – that there is an intimate, significant encounter taking place, this is an idea that Christians have always seen here. But there's more.

The vocative 'Woman' is used here for the sixth time. All of the women in John who have heard Jesus say 'Woman' to them in this way are currently unmarried, as far as we can tell. Certainly, they are alone.

This matters, because in a patriarchal world (and in many places today) any woman who had no male representative (father, husband, brother, adult son) was vulnerable, caught 'in-between', liable to exploitation and abuse. Be she widowed, divorced, unmarried, barren, the only real solution was marriage. This kind of marriage was (and is) often abused – see Tamar's story, found in Genesis 38, among others. In many parts of the world today, this is still the deal. The only real future is to marry the girl off, but due to the fallenness of man, these marriages can be quid

---

234. Daly-Denton, *Supposing Him to Be the Gardener.*

pro quo, toxic, abusive. Not always, but the pain of patriarchy is well-documented.

In all of the stories discussed in John, Jesus is standing before a vulnerable woman, and offering a solution that is different. Within the great overarching metaphor of the bridegroom searching for his bride, with woman representing our corporate identity, the people of God, the Church, we can locate ourselves in these stories. And in the new order that Jesus is creating, there is plenty of honour for these unmarried women. Now they have family, representation, care, provision and their own important place in the story, without having to marry. They often see things that men don't see; the Samaritan woman believes while Nicodemus does not, Mary Magdalene sees angels where Peter and John only saw grave clothes, and is the first to see the risen Christ himself. And none of them are compelled to marry in order to find their complete resolution. One of Christianity's innovations is the dignity of singleness for women.

This scene could have been the Hollywood ending, Mary and Jesus reunited in the garden as the sun rises, the risen Son having found (symbolically) his bride. Jesus and the Church, gazing into each other's eyes. For some Christians, this is the end of the story, this is the dominant posture of the Church, one of worship, intimacy and devotion. And yet, the story does not end here.

> Jesus said to her, 'Do not cling to me, for I have not yet ascended to the Father; but go to my brothers and say to them, "I am ascending to my Father and your Father, to my God and your God."'
>
> *(John 20:17)*

Gail O'Day suggests that 'cling' here communicates a broader range of meaning than mere physical holding. 'To hold onto something is to control, to own, to define, to manipulate, to manage, to co-opt for one's own ends.'[235] This, in Mary's commissioning, is a vital perspective on mission: 'Jesus cannot and will not be controlled.'[236]

We are going to see, in the climax of John's Gospel, three commissioning moments. This is the first, and Jesus tells Mary, 'Don't cling to me … go and tell.' Church is more than worship.

Mary Magdalene becomes the first in a very, very long line of single women who witness to the living Lord. Even today, as at most times in history, single women on cross-cultural mission vastly outnumber men. We must not miss that the first witness to the resurrection, the apostle to the apostles, the first sent one, is a woman. The key things defining an apostle are present in Mary's story: eyewitness to the resurrection, a personal commissioning by Christ.

At a time when a woman's witness was not considered valid in a court of law, Jesus chose a woman as witness to his resurrection.

Jesus' commission to Mary Magdalene is soaked in family language: 'Father … brothers'. Until this point in John, whenever Jesus has spoken of the Father it has been 'my Father'. Here, for the first time, he says, 'your Father'. The disciples, starting with Mary, are brought into the family by the power of the resurrection.

And so, we have man and woman, in the garden, early in the morning, as the darkness is passing and the light is dawning, on the first day of the week. Bridegroom and bride. Christ and the Church. God and his people. A new humanity. A new creation. A new beginning. A new family. Individually, Mary Magdalene is given a lasting, honourable legacy – we still know her name and celebrate her faith 2,000 years later! And corporately, the bride

---

235. O'Day, *The Word Disclosed*, p. 103.
236. Ibid.

of Christ is constituted as a family of mutual responsibility, of shame-removal, of apostolic commission, of protection for the vulnerable, a faithful bride.

Our pilgrimage is mission

Commissioning to mission is a uniquely Christian end to the story of the founder. In the major religions, the founder's legacy is captured in pilgrimage. In Islam, pilgrimage is one of the five pillars. Buddhists visit Bodhgaya, the place of Buddha's enlightenment. Jews focus on Jerusalem, their holy city. Hindus visit sacred mountains, rivers and festivals. In this way, the idea of ongoing quest, journey, aspiration is preserved from generation to generation. We understand that there is something beyond ourselves and beyond the local, something for which to strive. The idea of journey, of pursuit is enshrined and sacralised.

But Christianity does not celebrate pilgrimage. We do not have sacred sites to visit. Our Lord does not command reverence for the places his feet trod. Instead, the Risen One tells his disciples to go to the ends of the earth, to seek out new sites of significance, not revisit the old. We are commissioned outwards, not inwards; forwards, not backwards; towards the secular, not towards the sacred. Instead of returning to places made holy by miraculous phenomena, we are called to go to new places and make them holy through new miracles. The dynamics of pilgrimage are there for us – journey, cost, vulnerability, quest, a goal beyond our immediate, day-to-day lives, but our focus is towards the future, not the past. Our pilgrimage is mission. We seek renewed experience of God in the margins, not the centre, at the feet of the world, not its head, in the midst of the secular, not the hallowed. If John has shown us anything, he has shown us this. Jesus, the Sent One, come to make the Invisible visible, the Distant near, the Sacred accessible, is always on the move. He fulfils the Jewish pilgrim festivals (Tabernacles, Passover) in his own person. He is the Shepherd leading his sheep, calling us to follow him. He is the Way. Everything is movement. There is nothing static in God. And this missional energy is bequeathed to Mary, and to us; 'Do not cling to me ... but go ...'

The evening commissioning

> On the evening of that day, the first day of the week, the doors being locked where the disciples were for fear of the Jews, Jesus came and stood among them and said to them, 'Peace be with you.' When he had said this, he showed them his hands and his side. Then the disciples were glad when they saw the Lord. Jesus said to them again, 'Peace be with you. As the Father has sent me, even so I am sending you.' And when he had said this, he breathed on them and said to them, 'Receive the Holy Spirit.'
>
> *(John 20:19-22)*

In so many ways, John is reminding us here of Genesis 3:8. It's evening, the cool of the day, the time when God used to walk in the garden with the man and the woman. Now God has come to stand 'among them' in the upper room.

> When God came looking for Adam in the garden (Genesis 3:8), he and his wife heard the sound of him at the time of the evening breeze. Now, on the evening of the new creation's first day, a different wind sweeps through the room. The words for 'wind,' 'breath' and 'spirit' are the same (this is true in both Hebrew and Greek). This wind is the

healing breath of God's spirit, come to undo the long effects of primal rebellion.[237]

As Adam and Eve hid from the presence of the Lord from fear and shame, so now are the disciples hiding. Perhaps not just from the authorities. If I were Peter, knowing that I had failed my Lord and hearing that he was back from the dead, I too would be hiding – for fear of him!

And now, Jesus declares, 'As the Father has sent me, even so I am sending you.' This scene joins this story to the great overarching narrative of Scripture, to the original purposing of humankind. The commissioning of the disciples is not a surprise. Rather, it is the reissuing of the mission that was originally entrusted to humankind, in which Adam and Eve (and all that follow them) failed, and Christ himself has relaunched. 'The disciples are not just to represent Jesus … they are to re-present him, i.e. Jesus will be present in and through them in his Spirit as they fulfil their mission in the world.'[238]

And he breathes on them and says 'receive [my] Spirit'; just as he breathed originally on Adam and Eve.

The insufflation is plausibly to be understood as a renewal of the commission given to Adam. The allusion to Gen 2:7 suggests that Jesus is empowering his followers not with physical life, as with Adam, but with spiritual empowerment to do what Adam and others had failed to do …

Just as God's breathing into Adam made him alive and a part of the first creation, so Jesus' breathing into the disciples the Spirit might well be considered an act incorporating them into a stage of new creation, which Jesus had inaugurated already by his resurrection.[239]

237. Wright, *John for Everyone*, Kindle location 2648.
238. Kostenberger, 'Challenge', p. 191.
239. Beale, *A New Testament Biblical Theology*, p. 571-572.

Christine Amal Mallouhi (Lebanon) writes:

> The disciples were in a complex situation; they were a minority group cowering behind locked doors and due to their connection with Christ, who had just been executed as a common criminal, they were also implicated. They were hiding from the very people whom Jesus intended to send them to. The last thing that could have described them was 'peaceful', and the last place they wanted to go was outside, and the very last thing they wanted to do was to talk to anyone about Jesus and his teachings.[240]

For Mallouhi, the disciples are very much like the Christian minority in the Middle East today, who are 'hiding from the very people whom Jesus intended to send them to'. Jesus' double greeting of 'Peace be with you' is therefore vital for these frightened disciples. The death of Christ has achieved peace with God, and the calling of mission is to offer this peace to those who are currently waiting outside our locked rooms. This ministry of reconciliation is both vertical and horizontal, peace with God and peace with one another. In contexts, like Lebanon, where sectarian separation runs so deep, this commission can feel as overwhelming and terrifying today as it did to the disciples, locked in the upper room. Hence Jesus' gift of peace, and the breathing of the Holy Spirit, are indispensable if this commission is to be fulfilled.

He showed them his hands and side

Jesus' showing of his hands brought courage to the disciples. If the Lord has been wounded and yet is undeterred in his mission,

---

240. Mallouhi, 'Peacemaking as a Witness', Kindle location 7870.

we can draw strength from his example. He is not ashamed of his wounds, they are the proud battle scars of a victorious general. 'By his wounds we are healed'[241] is not just a mystical truth, but also a psychological one; his wounds bring confidence and courage to his fearful friends – they are healed of paralysing fear.

He also showed them his side. The way that Eve was created was that Adam was put into a 'deep sleep', and then Eve was taken from his side (Genesis 2:21). In the same way, Second Adam has been put into the deep sleep of death, and the bride, the 'woman' is taken from his side. The piercing of Christ brought forth the bride of Christ, and Jesus has the side-scar to prove it.

Fear is a very real enemy of mission. The wounds of Jesus are very real comfort. The breath of Jesus is very real empowering. The peace of Jesus is a very real gift.

John Stott (England) taught that this form of the Great Commission was the most crucial, yet the most neglected, because the most costly:

> The crucial form in which the Great Commission has been handed down to us (though it is the most neglected because it is the most costly) is the Johannine. Jesus had anticipated it in his prayer in the upper room which he said to the Father: 'As thou didst send me into the world, so I have sent them into the world' (John 17:18). Now, probably in the same upper room but after his death and resurrection, he turned his prayer-statement into a commission and said: 'As the Father has sent me, even so I send you' (John 20:21). In both of these sentences Jesus did more than draw a vague parallel between his mission and ours. Deliberately and precisely he made his mission the model of ours.[242]

---

241. See 1 Peter 2:24.
242. Stott, *Christian Mission*, p. 23.

It's so powerful. Throughout John we've seen how the Word is made flesh, we've seen Jesus' example, his courage, his humility, his wisdom, his pain. And now, at the end of the story, he says, 'As the Father has sent me, even so I am sending you.' Everything we have seen and reflected upon now becomes *our* responsibility, *our* calling. If he went to the margins, so do we. If he entered into dialogue, so do we. If he announced good news for the whole world, so do we. If he stood up to unjust systems of corrupt power, so do we. If he washed feet, so do we. If he strove for unity, so do we. If he suffered silently, so do we. If he identified with the outsider, so do we. And if he did it all in the power of the Spirit, so do we go in the power of that same Spirit. Grace Ji-Sun Kim (South Korea) agrees:

> As God sent the Son and Spirit to descend into humanity's darkness and despair, bringing the light of love and hope, we are called to descend into the places of greatest suffering in our communities. It is God's Spirit that guides us in our life-giving mission of mercy and justice, giving us the strength to love, the right words to say, and the power to heal.[243]

The third revealing

Jesus has risen, and revealed himself to his disciples twice. But now he will reveal himself to his disciples 'the third time' (21:14), the emphatic time, the decisive time.

> Just as day was breaking, Jesus stood on the shore; yet the disciples did not know that it was Jesus.
>
> *(John 21:4)*

---

243. Kim, *Embracing the Other*, p. 169.

> When they got out on land, they saw a charcoal fire in place, with fish laid out on it, and bread.
>
> *(John 21:9)*

For Peter, this scene is rich in significance. This is the exact lakeside where Jesus had first called him, 'Follow me' (Matthew 4:19). Now he stands again on the same shore, but the charcoal fire reminds him of the dark night of his betrayal, the only other time in John we hear about a charcoal fire, a direct textual allusion connecting these two stories. It is a symbol of his shame. *I stood by a charcoal fire and said 'I am not' three times.*

> Jesus said to them, 'Come and have breakfast.' Now none of the disciples dared ask him, 'Who are you?' They knew it was the Lord. Jesus came and took the bread and gave it to them, and so with the fish. This was now the third time that Jesus was revealed to the disciples after he was raised from the dead.
>
> *(John 21:12-14)*

We are again by the Sea of Tiberias (21:1), that provocative imperial name, and Jesus is again feeding people with abundant bread and fish, of miraculous origin and subversive implications. The taste and experience would certainly trigger their memory, back to 6:11, with its shepherding language and implications. Indeed, reading chapter 6 alongside chapter 21 makes sense for multiple textual reasons.

It is significant that Jesus is revealed over the breaking of bread. In Eden there was a meal that resulted in Adam and Eve's eyes being opened to their shame. Here on the beach, there is a meal in which the disciples' eyes are opened to recognise Jesus, and the removal of shame. You only break bread with friends. Jesus is telling them again – 'I know you let me down, but you really are my friends.' Here once again we see Jesus as host, welcoming the unworthy to his banquet. With mission as hospitality, Christ came to invite the hungry to feast, the unworthy to celebrate, the disillusioned to renewal. As with Jesus' great father David's welcome of Mephibosheth in 2 Samuel 9 (a name meaning 'from the mouth of shame') to share his royal table, covering his lameness and demonstrating to the world that this one-time son of his enemy was now welcomed to the family table, so here on the beach with the disciples, and especially Peter.

> When they had finished breakfast, Jesus said to Simon Peter, 'Simon, son of John, do you love me more than these?' He said to him, 'Yes, Lord; you know that I love you.' He said to him, 'Feed my lambs.' He said to him a second time, 'Simon, son of John, do you love me?' He said to him, 'Yes, Lord; you know that I love you.' He said to him, 'Tend my sheep.' He said to him the third time, 'Simon, son of John, do you love me?' Peter was grieved because he said to him the third time, 'Do you love me?' and he said to him, 'Lord, you know everything; you know that I love you.' Jesus said to him, 'Feed my sheep.'
>
> *(John 21:15-17)*

Three times Jesus recommissions Peter, an emphatic restoration making up for his three denials. A triple denial demands a triple restoration. Peter is not merely restored as a sheep, but called to be a shepherd, in the footsteps of Jesus who has shown himself decisively to be the Shepherd of Israel. This is extraordinary grace. We failed him as sheep, and now he calls us to be shepherds? Having so often trained ourselves to think in terms of 'You have been faithful with a few, so I entrust you with many',[244]

---

244. See Matthew 25:23.

these verses can be overwhelming for the struggling missionary. In this story, the narrative is, 'You have been unfaithful with a few, and yet I give you more. You have failed me as a sheep, and yet I am calling you to shepherding.' The grace of entrustment is always a surprising, tears-on-cheeks moment.

In my experience, these verses are powerful for worn out, burned out, exhausted, broken cross-cultural witnesses. We have all capitulated like Peter, and are in need of restoration. We all feel ashamed at how ineffective we have been, those moments of stepping into the high priest's courtyard in the middle of the night and failing in our courage. We all are painfully aware of our lack of impact, our inability to speak up, the reality that he is the 'I am' and we are the 'I am nots'.

And like Peter, we all need to be brought back to the beach, to be reminded of our call, and our friendship, and to have our shame taken away.

The Church is thrice commissioned. To weeping Mary, the word is, 'Do not cling to me . . . but go to my brothers.' To the fearful disciples, the word is, 'Peace be with you. As the Father has sent me, even so I am sending you.' To ashamed Peter, the word is, 'Feed my lambs' and then, 'Follow me' (21:19).

We too weep, with a tendency to cling – to want to stay at his feet in the garden. We too are afraid, with a tendency to hide inside our locked rooms. We too are ashamed, having failed our Lord so many times. And yet his voice, his commissioning, rings down the ages, across all nations, through each generation. His wounds inspire us. His Spirit empowers us. His tenderness compels us. This story must continue. This Word must be made flesh to all flesh. This light must shine in all darkness. This water must flow to all the thirsty. This bread must give life to all people. All his sheep must be gathered in.

And so we follow him.

Bibliography

'Abundant Africa: Our Decade to Shape the African Century' at https://abundant.africa (accessed 15.1.2024).

Adeney, Bernard T., *Strange Virtues: Ethics in a Multicultural World*, Leicester: Apollos, 1995.

Allen, Roland, *The Ministry of the Spirit: Selected Writings*, David M. Paton (ed.), Cambridge: Lutterworth Press, 2011.

Amaladoss, Michael S.J., *The Asian Jesus*, Chennai: IDCR/ISPCK, 2005.

Aquaro, George R.A., *Death by Envy: The Evil Eye and Envy in the Christian Tradition*, Lincoln, NE: iUniverse, 2004.

Ashton, John (ed.), *The Interpretation of John (Studies in New Testament Interpretation)*, Edinburgh: T&T Clark, 1997.

Aulen, Gustav, *Christus Victor: An Historical Study of the Three Main Types of the Idea of Atonement*, London: SPCK, reissued 2010.

Azumah, John, 'Incarnation and Translation in Islam and Christianity', pp. 61-78 in *Jesus and the Incarnation: Reflections of Christians from Islamic Contexts*, David Emmanuel Singh (ed.), Oxford: Regnum, 2011.

Azzazy, Mohammed F. and Azza Ezzat, 'The Sycamore in Ancient Egypt: Textual, Iconographic and Archaeopalynological Thoughts' 209-220 in *Liber Amicorum-Speculum Sidearm:*

Nut Astrophorus. Papers Presented to Alicia Marcella, Nadine Guilhou (ed.), Oxford: Archaeopress/Egyptology, 2016.

Bailey, Kenneth E., *Jesus through Middle Eastern Eyes: Cultural Studies in the Gospels,* London: SPCK, 2008.

Bailey, Kenneth E., *The Good Shepherd: A Thousand-Year Journey From Psalm 23 to the New Testament,* Downers Grove, IL: IVP, 2014.

Barclay, William, *The Gospel of Mark (Third Printing),* Edinburgh: St Andrew Press, 2009.

Barrosse, Thomas, 'The Seven Days of the New Creation in St. John's Gospel', *The Catholic Biblical Quarterly* 21, No. 4 (Oct. 1959): pp. 507-516.

Bauckham, Richard, *Gospel of Glory: Major Themes in Johannine Theology,* Grand Rapids, MI: Baker Academic, 2015.

Bauckham, Richard, *The Testimony of the Beloved Disciple: Narrative, History and Theology in the Gospel of John,* Grand Rapids, MI: Baker Academic, 2007.

Beale, Gregory K., *A New Testament Biblical Theology: The Unfolding of the Old Testament in the New,* Grand Rapids, MI: Baker Academic, 2011.

Bediako, Kwame, *Jesus and the Gospel in Africa: History and Experience (Theology in Africa Series),* New York: Orbis, 2004.

Bermejo-Rubio, Fernando, 'Jesus and the Anti-Roman Resistance: A Reassessment of the Arguments', *Journal for the Study of the Historical Jesus* 12 (2014): pp. 1-105.

Brown, Tricia Gates, *Spirit in the Writings of John: Johannine Pneumatology in Social-Scientific Perspective (Journal for the Study of the New Testament Supplement Series 253),* New York: T&T Clark, 2003.

Carroll, Seforosa, 'Coconut Theology', 532-551 in *Emerging Theologies from the Global South,* Mitri Raheb and Mark. A. Lamport (eds.), Eugene, OR: Wipf and Stock, 2023.

Carson, D.A., *The Gospel According to John* (Pillar New Testament Commentary), Leicester: Apollos, 1991.

Castells-Quintana, David and McDermott, Thomas K.J., 'Inequality and Climate Change: The Within-Countries Distributional Effects of Global Warming', 2023, https://ssrn.com/abstract=4357764 or http://dx.doi.org/10.2139/ssrn.4357764 (accessed 15.1.24).

Chacko, Biju, *Intercultural Christology in John's Gospel: A Subaltern Reading from India,* Minneapolis, MN: Fortress, 2022.

Chen, Yarong, *The Diffused Story of the Footwashing in John 13: A Textual Study of Bible Reception in Late Imperial China (Contrapuntal Readings of the Bible in World Christianity)*, Eugene, OR: Pickwick, 2021.

Chennattu, Rekha R.A., 'Women in the Mission of the Church', at http://www.sedos.org/english/chennattu.html (accessed 8.3.24).

Conde-Frazier, Elizabeth, 'Latina Evangelicas: A New Voice in Hispanic/Latina Theology', *Latin American Theology* 10 (2015): pp. 63-84.

Coorilos, Metropolitan Geevarghese, 'Ecology and Mission: Some Orthodox Theological Perspectives', pp. 134-147 in *Creation Care in Christian Mission,* Kapya J. Kaoma (ed.), Oxford: Regnum, 2015.

Coloe, Mary, 'The Nazarene King: Pilate's Title as the Key to John's Crucifixion', 839-848 in *The Death of Jesus in the Fourth Gospel,* Gilbert Van Belle (ed.), Bibliotheca Ephemeridium Theologicarum Lovaniensium 200, Leuven: Leuven University Press, 2007.

Cone, James, 'Whose Earth is it Anyway?' pp. 23-32 in Dieter Hessel and Larry Rasmussen (eds.), *Earth Habitat: Ecojustice and the Church's Response* Minneapolis, MN: Fortress, 2001.

Cruchley, Peter, '"Turning Whiteness Purple": Reflections on Decentering Whiteness in its Christian Colonial Missionary Mode', in *Deconstructing Whiteness, Empire and Mission,* Anthony G. Reddie and Carol Troupe (eds.), London: SCM, 2023.

Daly-Denton, Margaret, *John: An Earth Bible Commentary. Supposing Him to Be the Gardener,* London: T&T Clark, 2019.

Devenish, David, *What on Earth is the Church For? A Blueprint for the Future of Church-Based Mission and Social Action*, Milton Keynes: Authentic Media, 2005.

Doole, J. Andrew, 'To be "An Out-of-the-Synagoguer"', *JSNT*, Vol. 43, Issue 3, March 2021: pp. 389-410.

Dube, Musa W. and Staley, Jeffrey L. (eds.), *John and Postcolonialism: Travel, Space and Power,* Sheffield Academic Press, 2002.

Dube, Musa W., 'Reading for Decolonization (John 4.1-42)', pp. 51-75 in *John and Postcolonialism: Travel, Space and Power,* Musa W. Dude and Jeffrey L. Staley (eds.), Sheffield Academic Press, 2002.

Escobar, Samuel, 'Doing Theology on Christ's Road' Kindle loc 611-811 in *Global Theology in Evangelical Perspective: Exploring the Contextual Nature of Theology and Mission,* Jeffrey P. Greenmail and Gene L. Green (eds.), Downers Grove, IL: IVP Academic, 2012.

Evans, Julian, *God's Trees: Trees, Forests and Wood in the Bible.* Second Edition, Leominster: DayOne, 2018.

Fernandez, Eleazer S., 'Filipino Theology', pp. 316-335 in *Emerging Theologies from the Global South,* Mitri Raheb and Mark A. Lamport (eds.), Eugene, OR: Wipf and Stock, 2023.

Ford, David F., *The Gospel of John: A Theological Commentary,* Grand Rapids, MI: Baker Academic, 2021.

Francis, *Encyclical Letter Laudato Si' of the Holy Father Francis on Care for our Common Home,* 2015. https://www.vatican.va/content/francesco/en/encyclicals/documents/papa-francesco_20150524_enciclica-laudato-si.html (accessed 1.3.24).

Gench, Frances Taylor, *Encounters with Jesus (Studies in the Gospel of John),* Louisville, KY: Westminster John Knox, 2007.

Gener, Timoteo D. (ed.), *Asian Christian Theology: Evangelical Perspectives,* Carlisle: Langham, 2019.

George, Samuel, 'Theological Education as Missional Formation: Contributions of the World Council of Churches Ecumenical Disability Advocates Network', *International Review of Mission* 108, No. 1 (June 2019): pp. 8-17.

Gitari, David, *In Season and Out of Season,* Carlisle: Regnum, 1996.

Gonzales, Michelle A., 'Latina Feminist Theology', pp. 224-246 in *Emerging Theologies from the Global South,* Mitri Raheb and Mark A. Lamport (eds.), Eugene, OR: Wipf and Stock, 2023.

Greenman, Jeffrey P. and Green, Gene L., *Global Theology in Evangelical Perspective: Exploring the Contextual Nature of Theology and Mission,* Downers Grove, IL: IVP Academic, 2012.

Guardiola-Saenz, Leticia A., 'Border-crossing and its Redemptive Power in John 7.53-8.11: A Cultural Reading of Jesus and the Accused', pp. 129-152 in *John and Postcolonialism: Travel, Space and Power,* Musa W. Dube and Jeffrey L. Staley (eds.), Sheffield Academic Press, 2002.

Guyon, Jeanne, *Experiencing the Depths of Jesus Christ (Library of Spiritual Classics Volume 2),* Sargent, GA: SeedSowers, 1975.

Haddis, Makdes, *A Just Mission: Laying Down Power and Embracing Mutuality*, Downers Grove, MI: IVP, 2022.

Harper, Lisa Sharon, *The Very Good Gospel: How Everything Wrong Can be Made Right*. New York: WaterBrook, 2016.

Harries, Jim, 'The Case Against English in Africa and the Majority World, and its Implication for Christian Mission Today', Lecture Presented at OCMS on 21 June, 2022, www.youtube.com/watch?v=3fyEhrwQCdE (accessed 15.1.24).

Hayek, M. (ed.), *Ammar al-Basri: Apologie et Controverses,* Beirut: Dar al-Machreq, 1977.

Henry, Matthew, *Commentary: In One Volume,* Grand Rapids, MI: Zondervan, 1960.

Higton, Mike, 'Beyond Theological Self-Possession', pp. 13-27 in *Deconstructing Whiteness, Empire and Mission*, Anthony G. Reddie and Carol Troupe (eds.), London: SCM, 2023.

Hill, Graham Joseph, *Salt, Light and a City, Second Edition: Conformation – Ecclesiology for the Global Missional Community. Volume 2: Majority World Voices*, Eugene, OR: Wipf and Stock, 2020.

Hopley, Rosie, 'Violence Against Women' Churches That Change Communities seminar 2023, https://jubilee-plus.org/ctcc23/ (accessed 15.1.24).

Horsley, Richard A., *Jesus and Empire: The Kingdom of God and the New World Disorder,* Fortress Press, Minneapolis, MN: 2003.

Isaac, Munther, *The Other Side of the Wall: A Palestinian Christian Narrative of Lament and Hope,* Downers Grove, MI: IVP, 2020.

Jenkins, Philip, *The New Faces of Christianity: Believing the Bible in the Global South,* New York: Oxford University Press, 2006.

Johnson, Luke Timothy, *The Revelatory Body: Theology as Inductive Art,* Grand Rapids, MI: Eerdmans, 2004.

Joplin, Patricia Klindienst, 'Intolerable Language: Jesus and the Woman Taken in Adultery', pp. 226-237 in *Shadow of Spirit: Postmodernism and Religion,* Philippa Berry and Andrew Wernick (eds.), New York: Routledge, 1992.

Kaoma, Kapya J. (ed.), *Creation Care in Christian Mission,* Oxford: Regnum, 2015.

Kaoma, Kapya J., 'The Earth in the Mission of the Incarnate God', pp. 280-296 in *Creation Care in Christian Mission,* Kapya J. Kaoma (ed.), Oxford: Regnum, 2015.

Kanagaraj, Jey J., *John: A New Covenant Commentary,* Cambridge: Lutterworth Press, 2013.

Katanacho, Yohanna, *Reading the Gospel of John Through Palestinian Eyes*, Carlisle: Langham Preaching Resources, 2020.

Kaur, Suriander, '4 Incredible Christian Women Who Changed India', *Christianity Today*, 8 March 2023, https://www.christianitytoday.com/ct/2023/march-web-only/indian-christian-women-pandita-ramabai-cornelia-sorabji.html (accessed 1.12.23).

Keener, Craig S., *The Gospel of John: A Commentary*, Vol. 2, Grand Rapids, MI: Baker Academic, 2003.

Keener, Craig S., 'Sent Like Jesus: Johannine Missiology (John 20:21-21)', *Asian Journal of Pentecostal Studies* 12, No. 1 (Jan. 2009): pp. 21-45.

Keller, Timothy, *Center Church: Doing Balanced, Gospel-Centered Ministry in Your City*, Grand Rapids, MI: Zondervan, 2012.

Kim, Grace Ji-Sun, *Embracing the Other: The Transformative Spirit of Love*, Grand Rapids: Eerdmans, 2015.

Kim, Jean K., 'Adultery or Hybridity? Reading John 7.53-8.11 from a Postcolonial Context', pp. 111-128 in *John and Postcolonialism: Travel, Space and Power*, Musa W. Dube and Jeffrey L. Staley (eds.), Sheffield Academic Press, 2002.

Kim, Sean Seongkik, *The Spirituality of Following Jesus in John's Gospel: An Investigation of Akolouthein and Correlated Motifs*, Eugene, OR: Pickwick, 2017.

Kinoti, Hannah W., 'Well Being in African Society and in the Bible', pp. 112-122 in *The Bible in African Christianity* Hannah W. Kinoti and John M. Waliggo (eds.), Nairobi, Kenya: Acton, 1997.

Kitamori, Kazoh, *Theology of the Pain of God: The First Original Theology from Japan,* Eugene, OR: Wipe and Stock, 1965.

Kostenberger, Andreas J., 'The Challenge of a Systematized Biblical Theology of Mission: Missiological Insights from the Gospel of John', *Missiology: An International Review* 23, No. 4 (Oct. 1995): pp. 445-464.

Koyama, Kosuke, *Three Mile an Hour God,* London: SCM Press, 1979.

Kwiyani, Harvey, *Multicultural Kingdom: Ethnic Diversity, Mission and the Church*, London: SCM, 2020.

Liew, Tat-Siong Benny, 'Ambiguous Admittance: Consent and Descent in John's Community of "Upward" Mobility', pp. 193-224 in *John and Postcolonialism: Travel, Space and Power,* Musa W. Dube and Jeffrey L. Staley (eds.), Sheffield: Sheffield Academic Press, 2002.

Lim, David S., 'A Biblical Missiology of Kingdomization through Disciple Multiplication Movements of House Church Networks', pp. 79-92 in *Motus Dei: The Movement of God to Disciple the Nations*, Warwick Farah (ed.), Littleton, CO: William Carey Publishing, 2021.

Lim, David S., 'Contextualizing the Gospel in Ancestor-Venerating Cultures', Kindle location 7669-8406 in *The Gospel in Culture: Contextualization Issues through Asian Eyes*, Melba Padilla Maggay (ed.), Manila: OMF Literature and ISACC, 2013.

Maggay, Melba Padilla (ed.), *The Gospel in Culture: Contextualization Issues through Asian Eyes*, Manila: OMF Literature and ISACC, 2013.

Maggay, Melba, 'A Religion of Guilt Encounters a Religion of Power: Missiological Implications and Consequences', Kindle locations 390-1002 in *The Gospel in Culture: Contextualization Issues through Asian Eyes*, Melba Maggay (ed.), Manila: OMF Literature and ISACC, 2013.

Mallouhi, Christine M., 'Peacemaking as a Witness', Kindle location 7742-8037 in *Toward Respectful Understanding and Witness among Muslims: Essays in Honor of J. Dudley Woodberry*, Evelyne A. Reisacher (ed.), Pasadena, CA: William Carey Library, 2012.

Marcos, Sylvia, 'Teologia India: A Context Theology', pp. 269-288 in *Emerging Theologies from the Global South*, Mitri Rehab and Mark A. Lamport (ed.), Eugene, OR: Wipf and Stock, 2023.

Matenga, Jay, 'The Editorial', 2-5, *The Emancipation of Indigenous Theologies in Light of the Rise of World Christianity, ANVIL: Journal of Theology and Mission,* 39 No. 1, Oxford: Church Mission Society, 2023.

Matenga, Jay, 'Indigenous Relationship Ecologies: Space, Spirituality and Sharing', 2 November 2001, https://jaymatenga. com/pdfs/MatengaJ_IndigenousEcologies.pdf (accessed 1.12.23).

Matthew, Sam P., 'Early Contacts between Ancient India and the Western World: Implications for New Testament Background', pp. 157-188 in *In Master's Service: Reflections on Christian Ministry. In Honour of Rev. Dr. M. V. Abraham*, Abraham Philip (ed.), Kottayam: Marthoma Theological Seminary, 2011.

Mbiti, John S., 'Theological Impotence and the Universality of the Church', pp. 6-18 in *Mission Trends No. 3: Third World Theologies*, Gerald H. Anderson and Thomas F. Stransky (ed.), New York: Paulist Press, 1976.

Mbiti, John S., *Bible and Theology in African Christianity* Nairobi, Kenya: Oxford University Press, 1986.

McCullough, Andy, *Global Humility: Attitudes for Mission,* Welwyn Garden City: Malcolm Down, 2017.

McCullough, Andy, *The Bethlehem Story: Mission and Justice in the Margins of the World*, Eugene, OR: Resource Publications, 2021.

Mejudhon, Nanthachai, *Meekness: A New Approach to Christian Witness to the Thai People*, Unpublished Doctor of Missiology Thesis, Asbury Theological Seminary, Wilmore, Kentucky, USA, 1997.

Miguez, Nestor, Reiger, Joerg and Sung, Jung Mo, *Beyond the Spirit of Empire: Reclaiming Liberation Theology*, London: SCM Press, 2009.

Moffett, Samuel Hugh, *A History of Christianity in Asia. Volume Two 1500-1900*, Maryknoll: Orbis, 2005.

Moore, Stephen D., 'Are there Impurities in the Living Water that the Johannine Jesus Dispenses? Deconstruction, Feminism, and the Samaritan Woman (1993)', pp. 279-300 in *The Interpretation of John (Studies in New Testament Interpretation)*, John Ashton (ed.), Edinburgh: T&T Clark, 1997.

Motyer, Stephen, 'Jesus and the Marginalised in the Fourth Gospel', pp. 70-89 in Billington, Anthony, Lane, Tony & Turner, Max (eds.), *Mission and Meaning: Essays Presented to Peter Cotterell,* Carlisle: Paternoster, 1995.

Musk, Bill, *The Unseen Face of Islam: Sharing the Gospel with Ordinary Muslims at Street Level*, London: Monarch, 1989.

Muszczyński, Mariusz, *A Far Better Way: In Search of a New Understanding of Success*, trans: Natalia Klimczyk, College of Theology and Social Sciences in Warsaw, 2023.

Newbigin, Lesslie, *The Light has Come: An Exposition of the Fourth Gospel,* Grand Rapids, MI: Eerdmans, 1982.

Newbigin, Lesslie, *The Open Secret: An Introduction to the Theology of Mission*, Revised Edition, Grand Rapids, MI: Eerdmans, 1995.

Neyrey, Jerome H., "'I am the Door" (John 10:7,9): Jesus the Broker in the Fourth Gospel', *Catholic Biblical Quarterly* 69, No. 2 (2007): pp. 271-91.

Neyrey, Jerome H., *The Gospel of John (The New Cambridge Bible Commentary)*, Cambridge University Press, 2007.

Ngewa, Samuel, 'John', pp. 1277-1322 in *Africa Bible Commentary: A One-Volume Commentary Written by 70 African Scholars,* Tokunboh Adeyemo (eds.), Carlisle: Langham, 2006.

Nguyễn, Phanxicô Xaviê Văn Thuận, *Testimony of Hope: The Spiritual Exercises of Pope John Paul II*, trans. Julia Mary Darrenkamp and Anne Eileen Heffernan, Pauline Books and Media, 2000.

Niles, D.T., *This Jesus … Whereof We are Witnesses,* Philadelphia, PA: Westminster, 1965.

Niles, D.T., *Upon the Earth: The Mission of God and the Missionary Enterprise of the Churches*, London: Lutterworth Press, 1962.

Nothwehr, Dawn, 'For the Salvation of the Cosmos: The Church's Mission of Ecojustice', *International Bulletin of Mission Research* 43, No. 1 (2019): pp. 68-81.

O'Day, Gail R., *The Word Disclosed: John's Story and Narrative Preaching,* St Louis, MO: CBP Press, 1987.

Orobator, Agbonkhianmeghe E., *Theology Brewed in an African Pot,* Orbis, New York, 2009.

Padilla, C. Rene, 'Liberation Theology II', *The Reformed Journal* 33 (1983): pp. 14-18.

Padilla, C. Rene, *Mission Between the Times,* Grand Rapids, MI: Eerdmans, 1985.

Padilla DeBorst, Ruth, 'A New and Glorious Life', Plenary Session, Cape Town 2010, The Third Lausanne Congress on World Evangelization at https://www.youtube.com/watch?v=j_GhJwdneDk (accessed 15.1.24).

Pedersen, Else Marie Wiberg, Lam, Holger and Lodberg, Peter (eds.), *For All People: Global Theologies in Contexts: Essays in Honor of Viggo Mortensen*, Cambridge: Eerdmans, 2002.

Raheb, Mitri, *Faith in the Face of Empire: The Bible Through Palestinian Eyes*, New York: Orbis, 2014.

Raheb, Mitri and Lamport, Mark A. (eds.), *Emerging Theologies from the Global South*, Eugene, OR: Wipf and Stock, 2023.

Raheb, Viola, 'Middle Eastern Theologies', pp. 422-441 in *Emerging Theologies from the Global South*, Mitri Raheb and Mark A. Lamport (eds.), Eugene, OR: Wipf and Stock, 2023.

Raj, Udit, 'Cry of Christ', 11 January 2004, at http://www.countercurrents.org/dalit-uditraj110105.htm (accessed 15.1.24).

Reddie, Anthony G. and Troupe, Carol (eds.), *Deconstructing Whiteness, Empire and Mission,* London: SCM, 2023.

Reinhartz, Adele, 'The Gospel According to John', pp. 152-196 in *The Jewish Annotated New Testament: New Revised Standard*

Bible Translation, Amy-Jill Levine and Marc Zvi Brettler (eds.), Oxford: Oxford University Press, 2011.

Reisacher, Evelyne A. (ed.), *Toward Respectful Understanding and Witness among Muslims: Essays in Honor of J. Dudley Woodberry,* Pasadena, CA: William Carey Library, 2012.

Richards, E. Randolph and O'Brien, Brandon J., *Misreading Scripture with Western Eyes: Removing Cultural Blinders to Better Understand the Bible,* Downers Grove, MI: IVP, 2012.

Richards, E. Randolph and James, Richard, *Misreading Scripture with Individualist Eyes: Patronage, Honor, and Shame in the Biblical World,* Downers Grove, MI: IVP, 2020.

Robertson, S., 'Sonship in John's Gospel', *Asia Journal of Theology* 25, No. 2 (Oct. 2011): pp. 315-333.

Rodriguez, Jeannette, *'Tripuenteando:* Journey toward Identity, the Academy, and Solidarity', pp. 70-88 in *Feminist Intercultural Theology: Latina Explorations for a Just World,* Maria Pilar Aquino and Maria Jose Rosado-Nunes (eds.), Maryknoll, NY: Orbis, 2007.

Rihbany, Abraham Mitrie, *The Syrian Christ. Second Edition,* London: Andrew Melrose, 1920.

Sacks, Rabbi Jonathan, *Leviticus: The Book of Holiness. Covenant and Conversation,* Jerusalem: Maggid Books, 2015.

Sanneh, Lamin, 'Should Christianity be Missionary? An Appraisal and an Agenda', *Dialog: A Journal of Theology* 40 (2001): pp. 86-98.

Sanneh, Lamin, 'The Significance of the Translation Principle', Kindle location 297-467, in *Global Theology in Evangelical Perspective: Exploring the Contextual Nature of Theology and Mission,* Jeffrey P. Greenman and Gene L. Green (eds.), Downers Grove: IVP Academic, 2012.

Sanneh, Lamin, *Disciples of All Nations: Pillars of World Christianity*, Oxford: Studies in World Christianity, 2007.

Sattin, Anthony, *Nomads: The Wanderers who Shaped our World*, John Murray: London, 2022.

Schnackenburg, Rudolf, *Gospel According to St John: Commentary on Chapters 13-21 Vol. 3*, Chicago: Crossroad, 1983.

Schneiders, Sandra M., 'A Case Study: A Feminist Interpretation of John 4:1-42 (1991)', pp. 235-260 in *The Interpretation of John (Studies in New Testament Interpretation)*, John Ashton (ed.), Edinburgh: T&T Clark, 1997.

Schreiter, Robert J., 'Globalization, Postmodernity, and the New Catholicity', pp. 13-31 in *For All People: Global Theologies in Contexts: Essays in Honor of Viggo Mortensen*, Else Marie Wiberg Pedersen, Holger Lam, and Peter Lodberg (eds.), Cambridge: Eerdmans, 2002.

Segovia, Fernando F. and Mary Ann Tolbert (eds.), *Reading From this Place: Volume 1: Social Location and Biblical Interpretation in the United States*, Minneapolis, MN: Fortress, 1995.

Sempangi, F. Kefa with Barbara R. Thompson, *A Distant Grief*, Glendale, CA: G1 Regal Books, 1979.

Senior, Donald, 'The Johannine Theology of Mission', pp. 280-296 in *The Biblical Foundations for Mission*, Donald Senior and Carroll Stuhlmueller (eds.), Maryknoll, NY: Orbis, Fourth Printing, 1991.

Shafak, Elif, *The Island of Missing Trees*, London: Penguin, 2021.

Shanahan, Mike, 'Tree of life: How figs built the world and will help save it', *New Scientist*, 14 December 2016 at https://www.newscientist.com/article/mg23231041-100-the-roots-of-our-relationship-with-fig-trees-go-back-a-long-way/ (accessed 1.12.23).

Singh, David Emmanuel (ed)., *Jesus and the Incarnation: Reflections of Christians from Islamic Contexts*, Oxford: Regnum, 2011.

Singh, Sadhu Sundar, *At the Master's Feet*, trans. Arthur and Rebecca Parker, first published in 1922, Kindle edition by Living Bytes Publishing.

Stanley, Brian, *The World Missionary Conference, Edinburgh 1910* (Studies in the History of Christian Missions), Grand Rapids, MI: Eerdmans, 2009.

Stinton, Diane B., 'Jesus Christ, Living Water in Africa Today', pp. 425-443 in *The Oxford Handbook of Christology*, Francesca Aran Murphy (eds.), Oxford University Press, 2015.

Stott, John R.W., *Christian Mission in the Modern World*, London: Church Pastoral Aid Society, 1975.

Stott, John R.W., *The Contemporary Christian: Applying God's Word to Today's World*, Downers Grove, IL: IVP, 1992.

Stott, John R.W., *The Message of Ephesians (The Bible Speaks Today)*, Leicester: IVP, 1979.

Sugitharajah, R.S., *Asian Biblical Hermeneutics and Postcolonialism: Contesting the Interpretations*, Maryknoll, NY: Orbis, 1998.

Taylor, Dr and Mrs Howard, *The Spiritual Secret of Hudson Taylor,* New Kensington, PA: Whitaker House, 1997.

Taylor, John V., *The Growth of the Church in Buganda*, London: SCM Press, 1958.

Temple, William, *Readings in St. John's Gospel*, London: Macmillan, 1945.

Tennent, Timothy C., *Theology in the Context of World Christianity: How the Global Church Is Influencing the Way We Think about and Discuss Theology*, Grand Rapids, MI: Zondervan, 2007.

Thiong'o, Nguni wa, *A Grain of Wheat: Penguin Modern Classics*, London: Penguin, 2002.

Thomaskutty, Johnson, 'The Gospel of John', pp. 127-156 in *An Asian Introduction to the New Testament*, Johnson Thomaskutty (ed.), Minneapolis, MN: Fortress, 2022.

Thurman, Howard, *Jesus and the Disinherited,* Boston, MA: Beacon Press, 2022.

Tofaeno, Ama'amalele, *Ecotheology: AIGA, The Household of God. A Perspective from the Living Myths and Traditions of Samoa,* Erlangen, Germany: Erlangen Verla fur Mission und Oikumene, 2000.

Turaki, Yusufu, 'Ephesians', pp. 1451-1464 in *Africa Bible Commentary: A One-Volume Commentary Written by 70 African Scholars*, Tokunboh Adeyemo (ed.), Carlisle: Langham, 2006.

Tutu, Desmond, 'Foreword', in *Handbook of Theological Education in World Christianity: Theological Perspectives, Regional Surveys, Ecumenical Trends*, Dietrich Werner, David Esterline, Namsoon Kang and Roshva Raja (eds.), Oxford: Regnum Books International, 2010.

Valerio, Ruth, 'Why We are Not Stewards of the Environment', 18 January 2021, https://ruthvalerio.net/bibletheology/why-we-are-not-stewards-of-the-environment/ (accessed 15.1.24).

Vellanickal, Matthew, 'Evangelization in the Johannine Writings', pp. 121-168 in *Good News and Witness*, Lucien Legrand, J. Pathrapankal and Matthew Vellanickal (eds.), Bangalore: Theological Publications in India, 1973.

Volf, Miroslav, *Exclusion and Embrace: A Theological Exploration of Identity, Otherness and Reconciliation,* Nashville, TN: Abingdon, 1996.

Walls, Andrew F., 'The American Dimension in the History of the Missionary Movement', pp. 1-25 in *Earthen Vessels: American Evangelicals and Foreign Missions, 1880-1980,* Joel Carpenter and Wilbert R. Shenk (eds.), Grand Rapids, MI: Eerdmans, 1990.

Wan, Enoch, 'Jesus Christ for the Chinese: A Contextual Reflection', *Chinese Around the World,* July 2000: pp. 1-10.

Wan, Enoch, 'Tao – The Chinese Theology of God-Man', *His Dominion,* Spring 1985: pp. 24-27, Regina, Saskatchewan: Canadian Theological Seminary.

We Choose Abundant Life Group, *We Choose Abundant Life: Christians in the Middle East: Towards Renewed Theological, Social and Political Choices,* Beirut, 2021.

Weller, Paul, 'Coming Full Circle: Christianity, Empire, Whiteness, the Global Majority and the Struggles of Migrants and Refugees in the UK', pp. 173-192 in *Deconstructing Whiteness, Empire and Mission,* Anthony G. Reddie and Carol Troupe (eds.), London: SCM, 2023.

Werner, Dietrich, David Esterline, Namsoon Kang and Roshva Raja (eds.), *Handbook of Theological Education in World Christianity: Theological Perspectives, Regional Surveys, Ecumenical Trends,* Oxford: Regnum Books International, 2010.

Wesley, John, *Wesley's Explanatory Notes,* www.studylight.org/commentaries/eng/wen/2-kings-18.html (accessed 7.3.24).

White Jr, Lynn, 'The Historical Roots of our Ecologic Crisis', *Science* 155 No. 3767 (10 March 1967), pp. 1203-1207.

Williams, Rowan, 'Foreword', in *Sowing the Word: The Cultural Impact of the British and Foreign Bible Society, 1804-2004*, Stephen Batalden, Kathleen Cann and John Dean (eds.), Sheffield: Phoenix Press, 2004.

Williams, Rowan, *Writing in the Dust: After September 11*, Grand Rapids, MI: Eerdmans, 2002.

Witherington III, Ben, *The New Testament Story*, Grand Rapids, MI: Eerdmans, 2004.

Wright, Christopher J.H., *The Great Story and the Great Commission: Participating in the Biblical Drama of Mission*, Grand Rapids, MI: Baker Academic, 2023.

Wright, Tom, *How God Became King: Getting to the Heart of the Gospels*, London: SPCK, 2012.

Wright, Tom, *John for Everyone Part 2: Chapters 11-21* (New Testament for Everyone), London: SPCK, 2000.

Yeo, Khiok-Khng, *What Has Jerusalem to Do with Beijing? Biblical Interpretation from a Chinese Perspective* (Contrapuntal Readings of the Bible in World Christianity), Harrisburg, PA: Trinity Press International, 1998.

Yip, Ching-Wah Francis, 'Protestant Christianity and Popular Religion in China', *Ching Feng* 42.3-4 July-December 1999: pp. 130-156.